First Workshop on Linguistic Resources for Natural Language Processing (LR4NLP-2018)

Santa Fe, New Mexico, USA
20 August 2018

ISBN: 978-1-5108-6908-0

COLING 2018

The 27th International Conference on Computational Linguistics

Proceedings of the First Workshop on Linguistic Resources for Natural Language Processing (LR4NLP-2018)

August 20, 2018
Santa Fe, New Mexico, USA

Anabela Barreiro, Kristina Kocijan, Peter Machonis and Max Silberztein (eds.)

Proceedings of the First Workshop on
Linguistic Resources for Natural Language Processing

Preface

Linguists and developers of NLP software have been working separately for many years. Since stochastic methods, such as statistical and neural-network based parsers, have shown to be overwhelmingly successful in the software industry, NLP researchers have typically turned their focus towards technical issues specific to stochastic methods, such as improving recall and precision, and developing larger and larger training corpora. At the same time, linguists kept focusing on problems related to the development of exhaustive and precise resources that are mainly "neutral" vis-a-vis any NLP application, such as parsing and generating sentences.

However, recent progress in both fields has been reducing many of these differences, with large-coverage linguistic resources being used more and more by robust NLP software. For instance, NLP researchers now use large dictionaries of multiword units and expressions, and several linguistic experiments have shown the feasibility of using large phrase-structure grammars (a priori used for text parsing) in "generation" mode to automatically produce paraphrases of sentences that are described by these grammars.

The First Workshop on Linguistic Resources for Natural Language Processing (LR4NLP) of the 27th International Conference on Computational Linguistics (COLING 2018) held at Santa Fe, New Mexico, August 20, 2018, brought together participants interested in developing large-coverage linguistic resources and researchers with an interest in developing real-world Natural Language Processing (NLP) software. The presentations at the LR4NLP Workshop were organized into four sessions, as follows:

- Clash of the Titans: Linguistics vs. Statistics vs. Neural Networks

- May the Force Be with NooJ

- One for the Road: Monolingual Resources

- Language Resources Without Borders

The first session, Clash of the Titans: Linguistics vs. Statistics vs. Neural Networks, focused on linguistic and stochastic approaches and results. Our invited speaker, Mark Liberman, showed how semi-automatic analysis of large digital speech collections is transforming the science of phonetics, and offered exciting opportunities to researchers in other fields, such as the possibility of improving parsing algorithms by incorporating features from speech as well as text. He was followed by Silberztein, who presented a series of experiments aimed at evaluating reference corpora, such as the Open American National Corpus, and proposed a series of tasks to enhance them. Zhang & Moldovan then made an assessment on the limitations and strengths of neural net systems to rule-based systems on Semantic Textual Similarity by comparing its performance with traditional rule-based systems against the SemEval 2012 benchmark.

Several workshop participants have been using the NooJ software to develop the large-coverage linguistic resources needed by their NLP applications. NooJ was particularly germane to this workshop, because it is not only being used by linguists to develop resources in the form of electronic dictionaries, and morphological and syntactic grammars, but by computational linguists to parse and annotate large corpora, as well as by software engineers to develop NLP applications. Thus, we allocated the entire second session, May the Force Be with NooJ, to researchers using this platform. Machonis showed how a lexicon grammar dictionary of English phrasal verbs can be transformed into a NooJ dictionary, in order to accurately identify these structures in large corpora. Phrasal verbs are located by means of a grammar, and the results are then refined with a series of dictionaries, disambiguating grammars, and filters. Likewise, Kocijan et al. demonstrated how they use NooJ to detect and describe the major derivational processes used in the formation of perfective, imperfective, and bi-aspectual Croatian verbs. Annotated chains are exported into a format adequate for a web-based system and further used to enhance the aspectual and derivational information for each verb. Next, Boudhina & Fehri presented a rule-based system for disambiguating French locative verbs in order to accurately translate them into Arabic. They used the Dubois & Dubois Charlier French Verb dictionary, a set of French syntactic grammars, as well as a bilingual French-Arabic dictionary developed within the NooJ platform. Finally, Rodrigo et al. presented a NooJ application aimed at teaching Spanish as a foreign language to native speakers of Italian. Their presentation included an analysis of a journalistic corpus over a thirty-year time span focusing on adjectives used in the Argentine Rioplatense variety of Spanish.

In the third session, One for the Road: Monolingual Resources, researchers examined a variety of large-coverage, monolingual linguistic resources for NLP applications. Dorr & Voss described the linguistic resource STYLUS (SysTematicallY Derived Language USe), which they produced through extraction of a set of argument realizations from lexical-semantic representations for a range of 500 English verb classes. Their Verb Database contains a total of 9,525 entries and includes information about components of meaning and collocations. STYLUS enables systematic derivation of regular patterns of language usage without requiring manual annotation. Then, Gezmu et al. presented a corpus of contemporary Amharic, automatically tagged for morpho-syntactic information. Texts were collected from 25,199 documents from different domains and about 24 million orthographic words were tokenized. Malireddy et al. discussed a new summarization technique, called Telegraphic Summarization, that, instead of selecting whole sentences, picks short segments of text spread across sentences in order to build the resulting summary. They proposed a set of guidelines to create such summaries and annotated a gold corpus of 200 English short stories. Finally, Abera et al. described the procedures that were used for the creation of the first speech corpus of Tigrinya a Semitic language spoken in the Horn of Africa for speech recognition purposes.

The closing session, Language Resources Without Borders, focused on the development of large-coverage, multilingual linguistic resources for Machine Translation (MT). Abate et al. described the development of parallel corpora for five Ethiopian Languages Amharic, Tigrigna, Afan-Oromo, Wolaytta and Geez. The authors conducted statistical machine translation experiments for seven language pairs that showed that the morphological complexity of these languages has a negative impact on the performance of the translation, especially for the target languages. Then, using the FrameNet and SALSA corpora, Sikos & Padó examined English and German, highlighting how inferences can be made about cross-lingual frame applicability using a vector space model. They showed how multilingual vector representations of frames learned from manually annotated corpora can address the need of accessing broad-coverage resources for any language pair. Next, Zhai et al. presented a parallel multilingual oral corpus the TED Talks in English, French, and Chinese. The authors categorized and annotated translation relations, to distinguish literal translation from other translation techniques. They developed a classifier to automatically detect these relations, with the long-term objective being to have better semantic control when dealing with paraphrases or translational equivalencies. Tomokiyo et al. aimed at improving the Cesselin, a well-known, open source Japanese-French dictionary. They hypothesized that the degree of lexical similarity between results of MT into a third language might provide insight on how to better annotate proverbs, idiomatic constructions, and phrases containing quantifiers. To test this, they used Google Translate to translate both the Cesselin Japanese expressions and their French translations into English. Their results showed much promise, in particular for distinguishing normal usage from idiomatic examples. Barreiro & Batista presented a detailed analysis on Portuguese contractions in an aligned bilingual Portuguese-English corpus and argued that the choice to decompose contractions or not depended on their context, for which the occurrence of multiword units is key. Finally, Dhar et al. presented a newly created parallel corpus of English and code-mixed English-Hindi. Using 6,088 code-mixed English-Hindi sentences previously available, they created a parallel English corpus using human translators. They then presented a technique to augment run-of-the-mill MT approaches, which achieves superior translations without the need for specially designed translation systems, and which can be plugged into any existing MT system.

The common theme of all of the papers presented in this workshop was how to build large linguistic resources in the form of annotated corpora, dictionaries, and morphological and syntactic grammars that can be used by NLP applications. Linguists as well as Computational Linguists who work on NLP applications based on linguistic methods will find advanced, up-to-the-minute studies for these themes in this volume. We hope that readers will appreciate the importance of this volume, both for the intrinsic value of each linguistic formalization and the underlying methodology, as well as for the potential for developing automatic NLP applications.

Editors:
Anabela Barreiro, INESC-ID, Lisbon, Portugal
Kristina Kocijan, University of Zagreb, Zagreb, Croatia
Peter Machonis, Florida International University, Miami, USA
Max Silberztein, Université de Franche-Comté, Besançon, France

Organizers and Review Committee

Workshop Organizers

Anabela Barreiro, INESC-ID, Lisbon, Portugal
Kristina Kocijan, University of Zagreb, Croatia
Peter Machonis, Florida International University, USA
Max Silberztein, Université de Franche-Comté, France

Peer Review Committee

Program Committee Chair

Max Silberztein, Université de Franche-Comté, France

Jorge Baptista, University of Algarve, Portugal
Anabela Barreiro, INESC-ID Lisbon, Portugal
Xavier Blanco, Autonomous University of Barcelona, Spain
Nicoletta Calzolari, Istituto di Linguistica Computazionale, Italy
Christiane Fellbaum, Princeton University, USA
Héla Fehri, University of Sfax, Tunisia
Yuras Hetsevich, National Academy of Sciences, Belarus
Kristina Kocijan, University of Zagreb, Croatia
Mark Liberman, University of Pennsylvania, USA
Elena Lloret Pastor, Universidad de Alicante, Spain
Peter Machonis, Florida International University, USA
Slim Mesfar, Carthaga University, Tunisia
Simon Mille, Universitat Pompeu Fabra, Spain
Mario Monteleone, University of Salerno, Italy
Johanna Monti, University of Naples - L'Orientale, Italy
Bernard Scott, Logos Institute, USA

Invited Speaker

Mark Liberman, University of Pennsylvania, USA

Session Chairs

Anabela Barreiro, INESC-ID, Lisbon, Portugal
Kristina Kocijan, University of Zagreb, Croatia
Peter Machonis, Florida International University, USA
Max Silberztein, Université de Franche-Comté, France

Table of Contents

Corpus Phonetics: Past, Present, and Future
Mark Liberman 1

Using Linguistic Resources to Evaluate the Quality of Annotated Corpora
Max Silberztein 2

Rule-based vs. Neural Net Approaches to Semantic Textual Similarity
Linrui Zhang and Dan Moldovan 12

Linguistic Resources for Phrasal Verb Identification
Peter Machonis 18

Designing a Croatian Aspectual Derivatives Dictionary: Preliminary Stages
Kristina Kocijan, Krešimir Šojat and Dario Poljak 28

A Rule-Based System for Disambiguating French Locative Verbs and Their Translation into Arabic
Safa Boudhina and Héla Fehri 38

A Pedagogical Application of NooJ in Language Teaching: The Adjective in Spanish and Italian
Andrea Rodrigo, Mario Monteleone and Silvia Reyes 47

STYLUS: A Resource for Systematically Derived Language Usage
Bonnie Dorr and Clare Voss 57

Contemporary Amharic Corpus: Automatically Morpho-Syntactically Tagged Amharic Corpus
Andargachew Mekonnen Gezmu, Binyam Ephrem Seyoum, Michael Gasser and Andreas Nürnberger . . 65

Gold Corpus for Telegraphic Summarization
Chanakya Malireddy, Srivenkata N M Somisetty and Manish Shrivastava 71

Design of a Tigrinya Language Speech Corpus for Speech Recognition
Hafte Abera and Sebsibe H/Mariam 78

Parallel Corpora for bi-Directional Statistical Machine Translation for Seven Ethiopian Language Pairs
Solomon Teferra Abate, Michael Melese, Martha Yifiru Tachbelie, Million Meshesha, Solomon Atinafu, Wondwossen Mulugeta, Yaregal Assabie, Hafte Abera, Binyam Ephrem, Tewodros Abebe, Wondimagegnhue Tsegaye, Amanuel Lemma, Tsegaye Andargie and Seifedin Shifaw 83

Using Embeddings to Compare FrameNet Frames Across Languages
Jennifer Sikos and Sebastian Padó 91

Construction of a Multilingual Corpus Annotated with Translation Relations
Yuming Zhai, Aurélien Max and Anne Vilnat 102

Towards an Automatic Classification of Illustrative Examples in a Large Japanese-French Dictionary Obtained by OCR
Christian Boitet, Mathieu Mangeot and Mutsuko Tomokiyo 112

Contractions: To Align or Not to Align, That Is the Question
Anabela Barreiro and Fernando Batista 122

Enabling Code-Mixed Translation: Parallel Corpus Creation and MT Augmentation Approach
Mrinal Dhar, Vaibhav Kumar and Manish Shrivastava 131

Conference Program

Monday, August 20, 2018

9:00–10:30 **Session S1: Clash of the Titans: Linguistics vs. Statistics vs. Neural-nets**

9:10–9:50 *Corpus Phonetics: Past, Present, and Future*
Mark Liberman

9:50–10:10 *Using Linguistic Resources to Evaluate the Quality of Annotated Corpora*
Max Silberztein

10:10–10:30 *Rule-based vs. Neural Net Approaches to Semantic Textual Similarity*
Linrui Zhang and Dan Moldovan

11:00–12:20 **Session S2: May the Force Be with NooJ**

11:00–11:20 *Linguistic Resources for Phrasal Verb Identification*
Peter Machonis

11:20–11:40 *Designing a Croatian Aspectual Derivatives Dictionary: Preliminary Stages*
Kristina Kocijan, Krešimir Šojat and Dario Poljak

11:40–12:00 *A Rule-Based System for Disambiguating French Locative Verbs and Their Translation into Arabic*
Safa Boudhina and Héla Fehri

12:00–12:20 *A Pedagogical Application of NooJ in Language Teaching: The Adjective in Spanish and Italian*
Andrea Rodrigo, Mario Monteleone and Silvia Reyes

Monday, August 20, 2018 (continued)

14:00–15:20   Session S3: One for the Road: Monolingual Resources

14:00–14:20   *STYLUS: A Resource for Systematically Derived Language Usage*
Bonnie Dorr and Clare Voss

14:20–14:40   *Contemporary Amharic Corpus: Automatically Morpho-Syntactically Tagged Amharic Corpus*
Andargachew Mekonnen Gezmu, Binyam Ephrem Seyoum, Michael Gasser and Andreas Nürnberger

14:40–15:00   *Gold Corpus for Telegraphic Summarization*
Chanakya Malireddy, Srivenkata N M Somisetty and Manish Shrivastava

15:00–15:20   *Design of a Tigrinya Language Speech Corpus for Speech Recognition*
Hafte Abera and Sebsibe H/Mariam

16:00–18:00   Session S4: Language Resources without Borders

16:00–16:20   *Parallel Corpora for bi-Directional Statistical Machine Translation for Seven Ethiopian Language Pairs*
Solomon Teferra Abate, Michael Melese, Martha Yifiru Tachbelie, Million Meshesha, Solomon Atinafu, Wondwossen Mulugeta, Yaregal Assabie, Hafte Abera, Binyam Ephrem, Tewodros Abebe, Wondimagegnhue Tsegaye, Amanuel Lemma, Tsegaye Andargie and Seifedin Shifaw

16:20–16:40   *Using Embeddings to Compare FrameNet Frames Across Languages*
Jennifer Sikos and Sebastian Padó

16:40–17:00   *Construction of a Multilingual Corpus Annotated with Translation Relations*
Yuming Zhai, Aurélien Max and Anne Vilnat

17:00–17:20   *Towards an Automatic Classification of Illustrative Examples in a Large Japanese-French Dictionary Obtained by OCR*
Christian Boitet, Mathieu Mangeot and Mutsuko Tomokiyo

17:20–17:40   *Contractions: To Align or Not to Align, That Is the Question*
Anabela Barreiro and Fernando Batista

17:40–18:00   *Enabling Code-Mixed Translation: Parallel Corpus Creation and MT Augmentation Approach*
Mrinal Dhar, Vaibhav Kumar and Manish Shrivastava

Corpus Phonetics: Past, Present, and Future

Mark Liberman
Department of Linguistics
University of Pennsylvania
Philadelphia, PA, USA
`myl@cis.upenn.edu`

Invited Speaker

Abstract

Semi-automatic analysis of digital speech collections is transforming the science of phonetics, and offers interesting opportunities to researchers in other fields. Convenient search and analysis of large published bodies of recordings, transcripts, metadata, and annotations – as much as three or four orders of magnitude larger than a few decades ago – has created a trend towards "corpus phonetics," whose benefits include greatly increased researcher productivity, better coverage of variation in speech patterns, and essential support for reproducibility.

The results of this work include insight into theoretical questions at all levels of linguistic analysis, as well as applications in fields as diverse as psychology, sociology, medicine, and poetics, as well as within phonetics itself. Crucially, analytic inputs include annotation or categorization of speech recordings along many dimensions, from words and phrase structures to discourse structures, speaker attitudes, speaker demographics, and speech styles. Among the many near-term opportunities in this area we can single out the possibility of improving parsing algorithms by incorporating features from speech as well as text.

Biography

Mark Liberman is the Christopher H. Browne Professor of Linguistics at the University of Pennsylvania, as well as Professor of Computer and Information Science, Faculty Director of Ware College House, and Director of the Linguistic Data Consortium. Before moving to Penn, he was member of technical staff and head of the Linguistics Research Department at AT&T Bell Laboratories from 1975 to 1990. He is a fellow of the Linguistic Society of America and the American Association for the Advancement of Science, and co-editor of the Annual Review of Linguistics.

He received the Antonio Zampolli Prize from the European Language Resources Association in 2010, and the IEE James L. Flanagan Speech and Audio Processing Award in 2017.

His current research focuses on features of speech, language, and communicative interaction that are associated with neuropsychological categories and with relevant dimensions of variation in the population at large.

1

Using Linguistic Resources to
Evaluate the Quality of Annotated Corpora

Max Silberztein
Université de Franche-Comté
`max.silberztein@univ-fcomte.fr`

Abstract

Statistical and neural network based methods that compute their results by comparing a given text to be analyzed with a reference corpus assume that the reference corpus is complete and reliable enough. In this article, I conduct several experiments to verify this assumption and I suggest ways to improve these reference corpora by using carefully handcrafted linguistic resources.

1   Introduction

Nowadays, most Natural Language Processing (NLP) applications use stochastic methods that are, for example, statistical- or neural network-based, in order to analyze new texts. Analyzing a text involves thus comparing it with a "training" or reference corpus, which is a set of texts that have been either pre-analyzed manually or parsed automatically, and then checked by a linguist. Granted that the reference corpus and the text to analyze are similar enough, these methods produce satisfactory results.

Because natural languages contain infinite sets of sentences, these methods cannot just compare the text to be analyzed with the reference corpus directly at the sentence level. They rather process both the text and the reference corpus at the *wordform* level (i.e. contiguous sequences of letters). To analyze a sentence in a new text, they first look up how each wordform of the text was tagged in the reference corpus, and then they compare the context of the wordform in the text to be analyzed with similar ones in the reference corpus.

The basic assumption of these stochastic methods is that if the reference corpus is sufficiently large, the wordforms that constitute the text to be analyzed will contain enough occurrences to find identical, or at least similar, contexts. Reciprocally, if the reference corpus is too small or too different from the text to be analyzed, then the application will produce unreliable results. Therefore, evaluating the quality of an annotated corpus means answering the following questions:

- what is the minimum size of the annotated corpus needed to produce reliable analyses?

- how reliable is the information stored in an annotated corpus?

- how much information is missing in an annotated corpus, and how does the missing information affect the reliability of the analysis of new texts?

For this experiment, I have used the NooJ linguistic development environment[1] to study the *Slate* corpus included in the Open American National Corpus[2]. This sub-corpus, constituted by 4,531 articles/files, contains 4,302,120 wordforms. Each wordform is tagged according to the Penn tag set[3].

---

[1] NooJ is a free open-source linguistic development environment, distributed by the European Metashare platform, see (Silberztein, 2003) and (Silberztein, 2016).

[2] The Open American National Corpus (OANC) is a free corpus and can be downloaded at `www.anc.org`. We have looked at the Corpus of Contemporary American English (COCA), which has a subset that is free of charge: we will see in section 2 that it has problems related to vocabulary similar to those of the OANC. (Silberztein, 2016) has evaluated the reliability of the Penn treebank and found results similar to those discussed in section 4.

[3] In the OANC as well as in other annotated corpora such as the Penn treebank or the COCA, sequences of digits, punctuation characters and sequences that contain one or more dashes are also processed as linguistic units.

Proceedings of the First Workshop on Linguistic Resources for Natural Language Processing, pages 2–11
Santa Fe, New Mexico, USA, August 20, 2018.

2 Vocabulary Coverage

2.1 Stability of the vocabulary

As a first experiment, I split the *Slate* corpus into two files: Even.txt contains all the articles whose original filename ends with an even number (e.g. "ArticleIP_1554.txt"), whereas Odd.txt contains all the articles whose original filename ends with an odd number (e.g. "ArticleIP_1555.txt"). These two corpora are composed of intertwined articles, so that vocabulary differences cannot be blamed on chronological or structural considerations.

As Figure 1 shows,[4] almost half of the wordforms in the vocabulary of the total corpus either occur in Even.txt but not in Odd.txt or occur in Odd.txt but not in Even.txt. In other words, for half of the wordforms in the corpus' vocabulary, the fact that they occur or not appears to be a random accident. The fact that the vocabularies of two random subsets of this 4-million-wordform corpus are so different shows that this corpus is still too small to have a stabilized vocabulary.

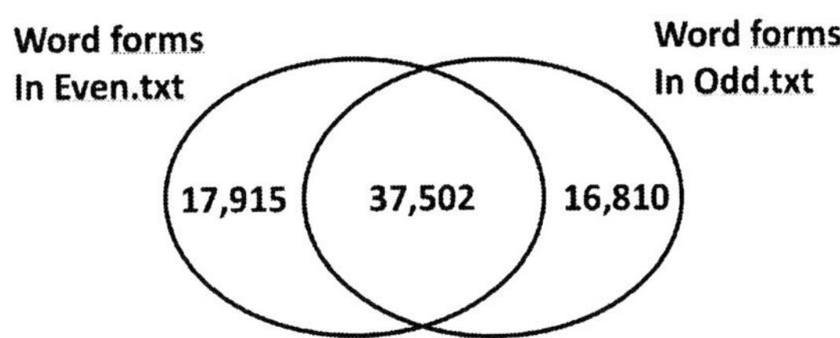

Figure 1. Vocabulary is unstable

Wordforms that occur in one sub-corpus but not in the other one, are not necessarily hapaxes or even rare wordforms: there are 4,824 wordforms that occur more than once in Even.txt, but never occur in Odd.txt, and there are 4,574 wordforms that occur more than once in Odd.txt, but never occur in Even.txt. The following are examples of wordforms that occur 10 times or more in one sub-corpus, but never occur in the other one:

- In Odd.txt: *cryptography* (12 occurrences), *mammary* (12), *predation* (12), *selector* (15), etc.
- In Even.txt: *irradiation* (13), *jelly* (17), *obsolescence* (11), *quintet* (16), *sturgeon* (10), etc.

The vocabulary covered by this 4-million-wordform corpus is still massively unstable, which indicates that the corpus size is much too small to cover a significant portion of the vocabulary.

2.2 Evolution of the vocabulary

As a second experiment, I studied the evolution of the size of the vocabulary in the full corpus. As we can see in Figure 2, the number of different wordforms (dashed line) first increases sharply and then settles down to a quasi-linear progression. That is not surprising because in a magazine, we expect to find a constant flow of new proper names (e.g. *Abbott*) and new typos (e.g. *achives*), as new articles are added to a corpus.

In NooJ, every element of the vocabulary is described by one, and only one, lexical entry. If a given wordform is polysemous, i.e. corresponds to more than one vocabulary element (e.g. *to milk* vs. *some milk*), then it is described by more than one lexical entry.

NooJ's Atomic Linguistic Units (ALUs) are either lexical entries (e.g. *eat*), inflected forms of a lexical entry (e.g. *eaten*) or derived forms of a lexical entry (e.g. *eatable*). NooJ handles affix ALUs (e.g. *re-*, *-ly*), simple ALUs (e.g. *table*), compound ALUs (e.g. *blue collars*, *in spite of*) as well as discontinuous ALUs (e.g. *turns ... off*, *took ... into account*). Note that contracted forms (e.g. *cannot*) and agglutinated forms (e.g. *autodialed*), very frequent in languages such as Arabic or German, are not ALUs: they are processed as sequences of ALUs.

---

[4] The total number of wordforms shown in Figure 1 is lower than 88,945, because we unified the forms that have different cases in the two sub-corpora. For instance, the wordform *Deductions* (only in Odd.txt) and the wordform *deductions* (only in Even.txt) are counted as one wordform.

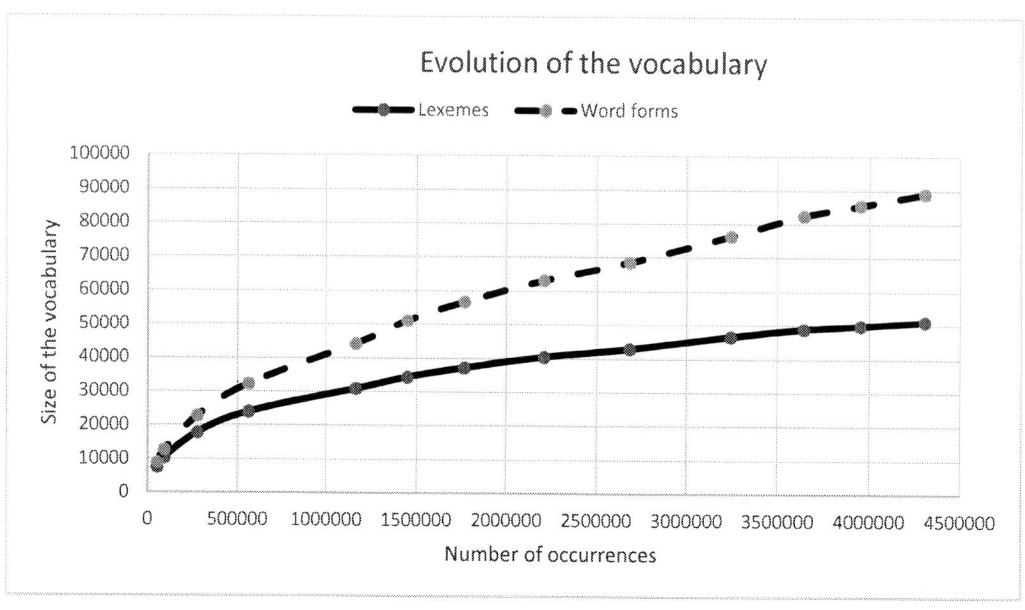

Figure 2. Evolution of the vocabulary

When evaluating the coverage of a reference corpus, it is important to distinguish ALUs from wordforms that have no or poor intrinsic linguistic value, such as numbers, uncategorized proper names and typos. To estimate the evolution of the vocabulary, I applied the English DELAS dictionary to the *Slate* corpus. The DELAS dictionary[5] represents standard English vocabulary, i.e. the vocabulary used in general newspapers and shared by most English speakers. It also includes non-basic terms such as *aardvark* (an African nocturnal animal) or *zugzwang* (a situation in chess), but it does not contain the millions of terms that can be found in scientific and technical vocabularies (e.g. the medical term *erythematosus*), nor terms used in regional variants all over the world (e.g. the Indian-English term *freeship*). The DELAS dictionary contains approximately 160,000 entries, which correspond to 300,000 inflected forms. Applying it to this corpus recognizes 51,072 wordforms, approximately a sixth of the standard vocabulary. Here are a few terms that never occur in the *Slate* corpus:

abominate, acarian, adjudicator, aeolian, aftereffect, agronomist, airlock, alternator, amphibian, anecdotic, apiculture, aquaculture, arachnid, astigmatism, atlas, autobiographic, aviator, awoken, axon, azimuth, etc.

The number of ALUs present in the corpus (solid line in Figure 2) grows slower and slower. By extrapolating it, I estimate that one would need to add at least 16 million wordforms to this 4-million-wordform corpus to get a decent 1/2 coverage of the standard vocabulary. Manually tagging such a large corpus — or even checking it after some automatic processing — would represent a considerable workload,[6] obviously implying a much larger project than simply constructing an English dictionary such as the DELAS.

Processing verbs correctly is crucial for any automatic parser because verbs impose strong constraints upon their contexts: for instance, as the verb *to sleep* is intransitive, one can deduce that any phrase that occurs right after it (e.g. *Joe slept last night*) has to be an adjunct rather than an argument (as in *Joe enjoyed last night*). Knowing that the verb *to declare* expects a subject that is a person, or an organization, allows automatic software to retrieve the pronoun's reference in the sentence: *They*

---

[5] The DELA family of dictionaries were created in the LADL laboratory, see (Courtois and Silberztein 1990; Klarsfeld 1991; Chrobot et al., 1999).

[6] 20 million wordforms to check, one second per check, 8-hours a day, 5-day a week, would take 3 years. By contrast, it takes between 6 and 9 months for a linguist to construct a NooJ module for a new language (that includes a DELAS-type dictionary).

declared an income, etc. However, if the reference corpus does not contain any occurrence of a verb, a statistical or neural-network based parser would have no means to deduce anything about its syntactic context nor its distributional restrictions, and therefore they would not be able to reliably process sentences that contain the verb.

The 4-million-wordform *Slate* corpus contains 12,534 wordforms tagged as verbal forms (tags VB, VBD, VBG, VBN, VBP or VBZ), which represents only a fifth of the 62,188 verbal forms processed by NooJ. Following are examples of verbs that never occur in the *Slate* corpus:

> *acerbate, acidify, actualize, adjure, administrate, adulate, adulterate, agglutinate, aggress, aliment, amputate, aphorize, appertain, arraign, approbate, asphyxiate*, etc.[7]

2.3 Compound words

In the *Slate* corpus, a few compound words that contain a hyphen have been tagged as units, e.g. "a-capella_JJ". But these same exact compounds, when spelled with a space character, were processed as sequences of two independent units, e.g. "a_DT capella_NN". At the same time, a large number of sequences that contain a hyphen, but are not compounds, have also been tagged as linguistic units, e.g.:

> *abide-and, abuse-suggesting, activity-regarded, adoption-related, Afghan-based*, etc.

Similarly, in the COCA, we can find *left-wing, wing-feathers* and *ultra-left-wing* tagged properly as ALUs, whereas *left wing, wing commander, wing nuts* are processed as sequences of two independent units. It seems that there is a systematic confusion between *compound ALUs* and sequences that contain a dash[8] in annotated corpora. In reality, most compounds do not contain a hyphen. For example, all occurrences of the adverb *as a matter of fact* have been tagged in the *Slate* corpus as:

As_IN a_DT matter_NN of_IN fact_NN

and in the COCA as:

as	as	ii
a	a	at1
matter	matter	nn1
of	of	jj32_nn132
fact	fact	nn1

This type of analysis makes it impossible for any NLP applications to process this adverb correctly. One would not want a MT system to translate this adverb word by word, nor a search engine to return these occurrences when a user is looking for the noun *matter*. In fact, a Web Semantic application should not even try to link these occurrences to the entities *dark matter* (2 occurrences), *gray matter* (2 occ.), *organic matter* (1 occ.) nor *reading matter* (1 occ.), etc.

NooJ's DELAC dictionary[9] contains over 70,000 compound nouns (e.g. *bulletin board*), adjectives (e.g. *alive and well*), adverbs (e.g. *in the line of fire*) and prepositions (e.g. *for the benefit of*). These entries correspond to approximately 250,000 inflected compound words. By applying the DELAC dictionary to the corpus, NooJ found 166,060 occurrences of compound forms, as seen in Figure 3.

These 166,060 compounds correspond to approximately 400,000 wordforms (i.e. 10% of the corpus) whose tags are either incorrect, or at least not relevant for any precise NLP application.

---

[7] Some of these forms do occur in the *Slate* corpus, but not as verbs. They have rather been tagged as adjectives, e.g. *actualized, amputated, arraigned*, etc.

[8] Silberztein (2016) presents a set of three criteria to distinguish between analyzable sequences of words and lexicalized multiword units: (1) the meaning of the whole cannot be completely computed from its components (e.g. a *green card* is much more than just a *card* that has a *green* color), (2) everyone uses the same term to name an entity (e.g. compare *a washing-machine* with *a clothes-cleaning device*), and (3) the transformational rules used to compute the relation between its components has some idiosyncratic constraints (compare the function of the adjective *presidential* in the two expressions: *presidential election* (*we elect the president, *presidents elect someone*) and *presidential race* (**we race the president, the presidents race against each other*)).

[9] Silberztein (1990) presents the first electronic dictionary for compounds (French DELAC), designed to be used by automatic NLP software. The English DELAC is presented in Chrobot et al. (1999).

These 166,060 occurrences represent 25,277 different compound forms, which amounts to only 10% of the English vocabulary. Standard terms such as the following never occur in the *Slate* corpus:

abandoned ship, access path, administrative district, aerosol spray, after hours, agglutinative language, air bed, album jacket, ammunition belt, anchor box, appeal court, aqueous humor, arc welder, assault charge, attitude problem, auction sale, aviator's ear, awareness campaign, axe to grind, azo dye, etc.

Moreover, most compound words actually found in the *Slate* corpus do not occur in all their forms: some nouns only occur in their singular form, whereas others only occur in their plural form. For instance, there are no occurrence of the singular forms of the following nouns:

absentee voters, access codes, additional charges, affinity groups, AID patients, Alsatian wines, amusement arcades, ancient civilizations, appetite suppressants, armed extremists, assembly operations, attack helicopters, audio guides, average wages, ax-grinders, etc.

Even if encountering an occurrence of any inflected or derived form for a lexical entry would allow an automatic system to correctly parse all its other inflected and derived forms, the *Slate* corpus only covers 10% of the compounds of the vocabulary. I estimate that one would need to add over 32 million wordforms to the corpus to get a decent 1/2 coverage of the English compounds.[10]

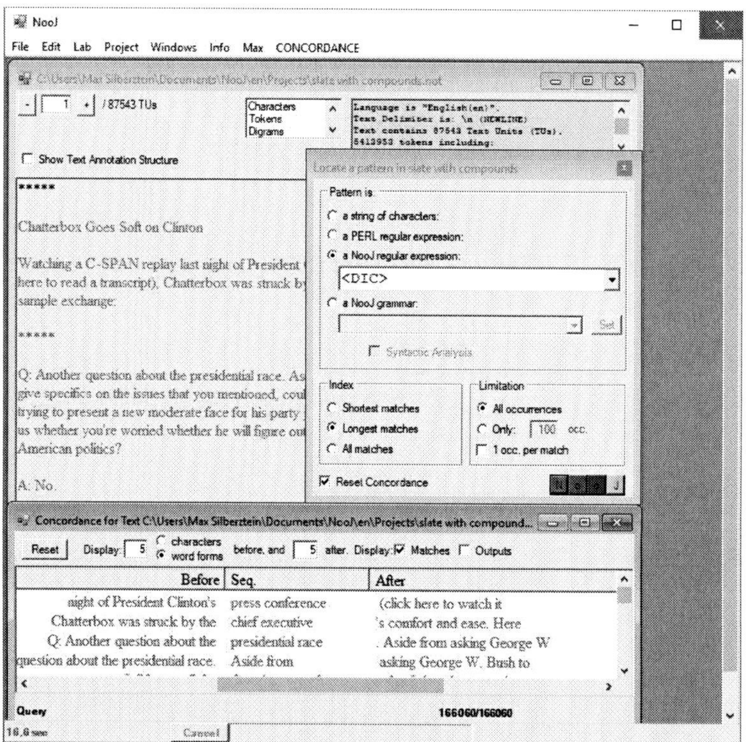

Figure 3. Compounds in the *Slate* corpus

2.4 Phrasal Verbs

Any precise NLP application must take into account all multiword units, even those that are discontinuous. Examples of discontinuous expressions include idiomatic expressions (e.g. *to read … the*

---

[10] 32 million wordforms to check, one second per check, 8-hours a day, 5-day a week, would take over 4 years. By contrast, it typically takes a year for a linguist to construct a DELAC-type dictionary.

riot act), verbs that have a frozen complement (e.g. *to take … into account*), phrasal verbs (e.g. *to turn … off*) and associations of predicative nouns and their corresponding support verb (e.g. *to take a (<E> | good | long | refreshing) shower*).

For this experiment, I applied NooJ's dictionary of phrasal verbs[11] to the *Slate* corpus. This dictionary contains 1,260 phrasal verbs, from *act out* (e.g. *Joe acted out the story*) to *zip up* (e.g. *Joe zipped up his jacket*). NooJ recognized over 12,000 occurrences[12] of verbal phrases, such as in:

… acting out their predictable roles in the…
… I would love to ask her out,…
… would have backed North Vietnam up…
… Warner still wanted to boss him around…
… We booted up and victory!…

However, less than 1/3 of the phrasal verbs described in the dictionary had one or more occurrences in the *Slate* corpus. For instance, phrasal verbs such as the following have no occurrence in the corpus: *argue down, bring about, cloud up, drag along, eye up, fasten up, goof up, hammer down*, etc.

3 Hapaxes

3.1 Wordforms and ALUs

In most applications that use statistical approaches (e.g. Economics, Medicine, Physics, etc.), hapaxes — i.e. statistical events that only occur once — are rightfully ignored as "accidents," as they behave like "noise," by polluting analysis results.

In linguistics, a hapax is a wordform that occurs only once in a reference corpus. There are reasons to ignore hapaxes during a text analysis since the unique syntactic context available cannot be used to make any reliable generalization. Following are examples of hapaxes that occur right after a verb in the OANC:

- an adjective, e.g. *… one cage is left* **unrattled***…*

- an adverb, e.g. … you touched **unerringly** on all the elements…

- a noun, e.g. that score still seemed **misogynous**…

- an organization name, e.g. the center caused **Medicare** to pay for hundreds…

- a person name, e.g. *Lewinsky told* **Jordan** *that…*

- a verbal form, e.g. the deal might **defang** last year's welfare reform…

- a foreign word, e.g. *they graduated* **magna** *cum laude…*
- or even a typo, e.g. *whipped mashed* **potatos** *and…*

It is only by taking into account multiple syntactic contexts for a wordform that one can hope to describe its behavior reliably. If a wordform in the text to be analyzed corresponds to a hapax in the reference corpus that occurs right after a verb, it would be very lucky if a statistical or neural-network based parser were tagging it correctly.

There are 31,275 different hapaxes in the *Slate* corpus, out of 88,945 different wordforms, i.e. a third of the vocabulary covered by the *Slate* corpus, which covers itself a sixth of the standard vocabulary. Consequently, statistical parsers that do not exclude hapaxes will produce unreliable results for up to one third of the wordforms present in the reference corpus' vocabulary.

---

[11] Peter Machonis is the author of the Lexicon-Grammar table for English Phrasal Verbs, which has been integrated into NooJ via a linked couple dictionary / grammar (Machonis, 2010).

[12] There are a few false-positives, i.e. phrasal verbs that were recognized but do not actually occur in the text, such as: *The Constitution grew out of a convention*; they represent less than 2% of the matches. Half of these errors could be avoided by using simple local grammars, such as giving priority to compounds (so that the recognition of the compound preposition *out of* would block the recognition of the phrasal verb *grew out* in the latter example).

7

3.2 Compound words

As we have seen previously, the OANC and the COCA (as most reference corpora) contain no special tags for compound words, which are nevertheless crucial for any precise NLP application. To automatically identify them, some researchers use statistical methods to try to locate colocations.[13] Their idea is that if, for instance, the two wordforms *nuclear* and *plant* occur together in a statistically meaningful way, one may deduce that the sequence *nuclear plant* corresponds to an English term. Even if one subscribes to this principle, statistical methods cannot deduce that a sequence of wordforms probably corresponds to a term if it occurs only once. In the *Slate* corpus, there are 9,007 compound words that only occur once, e.g.:

> *absent without leave, accident report, adhesive tape, after a fashion, age of reason, air support, alarm call, American plan, animal cracker, application process, artesian well, assault pistol, atomic power, automatic pilot, aversion therapy, away team, axe to grind*, etc.

If one removes these hapaxes from the list of compound words that occur in the corpus, the number of compound words that could theoretically be detected as co-locations is reduced to 25,277 − 9,007 = 16,270 occurrences, i.e. only 6% of the vocabulary.

Note that the colocation criterion does not really make any sense from a linguistic point of view. It is not because a sequence occurs often that it is necessarily an element of the English language vocabulary (e.g. the sequence *was in the* occurs 69 times), and reciprocally it is not because a sequence only occurs once in a corpus (e.g. *after a fashion*) that it is a lesser element of the English vocabulary. In the same manner that it would not make any sense to state that *alright* is not an element of English vocabulary because it only occurs once in the *Slate* corpus, it does not make sense to state that *artesian well* is not a term because it only occurs once in the same corpus.

3.3 Polysemy

To be reliable, statistical-based disambiguation techniques need to process units that are frequent enough. For example, in the *Slate* corpus, the wordform *that* is tagged 42,781 times as a subordinating conjunction (IN), out of 62,286 occurrences. It is then fair to predict that any of its occurrences has a 70% probability of being a subordinating conjunction.

However, if a corpus contains only one occurrence of a polysemous wordform, predicting its function in a new text can only produce unreliable results. For instance, the wordform *shrivelled* occurs only once in the *Slate* corpus:

> *... an orange that was, in Zercher's words, shrivelled and deformed...*

It has been correctly tagged as an adjective (JJ), but this is not a reason to deduce that this wordform will always function as an adjective, as one can see in sentence: *The lack of rain has shrivelled the crops.* In the *Slate* corpus, there are 2,285 wordforms that have two or more potential tags, but occur only once, e.g.:

> *aboveboard (adjective or adverb), accusative (adjective or noun), advert (noun or verb), aflame (adjective or adverb), agglomerate (adjective, noun or verb), airdrop (noun or verb), alright (adjective or adverb), amnesiac (adjective or noun), angora (adjective or noun), apologetics (singular or plural noun), aqueous, armour (noun or verb), astringent (adjective or noun), attic (adjective or noun), auburn (adjective or noun), Azerbaijani (adjective or noun)*, etc.

Any parser that processes these wordforms as monosemous (because they only occur once in the reference corpus) produces unreliable results.

---

13 See, for instance, the European PARSEME initiative `http://typo.uni-konstanz.de/parseme` and the program of the SIGLEX-MWE (Special Interest Group on Multiword Expressions) workshops
`http://multiword.sourceforge.net/PHITE.php?sitesig=MWE`.

4 Reliability

All statistical or neural-network based NLP applications that compare a reference corpus to the texts to analyze assume that the reference corpus can be relied upon: if the tags used to compute an analysis are incorrect, then one cannot expect these applications to produce perfect analyses. The fact that reference corpora contain errors is well known to NLP researchers.[14] Even though, I believe that the actual number of errors has been largely ignored or minimized.

The Open American National Corpus has been tagged by an enhanced version of GATE's ANNIE system,[15] using the Penn tag set. However, during this series of experiments, every superficial look at the *Slate* corpus[16] has uncovered mistakes. For instance, when looking at the form *that* in section 3.3., I found the following analyses for this wordform:

- 41,622 times as a subordinating conjunction (IN),

- 10,151 times as a Wh-determiner (WDT),

- 10,491 as a determiner (DT),

- 124 times as an adverb (RB).

All WDT (Wh-determiner) and RB (adverb) tags for the wordform *that* are incorrect: in fact, they correspond to pronoun uses of *that*. Here are a few examples of mistakes:

- Incorrect WDT: ... Publications that refuse to... phrase that describes this... stigma that came with...

- Incorrect RB: ... likes to boast that, ... to do just that, and delightfully ... know that, ...

Thus, at least 25% of the occurrences of the wordform *that* have been tagged incorrectly. There is a systematic confusion between Wh-determiners and pronouns (WDT instead of WP); occurrences of the wordform *that* that are followed by a period or a comma have been systematically tagged as adverbs. The "systematic" aspect of these mistakes in the corpus is unsettling, because it means that enlarging the corpus to 10 or even 100 million words will not enhance the usefulness of the statistical methods: there is no *really useful* information added to the corpus if it was added automatically. As a matter of fact, a superficial look at the full OANC corpus shows the same systematic mistakes as in the *Slate* sub-corpus, which suggests the use of automatic disambiguation rules.

If — as systematic mistakes imply — the tagger used automatic rules to disambiguate wordforms, it is essential that we are able to look at them, so that we can correct them. One may even argue that these automatic disambiguation rules could even be inserted directly in the final NLP application: in that case, the reference corpus becomes less and less useful.

To estimate the accuracy of the tags in the corpus, I have compiled a list of its 84,386 useful wordforms[17] associated with their tags, and parsed it with NooJ:

- Out of the 49,323 wordforms that were not tagged as proper names, 11,019 tags — i.e. over 20% — are considered as incorrect by NooJ. Examples of incorrect tags are:

> *abbreviate, abduct, abhor, abhors*, etc. (not nouns),
> *about, agonized, bible, cactus, California*, etc. (not adjectives)
> *expenditures, Japanese, many, initiatives, wimp*, etc. (not verbs)
> *anomaly, back, because, by, of, out, particular, upon*, etc. (not adverbs)

A number of derived or agglutinated forms have been tagged as ALUs, e.g.:

---

[14] See for instance Green and Manning (2010) about tagging errors in Arabic corpora, Kulick et al. (2011) and Volokh and Neumann (2011) about errors in tree-banks, and Dickinson (2015) about methods to detect the annotation errors.

[15] See `http://gate.ac.uk`.

[16] The Open American Corpus has been tagged

[17] Tags such as CD (Cardinal Number), LS (List item marker), POS (Possessive ending), SYM (symbol) and TO (to) are not useful in the sense that they do not add any information to the word they describe; they can be automatically added with simple SED-type replacements such as s/\([0-9]*\)/\1_CD/.

audienceless, autodialed, balancingly, bioremediation, barklike, etc.

However, there are good linguistic reasons to consider these wordforms to be analyzable sequences of two ALUs (i.e. two tags), in order to process prefixes such as *auto-, bio-* and suffixes such as *-less, -ly, -like* as ALUs themselves.

- Out of the 35,063 uppercase wordforms that have been associated with an Proper name (tagged NNP or NNPS), we also get a large number[18] of incorrect tags, e.g.:

Abacuses, Abandoned, ABATEMENT, Abattoir, Abbreviated, Ablaze,
Abnormal, Abolished, Abuse, Abstract, Accidental, ALMOST, etc.

The Penn tag set does not contain tags for typos: all uppercase typos were tagged as proper names (NNP or NNPS), e.g.: *Aconfession, Afew, AffairsThe, Allpolitics,* etc. Most other typos have been associated with a noun tag, e.g.:

absentionists (NNS), achives (NNS), accrossthe (NN), afteryou (NN), alwaysattend (NN), etc.

18,949 sequences that include the em dash[19] have been incorrectly processed as compound words, e.g. *aggression–that* (JJ), *believe–that* (JJ), *chance–a* (JJ), etc. Finally, one needs to mention that there are over 200 typos in the tags themselves, for instance:

a,DTn, believ_VBe, classi_JJc, di_VBDd, JFK-styl_NNPe, etc.

Adding the 10% irrelevant tags (e.g. "as_IN" in "as a matter of fact") to the 20% incorrectly tagged sequences that include a hyphen or an em dash (e.g. "minister—an_JJ") , to the 20% impossible tags (e.g. "many_VB"), as well as the typos, makes the *Slate* corpus unreliable at best.

5   Granularity of the linguistic information

Dictionaries for NLP applications actually need to associate their lexical entries with more information than just their part of speech. Nouns need to be classified in the very least as Human, Concrete or Abstract, because there are syntactic and semantic rules that do not apply in the same way to human, concrete or abstract noun phrases. Verbs need to be associated with a description of their subjects, prepositions and complements. For instance, in order to analyze correctly the following sentence:

The classroom burst into laughter

a computer program needs to know that the (compound) verb *to burst into laughter* expects a human subject, that *classroom* is not a human subject, and therefore it needs to activate a special analysis (e.g. metonymy) to process (e.g. index/link/translate/etc.) it.

In the previous evaluations, I counted wordforms as if each were representing all its corresponding ALUs: for instance, when the wordform *agent* occurs in the corpus, I counted it as if it represented two lexical entries: the person (in *a secret agent*), and the product (in *a bleaching agent*). But when parsing a text, NooJ produces over 2 potential analyses for each wordform in average. In consequence, if we were to take this linguistic information into account by enriching the tag set (e.g. add a +Human or +NonHuman feature for nouns, add a +Transitive or +Intransitive feature for verbs, distinguish between multiple meanings of each lexical entry, etc.), the coverage of the corpus would be half of our previous estimate.

---

[18] It is not possible to know if an uppercase word is or is not a proper name without a syntactic analysis of its context. For instance, "Black", "Carpenter", "Hope", etc. are common words as well as proper names, depending on their context. That said, by scanning over the list of the words tagged as proper names, I estimate that e at least 15% of them are mistakes.

[19] The em dash is represented by two consecutive dash characters in the OANC *Slate* corpus.

6   Conclusion and proposals

On the one hand, a large number of NLP applications rely on reference corpora to perform sophisticated analyses, such as intelligent search engines, automatic abstracts, information extraction, machine translation, etc. On the other hand, linguists have spent years carefully handcrafting a large quantity of linguistic resources. Using these resources could enhance reference corpora significantly:

- a first operation would be to compare the set of tagged wordforms in the reference corpus with the lexical entries in an English dictionary such as the DELAS; this operation would allow one to correct typos as well as "impossible" tags (e.g. *many* should never be tagged as a verb);

- a second operation would be to tag compound words (e.g. *as a matter of fact*) and discontinuous expressions (e.g. *ask … out*) already listed and described in dictionaries, as processing these linguistic units as a whole is crucial for any precise NLP application;

- a third operation would be to develop a set of simple local grammars to correct tags in the text that are not compatible with the English grammar (e.g. *that* should not be tagged as a Wh-determiner in *phrase that describes this*). These local grammars could even replace the meaningless algorithms (e.g. *that* before a comma tagged as an adverb) used to tag the reference corpus;

- a fourth, more ambitious project would be to enhance the tag set in order to distinguish human, concrete and abstract nouns, as well as to classify verbs according to their complements. That would allow sophisticated NLP applications such as Information Extraction and MT software to be trained on a semantic-rich tagged corpus.

References

Agata Chrobot, Blandine Courtois, Marie Hamani, Maurice Gross, Katia Zellagui. 1999. *Dictionnaire Electronique DELAC anglais : noms composés*. Technical Report #59, LADL, Université Paris 7: Paris, France.

Blandine Courtois and Max Silberztein (editors). 1990. *Les dictionnaires électroniques du français*. Larousse: Paris, France.

Markus Dickinson. 2015. Detection of Annotation Errors in Corpora. In *Language & Linguistics Compass*, vol 9, Issue 3. Wiley Online Library, https://doi.org/10.1111/lnc3.12129.

Spence Green and Christopher Manning. 2010. Better Arabic parsing: Baselines, evaluations, and analysis. In *Proceedings of the 23rd International Confeence on Computational Linguistics* (COLING), pages 394-402.

Gaby Klarsfeld. 1991. *Dictionnaire morphologique de l'anglais*. Technical Report, LADL, Université Paris 7: Paris, France.

Seth Kulick, Ann Bies, Justin Mott. 2011. Further Developments in Treebank Error Detection Using Derivation Trees. In *Proceedings of the 49th Annual Meeting of the Association for Computational Linguistics: Human Language Technologies*, Association for Computational Linguistics, pages 693–698, Portland, Oregon, USA.

Peter Machonis. 2010. English Phrasal Verbs: from Lexicon-Grammar to Natural Language Processing. *Southern Journal of Linguistics*, vol. 34, n01: 21-48.

Max Silberztein. 2003. *The NooJ Manual*. Available for download at www.nooj-association.org.

Max Silberztein. 1990. Le dictionnaire électronique DELAC. In Les dictionnaires électroniques du français. Larousse: Paris, France.

Max Silberztein. 2016. *Formalizing Natural Languages: the NooJ Approach*. Cognitive Science Series. Wiley-ISTE: London, UK.

Alexander Volokh, Günter Neumann. 2011. Automatic detection and correction of errors in dependency tree-banks. In *Proceedings of the 49th Annual Meeting of the Association for Computational Linguistics: Human Language Technology*: short papers, vol. 2, pages 346-350.

Rule-based vs. Neural Net Approach to
Semantic Textual Similarity

Linrui Zhang
The University of Texas at Dallas
800 West Campbell Road; MS EC31,
Richardson, TX 75080 U.S.A
Linrui.zhang@utdallas.edu

Dan Moldovan
The University of Texas at Dallas
800 West Campbell Road; MS EC31,
Richardson, TX 75080 U.S.A
moldovan@hlt.utdallas.edu

Abstract

This paper presents a neural net approach to determine Semantic Textual Similarity (STS) using attention-based bidirectional Long Short-Term Memory Networks (Bi-LSTM). To this date, most of the traditional STS systems were rule-based that built on top of excessive use of linguistic features and resources. In this paper, we present an end-to-end attention-based Bi-LSTM neural network system that solely takes word-level features, without expensive, feature engineering work or the usage of external resources. By comparing its performance with traditional rule-based systems against the SemEval 2012 benchmark, we make an assessment on the limitations and strengths of neural net systems as opposed to rule-based systems on STS.

1 Introduction

Semantic Textual Similarity (STS) is the task of determining the resemblance of the meanings between two sentences (Agirre et al., 2012; Agirre et al., 2013; Agirre et al., 2014; Agirre et al., 2015; Agirre et al., 2016; Cer et al., 2017). For the sentence pairs below, on a scale from 0 to 5, (1) is very similar [5.0], (2) is somewhat similar [3.0] and (3) is not similar [0.2]:

1. Someone is removing the scales from the fish.

   A person is descaling a fish.

2. A woman is chopping an herb.

   A man is finely chopping a green substance.

3. The woman is smoking.

   The man is walking.

In STS tasks, the performance of traditional models relies highly on the usage of linguistic resources and hand-crafted features. For example, in SemEval 2012 Task 06: A Pilot on Semantic Textual Similarity (Agirre et al., 2012), the top three performers (Šarić et al., 2012; Bär et al., 2012; Banea et al., 2012) all derived knowledge from WordNet, Wikipedia and other large corpora. In particular, Banea et al. built the models from 6 million Wikipedia articles and more than 9.5 million hyperlinks; Bär et al. used Wiktionary, which contains over 3 million entries; and Šarić et al. used The New York Times Annotated Corpus that contains over 1.8 million news articles. Blanco and Moldovan (2013) proposed a model with semantic representation of sentences, which was considered to use the smallest external resources and features in 2015. However, their model still required WordNet with approximately 120,000 synsets and a semantic parser.

Complex neural network architectures are being increasingly used for learning to compute the semantic resemblances among natural language texts. To this date, there are two end-to-end neural network models proposed for STS tasks (Shao, 2017; Prijatelj et al., 2017), and both of them followed a standard sentence pair modeling neural network architecture that contains three components: a word embedding

Proceedings of the First Workshop on Linguistic Resources for Natural Language Processing, pages 12–17
Santa Fe, New Mexico, USA, August 20, 2018.

component that transforms words into word vectors, a sentence embedding component that takes word vectors as input and encodes the sentence into a single vector that represents the semantic meanings of the original sentence, and a comparator component that evaluates the similarity between sentence vectors and generates a similarity score.

In this paper, we modified and improved the modals proposed by Prijatelj et al. (2017) and Shao (2017), and proposed a Bi-LSTM neural network model as the representative of the neural net approach and evaluated it on the SemEval 2012 dataset. In the experimental section, we compared our system with the top three performers in SemEval 2012 using traditional rule-based models. Because neither Shao nor Prijatelj et al. considered attention mechanisms (Yang et al., 2016) in their systems, we specifically applied attention mechanisms to improve the performance of our system.

The goal of the paper is to illustrate that with well-designed neural network models, we can achieve competitive results (compared to traditional rule-based models) without expensive feature engineering work and external resources. We also make an assessment on the limitations of neural net systems as opposed to rule-based systems on STS.

2   Related Work

Determining textual similarity is relatively new as a stand-alone task since SemEval-2012, but it is often a component of NLP applications such as information retrieval, paraphrase recognition, grading answers to questions and many other tasks. In this section, we only list the works that are involved in our evaluation systems: the top performers in SemEval 2012 and recent neural network-based approaches in SemEval 2017.

The performance of the rule-based models (Šarić et al., 2012; Bär et al., 2012; Banea et al., 2012) mostly rely on word pairings and knowledge derived from large corpora, e.g., Wikipedia. Regardless of details, each word in $sent_1$ is paired with the word in $sent_2$ that is most similar according to some similarity measure. Then, all similarities are added and normalized by the length of $sent_1$ to obtain the similarity score from $sent_1$ to $sent_2$. The process is repeated to obtain the similarity score from $sent_2$ to $sent_1$, and both scores are then averaged to determine the overall textual similarity. Several word to word similarity measures are often combined with other shallow features (e.g. n-gram overlap, syntactic dependencies) to obtain the final similarity score.

Shao (2017) proposed a simple convolutional neural network (CNN) models for STS. He used a CNN as the sentence embedding component to encode the original sentences into sentence-level vectors and generated a semantic difference vector by concatenating the element-wise absolute difference and the element-wise multiplication of the corresponding sentence vectors. He then passed the semantic difference vector into a fully connected neural network to perform regression to generate the similarity score on a continuous inclusive scale from 0 to 5. His model ranked 3rd on the primary track of SemEval 2017.

Prijatelj et al. (2017) wrote a survey on neural networks for semantic textual similarity. The framework of their model is similar to Shao's, but they explored various neural network architectures, from simple to complex, and reported the results of applying the combination of these neural network models within this framework.

3   System Description

Figure 1 provides an overview of our neural network-based model. The sentence pairs first pass through a pre-processing step described in subsection 3.1 to generate word embeddings. The attention-based Bi-LSTM models transform the word embeddings into sentence-level vectors described in subsection 3.2. In subsection 3.3, we use the same semantic difference vector as Shao to represent the semantic difference between the sentence-level vectors. Lastly, we pass the semantic difference vector into fully connected neural networks to generate the similarity score between the original sentence pairs.

3.1   Pre-processing

We first applied a simple NLP pipeline to the input sentences to tokenize them, remove punctuations and lower-case all the tokens. Second, we looked up the word embeddings from the pretrained 50-dimension GloVe vectors, and set non-existing words to zero vector. Third, we enhanced the word embeddings by adding a true/false (1/0) flag to them if the corresponding word appears in both sentences. Lastly, we unified the length of the inputs by padding the sentences.

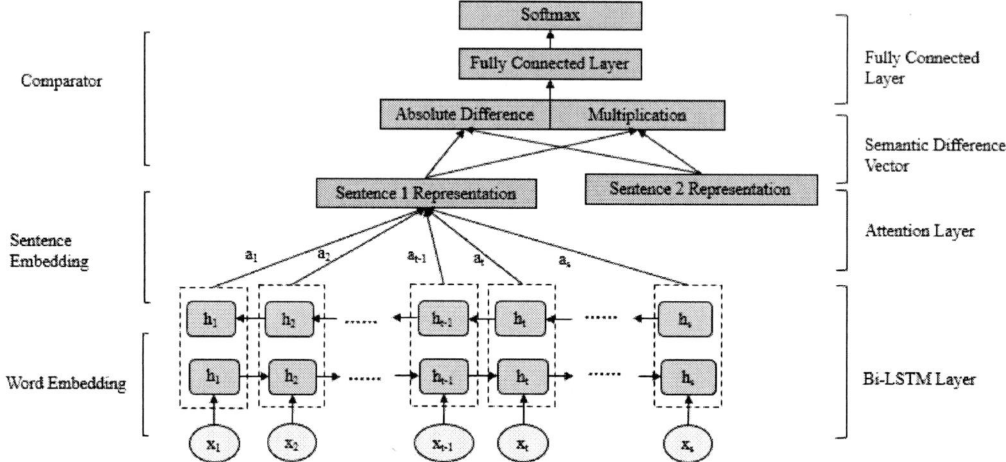

Figure 1: The structure of attention-based Bi-LSTM network for Semantic Textual Similarity.

3.2 Attention-based LSTM

Since sentences are sequences of words, and the order of the words matters, it is natural to use LSTMs (Hochreiter and Schmidhuber, 1997) to encode sentences into vectors. However, sometimes the backward sequence contains useful information as well, especially for long and unstructured sentences. Because of this, Irsoy and Cardie (2014) proposed Deep Bidirectional RNNs that can make predictions based on future words by having the RNN model read through the sentence backwards. In this section, we will first introduce a regular LSTM network and then extend it into a Bi-LSTM. At the end of this section, we will apply attention mechanisms to improve the performance of the system.

The traditional LSTM unit is defined by 5 components: an input gate, a forget gate, an output gate, a new memory generation cell and a final memory cell.

The input gate is to decide if the input x_t is worth being preserved based on the input word x_t and the past hidden state h_{t-1}.

$$i_t = \sigma(W^{(i)}x_t + U^{(i)}h_{t-1}) \tag{1}$$

The forget gate f_t makes an assessment on whether the past memory cell is useful to compute the current memory cell.

$$f_t = \sigma(w^{(f)}x_t + U^{(f)}h_{t-1}) \tag{2}$$

The output gate is to separate the final memory c_t from the hidden state h_t.

$$o_t = \sigma(W^{(o)}x_t + U^{(o)}h_{t-1}) \tag{3}$$

The new memory generation cell is used to generate a new memory $\tilde{c}_t$ by input work x_t and the past hidden state h_{t-1}.

$$\tilde{c}_t = \tanh(W^{(c)}x_t + U^{(c)}h_{t-1}) \tag{4}$$

The final memory cell produces the final memory c_t by summing the advice of the forget gate f_t and input gate i_t.

$$c_t = f_t \cdot c_{t-1} + i_t \cdot \tilde{c}_t \tag{5}$$

14

$$h_t = o_t \cdot tanh(c_t) \tag{6}$$

A Bi-LSTM could be viewed as a network that maintains two hidden LSTM layers together, at each time-step t, one for the forward propagation and another for the backward propagation. The final classification results are generated through the combination of the score results produced by both hidden layers. The mathematical representation of a simplified Bi-LSTM is shown as follows:

$$\vec{h}_t = f(\vec{W}x_t + \vec{V}\vec{h}_{t-1} + \vec{b}) \tag{7}$$

$$\overleftarrow{h}_t = f(\overleftarrow{W}x_t + \overleftarrow{V}\overleftarrow{h}_{t-1} + \overleftarrow{b}) \tag{8}$$

$$\hat{y}_t = g(Uh_t + c) = g(U[\vec{h}_{t-1}; \overleftarrow{h}_{t-1}] + c) \tag{9}$$

where $\hat{y}_t$ is the final predication. The symbols $\rightarrow$ and $\leftarrow$ are indicating directions. The rest of the terms are defined the same as in regular LSTM neural networks. W, U are weight matrices that are associated with input x_t and hidden states h_t. U is used to combine the two hidden LSTM layers together, b and c are bias term. $g(x)$ and $f(x)$ are activation functions.

Not all words contribute equally to the representation of the sentence meaning; thus, we extract words that are more informative to the sentence and aggregate these words to the sentence-level vector by applying the attention mechanism. Specifically:

First, we feed the hidden state h_t through a one-layer MLP to get u_t, and u_t could be viewed as a hidden representation of h_t.

$$u_t = tanh(Wh_t + b) \tag{10}$$

Second, we multiply u_t with a context vector u_w, and normalized the results through a softmax function to get the importance weight a_t of each hidden state h_t. The context vector could be seen as a high-level vector to select informative word in the sentence (Sukhbaatar et al., 2015) and it will be jointly learned during the training process.

$$a_t = \frac{exp(u_t^T u_w)}{\sum_t exp(u_t^T u_w)} \tag{11}$$

Lastly, the final state S is a sum over of the hidden states and its the importance weights.

$$S = \sum_t a_t h_t \tag{12}$$

3.3   Semantic Difference of Sentences

We used the same semantic difference vector as Shao, by concatenating the element-wise absolute difference and the element-wise multiplication of the corresponding sentence-level embedding pairs.

The generated semantic difference vector is passed through a two-layer fully connected neural networks with a softmax function as the output layer and generated a probabilistic distribution over the six similarity labels used in the SemEval 2012 task. We multiplied it with a constant matrix with integers from 0 to 5 to transfer the probabilistic distribution into a float number as the final semantic similarity score between the original sentence pairs.

4   Experiment

4.1   Corpus

We evaluated our system on the corpora used in SemEval 2012 Task 06: A Pilot on Semantic Textual Similarity. It contains five corpora: (1) MSRvid, short sentences for video descriptions; (2) MSRpar, long sentences of paraphrases; (3) SMTeuroparl, output of machine translation systems and reference translations; (4) OnWN, OntoNotes and WordNet glosses; and (5) SMTnews, output of machine translation systems in the news domain and gold translations. In corpus (1) to (3), both training and testing data are provided, and corpus (4) and (5) are surprise data (new domain data) and only testing data are provided. For more details about the corpus, please refer to Agirre et al. (2012).

We followed the training and testing splits of the original corpus. Since corpus (4) and (5) do not have corresponding training data, we used the training data of corpus (2) as the training data for corpus (4) since both corpus contains long and hard to parse sentences, and we used the training data of corpus (3) as the training data for corpus (5), since both corpus contains ungrammatical sentences.

4.2   Experiment Results

We used the Pearson correlation coefficient to evaluate the performance. We introduced two neural network models: a regular LSTM model and a Bi-LSTM model and, for each model, we also demonstrated their performance with attention mechanisms. Table 1 shows the results of the neural network-based systems and the traditional rule-based systems on in-domain data (corpus 1 to 3) and out-of-domain data (corpus 4 and 5).

System		MSRvid	MSRpar	SMTeuroparl	OnWN	SMTnews
LSTM	Basic	0.7774	0.5278	0.2787	0.4519	0.2071
	+attention	0.7851	0.5891	0.3492	0.4773	0.2635
Bi-LSTM	Basic	0.7661	0.5258	0.3993	0.4591	0.3298
	+attention	0.7762	0.6210	0.4368	0.5607	0.3976
Bär et al., 2012		0.8739	0.6830	0.5280	0.6641	0.4937
Šarić et al., 2012		0.8620	0.6985	0.3612	0.7049	0.4683
Banea et al., 2012		0.8750	0.5353	0.4203	0.6715	0.4033

Table 1: The Person correlation coefficient of our system and the top three performers in SemEval 2012 benchmark.

4.3   Results Analysis

From the results, we could observe that: (1) The overall performance of the rule-based model is still slightly better than the neural network-based approach. However, we must note that the neural network models are end-to-end models that do not use complicated linguistic features and resources. (2) The neural network-based approaches are better at handling long sentences, whereas the rule-based systems are good at handling short sentences. The reason is that the performance of the traditional rule-based models greatly relies on the extraction of features, however, long sentences are usually hard to parse. The errors that occur in the feature extraction step will propagate until the end and decrease the performance of the system. Whereas the neural network models only take word-level features and do end-to-end training, so they do not have this "error propagation" issue. Besides, since we add attention mechanisms, the system could aggregate the influence of the informative words and ignore the unimportant words in long sentences. From the results we observe that our system beats the third-ranked performer on the MSRpar corpus, and the second- and third-ranked performers on the SMTeuroparl corpus, which contains mainly long sentences. (3) The regular LSTM model performs poorly on the SMTeuroparl corpus, but the Bi-LSTM dramatically increases the performance (ranking just after the top performer with rule-based systems). The reason is that in the SMTeuroparl corpus, one sentence in the sentence pair is usually ungrammatical. Regular LSTM can only capture the forward sequential information of sentences, so it will miss some information if the sentences are unstructured. However, the Bi-LSTM model can compensate for this missing information by capturing the backward sequential information as well, and this makes the system more robust when handling ungrammatical sentences. (4) The traditional rule-based models show a huge advantage over neural network-based models on new domain datasets. The reason is that the neural-network models are supervised models that mostly depend on the training data, and when transferred to new domains lacking training data, the performance of the system drops dramatically. On the other hand, rule-based systems rely mostly on word pairings and linguistic resources that are not as dependent on training data.

References

Eneko Agirre, Mona Diab, Daniel Cer, and Aitor Gonzalez-Agirre. 2012. Semeval-2012 task 6: A pilot on semantic textual similarity. In Proceedings of the First Joint Conference on Lexical and Computational Semantics Volume

1: *Proceedings of the main conference and the shared task, and Volume 2: Proceedings of the Sixth International Workshop on Semantic Evaluation*, pages 385–393. Association for Computational Linguistics.

Eneko Agirre, Daniel Cer, Mona Diab, Aitor Gonzalez-Agirre, and Weiwei Guo. 2013. * sem 2013 shared task: Semantic textual similarity. In Second Joint Conference on Lexical and Computational Semantics (* SEM), Volume 1: *Proceedings of the Main Conference and the Shared Task: Semantic Textual Similarity*, volume 1, pages 32–43.

Eneko Agirre, Carmen Banea, Claire Cardie, Daniel Cer, Mona Diab, Aitor Gonzalez-Agirre, Weiwei Guo, Rada Mihalcea, German Rigau, and Janyce Wiebe. 2014. Semeval-2014 task 10: Multilingual semantic textual similarity. In *Proceedings of the 8th international workshop on semantic evaluation (SemEval 2014)*, pages 81–91.

Eneko Agirre, Carmen Banea, Claire Cardie, Daniel Cer, Mona Diab, Aitor Gonzalez-Agirre, Weiwei Guo, Inigo Lopez-Gazpio, Montse Maritxalar, Rada Mihalcea, et al. 2015. Semeval-2015 task 2: Semantic textual similarity, english, spanish and pilot on interpretability. In *Proceedings of the 9th international workshop on semantic evaluation (SemEval 2015)*, pages 252–263.

Eneko Agirre, Carmen Banea, Daniel Cer, Mona Diab, Aitor Gonzalez-Agirre, Rada Mihalcea, German Rigau, and Janyce Wiebe. 2016. Semeval-2016 task 1: Semantic textual similarity, monolingual and cross-lingual evaluation. In *Proceedings of the 10th International Workshop on Semantic Evaluation (SemEval-2016)*, pages 497–511.

Carmen Banea, Samer Hassan, Michael Mohler, and Rada Mihalcea. 2012. Unt: A supervised synergistic approach to semantic text similarity. In *Proceedings of the First Joint Conference on Lexical and Computational Semantics-Volume 1: Proceedings of the main conference and the shared task, and Volume 2: Proceedings of the Sixth International Workshop on Semantic Evaluation*, pages 635–642. Association for Computational Linguistics.

Daniel Bär, Chris Biemann, Iryna Gurevych, and Torsten Zesch. 2012. Ukp: Computing semantic textual similarity by combining multiple content similarity measures. In *Proceedings of the First Joint Conference on Lexical and Computational Semantics-Volume 1: Proceedings of the main conference and the shared task, and Volume 2: Proceedings of the Sixth International Workshop on Semantic Evaluation*, pages 435–440. Association for Computational Linguistics.

Eduardo Blanco and Dan Moldovan. 2013. A semantically enhanced approach to determine textual similarity. In *Proceedings of the 2013 Conference on Empirical Methods in Natural Language Processing*, pages 1235–1245.

Daniel Cer, Mona Diab, Eneko Agirre, Inigo Lopez-Gazpio, and Lucia Specia. 2017. Semeval-2017 task 1: Semantic textual similarity-multilingual and cross-lingual focused evaluation. *arXiv preprint* arXiv:1708.00055.

Sepp Hochreiter and Jurgen Schmidhuber. 1997. Long short-term memory. *Neural computation*, 9(8):1735–1780.

Ozan Irsoy and Claire Cardie. 2014. Opinion mining with deep recurrent neural networks. In *Proceedings of the 2014 conference on empirical methods in natural language processing (EMNLP)*, pages 720–728.

Derek S Prijatelj, Jonathan Ventura, and Jugal Kalita. 2017. Neural networks for semantic textual similarity. In *Proceedings of the 14th International Conference on Natural Language Processing*, pages 456-465.

Frane Šarić, Goran Glavaš, Mladen Karan, Jan Šnajder, and Bojana Dalbelo Bašić. 2012. Takelab: Systems for measuring semantic text similarity. In *Proceedings of the First Joint Conference on Lexical and Computational Semantics-Volume 1: Proceedings of the main conference and the shared task, and Volume 2: Proceedings of the Sixth International Workshop on Semantic Evaluation*, pages 441–448. Association for Computational Linguistics.

Yang Shao. 2017. Hcti at semeval-2017 task 1: Use convolutional neural network to evaluate semantic textual similarity. In *Proceedings of the 11th International Workshop on Semantic Evaluation (SemEval-2017)*, pages 130–133.

Sainbayar Sukhbaatar, Arthur Szlam, Jason Weston, and Rob Fergus. 2015. End-to-end memory networks. In *Advances in neural information processing systems*, Montréal, Canada, pages 2440–2448.

Zichao Yang, Diyi Yang, Chris Dyer, Xiaodong He, Alex Smola, and Eduard Hovy. 2016. Hierarchical attention networks for document classification. *In Proceedings of the 2016 Conference of the North American Chapter of the Association for Computational Linguistics: Human Language Technologies,* pages 1480–1489.

Linguistic Resources for Phrasal Verb Identification

Peter A. Machonis
Florida International University
Dept. of Modern Languages
11200 SW 8th Street
Miami, FL 33199 USA
machonis@fiu.edu

Abstract

This paper shows how a lexicon grammar dictionary of English phrasal verbs (PV) can be transformed into an electronic dictionary, in order to accurately identify PV in large corpora within the linguistic development environment, NooJ. The NooJ program is an alternative to statistical methods commonly used in NLP: all PV are listed in a dictionary and then located by means of a PV grammar in both continuous and discontinuous format. Results are then refined with a series of dictionaries, disambiguating grammars, filters, and other linguistics resources. The main advantage of such a program is that all PV can be identified in any corpus. The only drawback is that PV not listed in the dictionary (e.g., archaic forms, recent neologisms) are not identified; however, new PV can easily be added to the electronic dictionary, which is freely available to all.

1   Introduction

Although described as early as the 1700's, English phrasal verbs (PV) or verb-particle combinations, such as *figure out, look up, turn on*, etc. have long been considered a characteristic trait of the English language and are to this day one of the most difficult features of English to master for non-native speakers. PV began attracting the attention of linguists in the early 1900's with Kennedy's (1920) classic study. Many have reiterated his historical analysis, such as Konishi (1958:122), who also finds a steady growth of these combinations after Old English, a slight drop during the Age of Reason – with authors such as Dryden and Johnson who avoided such "grammatical irregularities" – followed by a new expansion in the 19th century.

A renewal of interest in PV arose in the 1970's, with the works of Bolinger (1971:xi), who associated PV with a "creativeness that surpasses anything else in our language" and Fraser (1976), who first presented detailed descriptions of PV transformations. In particular, he studied constraints on particle position. Although many PV allow movement (*figure out the answer, figure the answer out*), if the direct object is a pronoun, it can only appear before the particle (*figure it out, *figure out it*). Fraser (1976:19) also showed that some PV idioms prohibit particle movement (e.g., *dance up a storm, *dance a storm up*) whereas others permit movement (e.g., *turn back the clock* or *turn the clock back*).

More recently, Hampe (2002), in her corpus-based study of semantic redundancy in English, suggests that compositional PV can function as an "index of emotional involvement of the speaker," and today, linguists and computer scientists debate the status of compositional vs. idiomatic PV. Whereas idiomatic PV, such *break up the audience* "cause to laugh" or *burn out the teacher* "exhaust," cannot be derived from the meaning of the verb plus particle and must be clearly listed in the lexicon, compositional PV, such as *drink up the milk* or *boot up the computer*, can be derived from the meaning of the regular verb. In this case, the particle simply functions as an intensifier (e.g., *rev up the engine*), aspect marker (e.g., *lock up the car*), or an adverbial noting direction (e.g., *drive up prices*). Although these are strong arguments in favor of separating compositional from idiomatic PV, Machonis (2009) suggests a disadvantage of treating compositional PV separately from frozen ones in that simple verb entries can become enormously complex when all English particles – Fraser (1976) lists fifteen different particles – are taken into account.

Proceedings of the First Workshop on Linguistic Resources for Natural Language Processing, pages 18–27
Santa Fe, New Mexico, USA, August 20, 2018.

PV present one of the thorniest problems for Natural Language Processing; in fact, Sag et al. (2002: 14) state multiword expressions "constitute a key problem that must be resolved in order for linguistically precise NLP to succeed." This paper shows how a lexicon grammar dictionary can be transformed into an electronic dictionary, in order to correctly identify PV, both continuous and discontinuous, in large corpora, using multiple algorithms and filters within the linguistic development environment, NooJ (Silberztein, 2016).

2 Using NooJ for Automatic PV Recognition

2.1 Previous Work

Previous studies using NooJ (Machonis, 2010; 2012; 2016), showed that the automatic recognition of PV proved to be far more complex than for other multiword expressions due to three main factors: (1) their possible discontinuous nature (e.g., *let out the dogs* ⇔ *let the dogs out*), (2) their confusion with verbs followed by simple prepositions (e.g., *Do you remember what I asked you in Rome?* (verb + prepositional phrase) vs. *Did you ask the prince in when he arrived?* (PV)), and (3) genuine ambiguity only resolvable from context (e.g., *Her neighbor was looking over the broken fence*, which can mean either "looking above the fence" (preposition) or "examining the fence" (PV)). Even with disambiguating grammars, adverbial and adjectival expression filters, and idiom dictionaries, our previous PV studies using NooJ achieved only 88% precision with written texts and 78% precision with an oral corpus, with most of the noise coming from the particles *in* and *on*, which are fairly tricky to distinguish automatically from prepositions (e.g. *had a strange smile on her thin lips* vs. *had her hat and jacket on*), even with the disambiguation grammars, filters, and extra dictionaries mentioned above.

2.2 Using Lexicon Grammar Tables in Tandem with NooJ

The NooJ platform is a freeware linguistic development environment that can be downloaded from http://www.nooj4nlp.net/, which allows linguists to describe several levels of linguistic phenomena and then apply formalized descriptions to any corpus of texts. Instead of relying on a part of speech tagger that obligatorily produces a certain percentage of tagging mistakes, NooJ uses a Text Annotation Structure (TAS) that holds all unsolved ambiguities. Furthermore, these annotations, as opposed to tags, can represent discontinuous linguistic units, such as PV (Silberztein, 2016).

Lexicon grammar (Gross, 1994; 1996) accentuates the reproducibility of linguistic data in the form of exhaustive tables or matrices, which contain both lexical and syntactic information. For example, each verb in a table would be discussed by a team of linguists and marked as plus (+) or minus (-) for all possible complements and relevant transformations. This descriptive approach to syntax showed the enormous complexity of language and challenged the Chomskian model (Gross, 1979).

Our original PV tables included 700 entries of transitive and neutral PV[1] with the particle *up*, 200 with *out*, and 300 entries with other particles, such as *away, back, down, in, off, on, over* (300 entries). These tables are manually constructed and a sample is given in Table 1. The first two columns represent potential subjects, N_0, which can be human, non-human, or both. This is followed by the verb, the particle, and an example of a direct object, N_1. The direct object is also classified as human, non-human, or both, although only one example is given. The next column, $N_0\,V\,N_1$, takes into consideration cases where the verb can have a similar meaning, even if the particle is not used. A plus indicates that the PV can be used without the particle: e.g., *The chef beat up the eggs* ⇔ *The chef beat the eggs*. These would be considered compositional PV, since the verb keeps its regular meaning, but the particle is merely viewed as an intensifier or aspect marker, as explained in the introduction. The next column, $N_1\,V\,Part$, identifies neutral verbs, with a plus in that column indicating that the verb has both a transitive and intransitive linked use: e.g., *She booted up the computer* ⇔ *The computer booted up*. Finally, a plus in the $N_1\,V$ column signifies that the verb can be neutral, even if the particle is not expressed: e.g., *The building blew, The water boiled, The computer booted*. The last column gives a synonym for the PV. Note that different meanings of the same PV (e.g., *beat up, blow up, bolster up*) necessitate different values in the lexicon grammar.

---

[1] Transitive PV take a direct object and have no intransitive: e.g., *The bully beat up the child*, but not **The bully beat up* nor **The child beat up*. Neutral PV (also referred to as ergative PV) take a direct object, which could also function as the subject: e.g., *The terrorists blew up the building* ⇔ *The building blew up*). For more information on neutral or ergative verbs within a lexicon grammar framework, see Machonis (1997).

Z_0 = N : Nhum	Z_0 = N : N-hum	Verb	Particle	Example of N_1	Z_1 = N : Nhum	Z_1 = N : N-hum	N_0 V N_1	N_1 V Part	N_1 V	Synonym
+	+	beam	up	the aliens	+	+	-	+	-	transport by energy
+	+	bear	up	the weight	+	+	+	-	-	support
+	+	beat	up	the door	-	+	-	-	-	damage
+	+	beat	up	the eggs	-	+	+	-	-	beat
+	-	beat	up	the child	+	-	+	-	-	attack physically & hurt
+	+	beef	up	the proposal	-	+	-	-	-	strengthen
+	+	bend	up	the credit card	-	+	+	-	-	bend completely
+	-	bind	up	the wound	+	+	+	-	-	put bandage on
+	+	block	up	the sink	-	+	+	+	-	obstruct
+	+	blow	up	the balloons	-	+	-	-	-	inflate
+	+	blow	up	the building	+	+	-	+	+	explode
+	+	blow	up	the photo	-	+	-	-	-	enlarge
+	+	blow	up	the scandal	-	+	-	+	-	exaggerate
+	-	boil	up	some water	-	+	+	-	+	boil
+	+	bolster	up	Max	+	+	+	-	-	give hope to
+	+	bolster	up	the theory	-	+	-	-	-	support
+	+	boot	up	the computer	-	+	+	+	+	start

Table 1: Sample Lexicon Grammar Table: Phrasal Verbs with the Particle *up*

Figure 1 below is a sample of the NooJ PV Dictionary, which mirrors all of the syntactic information contained within the highlighted area of the lexicon grammar entry in Table 1 above. As can be seen, there is also a French translation of the English PV in the NooJ dictionary. The NooJ PV Grammar in Figure 2 works in tandem with this dictionary to annotate PV in large corpora. The bottom portion of the graph represents the path for continuous PV, while the top portion of the graph represents the path for identifying discontinuous PV, i.e., with a noun phrase and optional adverb inserted between the verb and the particle. The noun phrase has an embedded NP structure, which is explained further in 3.1. Most importantly, the PV grammar uses the NooJ functionality *$THIS=$V$Part*, which assures that a particular particle must be associated with a specific verb in the PV dictionary in order for it to be recognized as a PV. That is, NooJ only recognizes verb-particle combinations listed in the PV dictionary, not simply any verb that can be part of a PV followed by any particle.

NooJ Community Edition   — □ ✕

File   Edit   Lab   Project   Windows   Info   DICTIONARY

Entry	S-Lemma	C..	FLX	FR	N1example	Part	synonym	SynSem
beef	beef	V	ASK	renf...	the proposal	up	strengthen	PV+FXC+N0Hum+N0NHum+N1NHum
bend	bend	V	BEND	tordre	the credit card	up	bend completely	PV+FXC+N0Hum+N0NHum+N1NHum+NoPart
bind	bind	V	FIND	bander	the wound	up	put bandage on	PV+FXC+N0Hum+N1Hum+N1NHum+NoPart
block	block	V	ASK	obst...	the sink	up	obstruct	PV+FXC+N0Hum+N0NHum+N1NHum+NoPart+N1VPart
blow	blow	V	BLOW	agra...	the photo	up	enlarge	PV+FXC+N0Hum+N0NHum+N1NHum
blow	blow	V	BLOW	exag...	the scandal	up	exaggerate	PV+FXC+N0Hum+N0NHum+N1NHum+N1VPart
blow	blow	V	BLOW	expl...	the building	up	explode	PV+FXC+N0Hum+N0NHum+N1Hum+N1NHum+N1VPart+N1V
blow	blow	V	BLOW	gonfler	the balloons	up	inflate	PV+FXC+N0Hum+N0NHum+N1NHum
boil	boil	V	ASK	boui...	some water	up	boil	PV+FXC+N0Hum+N1NHum+NoPart+N1V

0.8 sec   Cancel

Figure 1: NooJ PV Dictionary Showing Highlighted Area of Lexicon Grammar in Table 1

In addition to the PV grammar and dictionary that work together to identify PV in large corpora, we had to add other types of resources to remove noise. These include three disambiguation grammars, which examine the immediately preceding and following environments of potential PV, and eliminate nouns that are mistaken for verbs (e.g., *take a **run down** to Spain* ≠ *run down*, *his **hands** still in his pockets* ≠ *hand in*), prepositions that are identified as PV (*what a comfort I **take in** it* ≠ *take in*), and prepositions that introduce locative expressions (***asked you in Rome***). We have also written adverbial and adjectival expression filters and idiom dictionaries that identify certain fixed expressions as "unambiguous" and thus cannot be given the TAS of PV (e.g., ***asked <u>in a low tone</u>*** ≠ *ask in*, ***put on <u>one's guard</u>*** ≠ *put on*, ***<u>take an interest in</u>*** ≠ *take in*). The underlined expressions in the examples represent fixed expressions, which consequently cannot be part of a candidate PV string. The goal of these extra grammars and dictionaries is to remove noise without creating silence. More details on these resources are described in Machonis (2016).

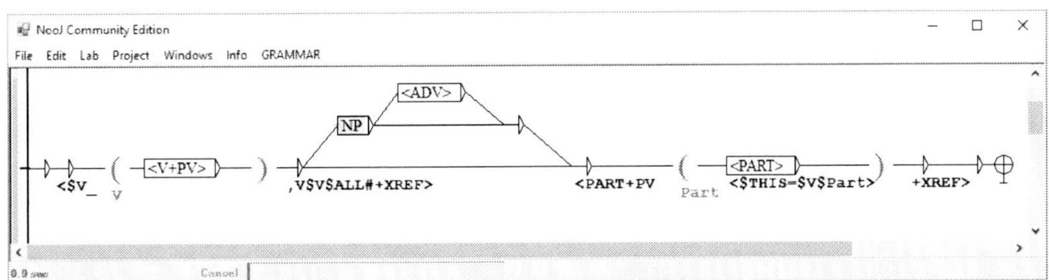

Figure 2: NooJ PV Grammar

This PV Grammar is fairly accurate, and with the recent improvements made (see section 3), can now correctly identify many discontinuous PV involving two, three, or four word forms, such as the following from our sample corpora – the 1881 Henry James novel *The Portrait of a Lady* (233,102 word forms) and an oral corpus consisting of 25 transcribed *Larry King Live* programs from January 2000 (228,950 word forms):

> She had **reasoned** the matter well **out**, (*Portrait of a Lady*)
> Shall I **show** the gentleman **up**, ma'am?
> Mayor Ed Koch **has** a great new book **out** (*Larry King Live*)
> We now know that they **tracked** it all the way **down** and then back up
> That really **turned** the national economy **around**

3   Improvements to Original Grammar

To improve precision while avoiding noise, refinements were made to the original 2010 NooJ PV grammar. In this section, we present some of these enhancements.

3.1   PV Grammar

One of the first things we did was to limit the embedded NP node in the PV grammar (Figure 2). While the original NP node (Figure 3) could accept a variety of noun phrases, the refined NP node (Figure 4) and DET node (Figure 5) within the present grammar restrict the type of NP allowed. For example, the sentence *he **had found out*** was previously annotated as a PV[2], i.e., *had* NP *out*, as in the example above, ***has** a great new book **out***. Now, since *found* does not have an article associated with the singular form, the verb in the sentence *he **had found out*** is no longer annotated as a PV, while the phrase ***has** a great new book **out***, where the singular NP is introduced with a determiner, still is. The new NP node is also able to identify PV originally overlooked, such as the following from our oral corpus: *and I **checked** all this **out***. Other PV noise removed by the new grammar includes the following from *Portrait of a Lady*:

> with Pansy's little **figure** marching **up** the middle of
> the band of tapestry Pansy **had** left **on** the table.
> on the contrary, he **had** only let **out** sail.

---

[2] Although *found* is generally the past tense or past participle of the verb *find*, it can also be the present tense of the verb *found*, an adjective (*found materials*), or a noun (*they earn so much a week and found* "food and lodging in addition to pay"). NooJ recognizes all of these possibilities in the TAS.

The expression *let out*, however, is correctly identified as a PV in this last example. While disambiguation grammars and idiom dictionaries are able to remove noise automatically in NooJ, avoiding improper noun phrases is an important first step. In fact, the original 2010 PV grammar used a punctuation node after the particle to identify all discontinuous PV, which severely limited the recall of discontinuous PV. This new grammar without the punctuation node, however, had the disadvantage of identifying many prepositional phrases involving overlapping particles and prepositions as PV, which created a real difficulty for processing PV. Consequently, we added a series of disambiguation grammars.

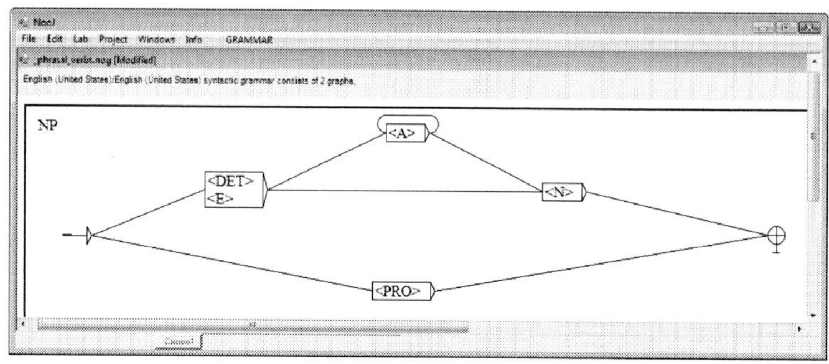

Figure 3: Original NP Node in NooJ PV Grammar

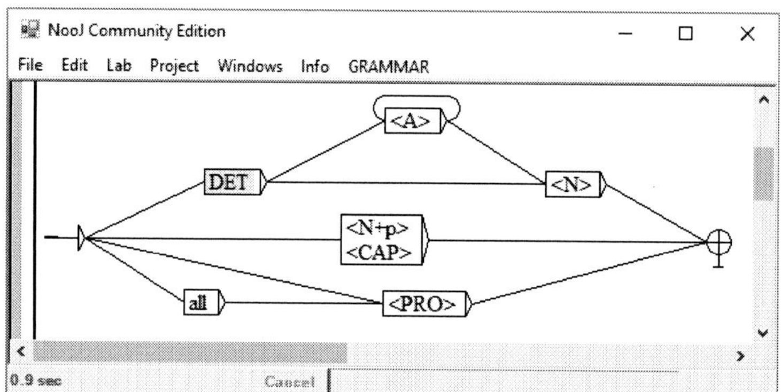

Figure 4: Revised NP Node in NooJ PV Grammar

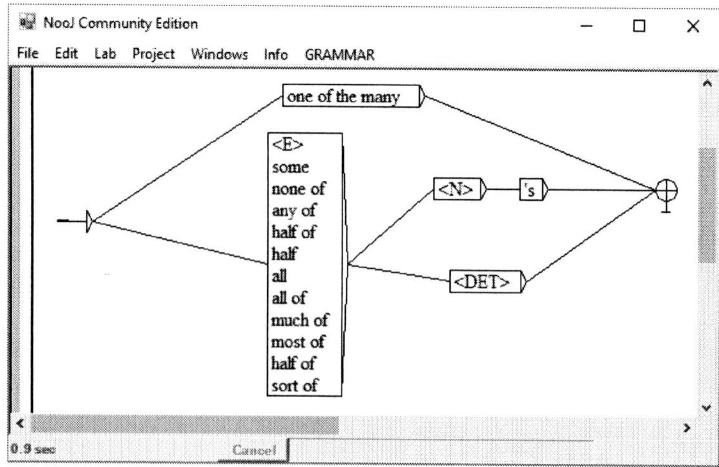

Figure 5: New DET Node in NooJ PV Grammar

3.2 Disambiguation Grammars

After a PV analysis, the TAS can be automatically modified by any of three PV disambiguation grammars, described in more detail in Machonis (2016), which specify certain structures that are **not** to be assigned PV status. The first grammar examines the environment to the right of a candidate PV string. This syntactically motivated grammar states that if the PV occurs with a pronoun object, the PV must be in the discontinuous format (e.g., *figure it out, look him up, take them away*). Thus if an object pronoun follows a supposed particle, it must be a preposition, as in the following: *what sort of pressure is* **put on** *them back in Cuba.* The first disambiguation grammar specifies that this instance of *put on* (e.g., *put on my T-shirt*) is not a PV. The PV *put on* is very common is our oral corpus (e.g., *put on nine pounds, put on my wedding dress, put on a prayer shawl, put my jeans on*), yet shows enormous potential for overlapping with prepositional phrases.

The second disambiguation grammar identifies verbs that are nouns by examining the environment to the left of a hypothetical PV. In essence, if a determiner or adjective appears immediately before the hypothetical PV, then this second disambiguation grammar correctly assumes that it is a noun and removes the PV status from the TAS. This grammar successfully eliminates much noise derived from PV that overlap with nouns, such as *break in, check out, cheer up, figure out, hand in, head up, play out, sort out, take up, time in.* etc.

Our third disambiguation grammar examines the environment to the right of a candidate PV string, but specifically focuses on prepositions introducing locative prepositional phrases that are clearly not part of a PV. This third disambiguation grammar makes use of a supplemental Locative Dictionary, which contains some frequent locatives found in our corpora, such as *church, library, sitting-room*, as well as place names such as *London, Paris, Rome.* These nouns are all marked as N+Loc and the PV status is automatically removed from the TAS by this grammar. For example, the place names *China* and *New Hampshire*, recently added to the Locative Dictionary, assure that the following sentences are not considered PV:

> We will be **doing** it again **in** New Hampshire.
> The Democrats **have** a big dispute **on** China.

Not all locative expressions have to be added to the dictionary, since some noise is already avoided by means of the new NP node in the PV grammar mentioned in 3.1 above. For example, the following represent cases of noise recently removed from our transcribed *Larry King Live* corpus. That is, the singular noun *place* does not have a determiner and the potential PV *take something in* is no longer recognized as a PV in these cases:

> that trial is going to **take** place **in** Albany
> process that's about to **take** place **in** Florida,
> effort that will have to **take** place **in** the Pacific Ocean

3.3 Avoiding Idiom / Phrasal Verb Overlap

Although PV, as multiword expressions, are idioms in themselves, another problem we face in trying to accurately identify PV in large corpora is the overlap of certain idiomatic expressions with PV. For example, idioms that contain prepositions, such as *in, off,* and *on*, can easily be mistaken for PV in our corpora:

> asked her **in a low tone** $\neq$ PV **ask in**
> **put** the girl **on her guard** $\neq$ PV **put on**
> **take an interest in** her $\neq$ PV **take in**

Among the additional lexical resources incorporated into NooJ, we have an Adverbials Grammar which identifies expressions such as *at one time, in a low tone, in her lap, on one's mind*, etc. as unambiguous adverbs (ADV+UNAMB). Consequently, neither the noun/verb (*time*), nor the preposition (*in, on*) can be associated with a PV.

Another grammar identifies a few idioms that also appear with certain support verbs such as *have*, *put*, and *take*, but can create noise when they are identified as PV (e.g., *have* NP *on*, *put* NP *on*, *take* NP *off*). This Adjectivals Grammar labels certain expressions as unambiguous adjectives (A+UNAMB) and consequently eliminates PV noise from sentences such as:

she **had** been much <u>on her guard</u>
the airport has already **put** grief counselors <u>on duty</u> here
was waiting to **take** him <u>off his guard</u>.

We have also incorporated into our PV analysis a larger dictionary of simple *Prep C_i* idioms that do not have multiple modifiers, such as *in a haze, in the clouds, off duty, on a collision course, out of the question, over the top*, etc. These are assigned the notation A+PrepC1+UNAMB, thus avoiding noise with potential PV using the particles *in, off, on, out, over*. For example, the expression *on pins and needles* is no longer confused with the PV *keep something on* in the following sentence from *Portrait of a Lady*: *Your relations with him, while he was here,* **kept** me <u>*on pins and needles*</u>.

Finally, there are two dictionaries that work in tandem with grammars that target more complex idiomatic expressions such as *keep an eye on, take an interest in, take great pleasure in, have an opinion on, put blame on, take part in*, etc. where the frozen noun can take a variety of determiners and modifiers (Idiom1). Another dictionary lists expressions such as *turn one's back on, turn one's back against*, etc. (Idiom2). These two dictionaries work together with grammars that first identify these idioms. For example, the Idiom1 Grammar in Figure 6 annotates the expression *put the blame on* as V+Idiom1, DET, N+Idiom, PREP+Idiom. Then the Idiom Disambiguation Grammar (Figure 7) removes any potential PV from the TAS with the "this is not a PV" notation <!V+PV>, thus avoiding noise with the true PV *put something on*.

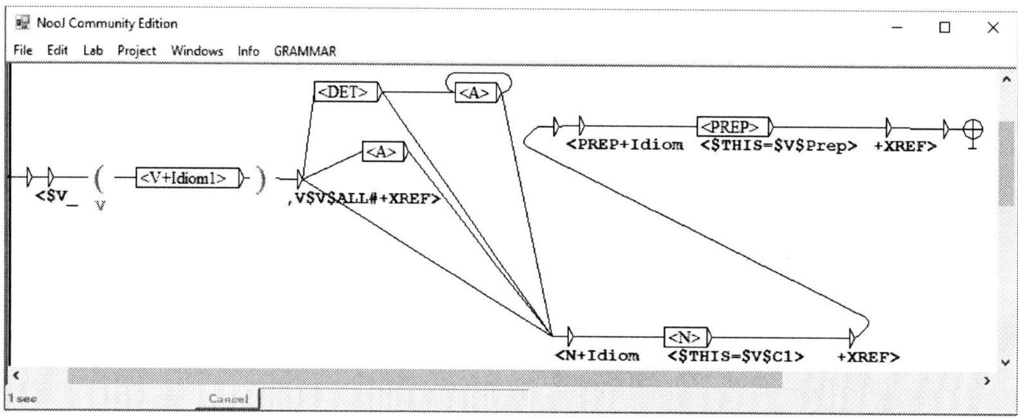

Figure 6: Verbal Idiom1 Grammar

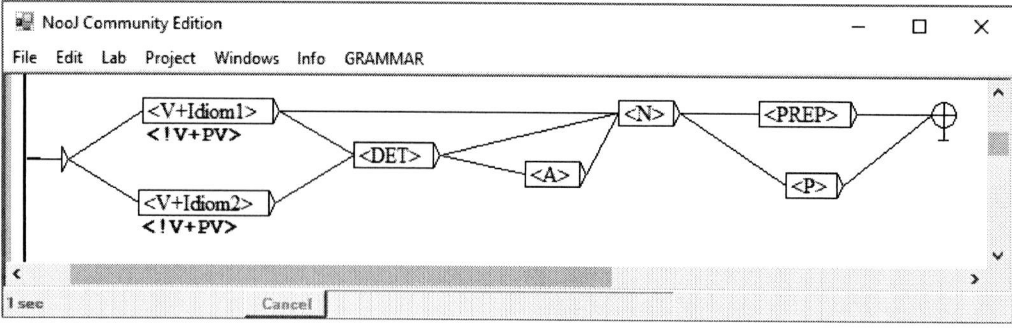

Figure 7: Idiom Disambiguation Grammar

As can be seen, most of the potential noise created by idiomatic expressions comes from the prepositions *in* and *on*, especially when used with high frequency verbs such as *keep, have, put, take,* and *turn.*

4   Results and Future Work

In Table 2, we present an indication of improvements made to our overall PV analysis using the two sample texts – the 1881 novel *The Portrait of a Lady* (233,102 word forms) and the 2000 oral corpus of transcribed *Larry King Live* programs (228,950 word forms). The year 2010 represents the output of our original grammar with punctuation node that overlooked many discontinuous PV. The year 2016 represents results when the punctuation node was removed from the PV Grammar and the three disambiguation grammars were added. The 2018 results represent more recent modifications to the PV Grammar, along with fine-tuning of the adverbial and adjectival expression filters and auxiliary dictionaries within NooJ. The first column represents the overall number of PV strings identified by NooJ. If a PV was automatically removed by a disambiguation grammar or other filter, it was not counted. Of the potential PV strings identified, the next two columns represent correct continuous and discontinuous PV manually verified. The next two columns represent noise, either prepositions that were incorrectly annotated as particles and part of a PV, or other PV misidentifications due to nouns mistaken for verbs (e.g., *I should spend the **evening** out*), verbs for nouns (to **make** her <u>reach</u> out a hand), etc. The last column represents precision: True Positives / (True Positives + False Positives).

As can be seen, the number of PV automatically identified by NooJ has grown since we first started this long-term project, mainly because many discontinuous PV were not annotated due to the punctuation node requirement of the initial grammar. If this change also created much noise (false positives, incorrect PV) in our 2016 analysis, with recent changes to the PV Grammar, the addition of idiom dictionaries, and the tweaking of disambiguating grammars and other linguistics resources, precision has greatly improved, especially with our literature sample. Precision is still a major problem with our oral corpus, however, chiefly due to the noise created by the prepositions *in* and *on*. In fact, precision can be greatly improved by removing all PV with the particles *in* and *on* from the NooJ dictionary. While this does not accomplish the main NLP goal of annotating every PV in a large corpus, our resource could serve as a springboard for a purely linguistic endeavor, such as analyzing the evolution of PV throughout the history of the English language.

TEXT	Potential PV strings identified by NooJ	Correct PV (continuous)	Correct PV (discontinuous)	Incorrect PV (Prepositions)	Incorrect PV (Misidentifications)	Percentage of incorrect	PRECISION: Percentage of PV correctly identified
Portrait of a Lady (2010)	583	405	83	44	51	16.30%	83.70%
Portrait of a Lady (2016)	658	426	152	62	18	12.16%	87.84%
Portrait of a Lady (2018)	636	426	152	55	3	9.12%	90.88%
Larry King Live (2010)	614	424	102	53	35	14.33%	85.67%
Larry King Live (2016)	800	451	172	136	39	21.88%	77.88%
Larry King Live (2018)	730	452	169	97	12	14.93%	85.07%

Table 2: Comparison of PV Identification in 2010 & 2016 Studies vs. Today

Thim (2012:201-5), in his detailed PV study highlights "the little attention Late Modern English – in particular the 19th century – has received." "Most of the 19th century is not covered at all," he states. A work in progress actually involves reducing the NooJ dictionary to include only six particles (*out, up, down, away, back, off*) instead of twelve, which has helped us achieve 98% precision in an analysis of *The Portrait of a Lady*. In order to get a better idea of the evolution of PV in Late Modern English, we plan to use the NooJ PV Grammar, with a limited PV Dictionary, to analyze numerous 19th century texts from a variety of authors, both American (Herman Melville, James Fenimore Cooper, Washington Irving, Nathaniel Hawthorne, Harriet Beecher Stowe, Mark Twain, Edith Wharton) and British (Charles Dickens, Jane Austen, Walter Scott, the Bronte sisters, George Eliot, Thomas Hardy, Oscar Wilde).

Previously, Hiltunen (1994:135) examined English texts limiting his searches to these six typical particles representing three levels of PV frequency: high (*out, up*), mid (*down, away*), and low (*back, off*). By doing the same, we could get an accurate snapshot of PV usage, although limited to these six particles, in numerous 19th century novels with improved precision. In fact, our dictionary and grammar could become very useful instruments to automatically measure PV usage in different genres – novels, plays, nonfiction, technical material, daily life texts (e.g., news articles, blogs), etc. – and at different periods in the history of the English language.

In conclusion, the NooJ PV dictionary and grammar are great resources for identifying this most difficult, characteristic feature of the English language. While PV are indeed a "pain in the neck for NLP," what we have described is a reliable first step in accurately identifying them in large corpora, while automatically removing as much noise as possible. As we have seen in this paper, incorporating other idioms in an NLP analysis greatly helps to alleviate this noise. And although certain prepositions still create a fair amount of noise, many of these problems can eventually be resolved when we are able to build a NooJ grammar to recognize entire English sentences, another future goal.

References

Dwight Bolinger. 1971. *The Phrasal Verb in English*. Harvard University Press, Cambridge, MA.

Bruce Fraser. 1976. *The Verb-Particle Combination in English*. Academic Press, New York, NY.

Maurice Gross. 1979. On the failure of generative grammar. *Language* 55(4):859-885.

Maurice Gross. 1994. Constructing Lexicon grammars. In Beryl T. (Sue) Atkins & Antonio Zampolli (eds.), *Computational Approaches to the Lexicon*, 213-263. Oxford University Press, Oxford, UK.

Maurice Gross. 1996. Lexicon Grammar. In Keith Brown & Jim Miller (eds.), *Concise Encyclopedia of Syntactic Theories*, 244-258. Elsevier, New York, NY.

Beate Hampe. 2002. *Superlative Verbs: A corpus-based study of semantic redundancy in English verb-particle constructions*. Gunter Narr Verlag, Tübingen, Germany.

Risto Hiltunen. 1994. On Phrasal Verbs in Early Modern English: Notes on Lexis and Style. In Dieter Kastovsky (ed.), *Studies in Early Modern English*, 129-140. Mouton de Gruyter, Berlin, Germany.

Arthur Garfield Kennedy. 1920. *The Modern English Verb-adverb Combination*. Stanford University Press, Stanford, CA.

Tomoshichi Konishi. 1958. The growth of the verb-adverb combination in English: A brief sketch. In Kazuo Araki, Taiichiro Egawa, Toshiko Oyama & Minoru Yasui (eds.), *Studies in English grammar and linguistics: A miscellany in honour of Takanobu Otsuka*, 117-128. Kenkyusha, Tokyo, Japan.

Peter A. Machonis. 1997. Neutral verbs in English: A preliminary classification. *Lingvisticæ Investigationes* 21(2):293-320.

Peter A. Machonis. 2009. Compositional phrasal verbs with *up*: Direction, aspect, intensity. *Lingvisticae Investigationes* 32(2):253-264.

Peter A. Machonis. 2010. English Phrasal Verbs: from Lexicon Grammar to Natural Language Processing. *Southern Journal of Linguistics* 34(1):21-48.

Peter A. Machonis. 2012. *Sorting* NooJ *out to take* Multiword Expressions *into account*. In Kristina Vučković, Božo Bekavac, & Max Silberztein (eds.), *Automatic Processing of Various Levels of Linguistic Phenomena: Selected Papers from the NooJ 2011 International Conference*, 152-165. Cambridge Scholars Publishing, Newcastle upon Tyne, UK

Peter A. Machonis. 2016. Phrasal Verb Disambiguating Grammars: Cutting Out Noise Automatically. In Linda Barone, Max Silberztein, & Mario Monteleone (eds.), *Automatic Processing of Natural-Language Electronic Texts with NooJ*, 169-181. Springer International Publishing AG, Cham, Switzerland.

NooJ: A Linguistic Development Environment. http://www.nooj4nlp.net/

Ivan A. Sag, Timothy Baldwin, Francis Bond, Ann Copestake & Dan Flickinger. 2002. Multiword expressions: A pain in the neck for NLP. *Proceedings of the Third International Conference on Intelligent Text Processing and Computational Linguistics*, 1-15. CICLING, Mexico City, Mexico.

Max Silberztein. 2016. *Formalizing Natural Languages: The NooJ Approach.* Wiley ISTE, London, UK.

Stephan Thim. 2012. *Phrasal Verbs: The English Verb-Particle Construction and Its History.* Walter de Gruyter, Berlin, Germany.

Designing a Croatian Aspectual Derivatives Dictionary: Preliminary Stages

Kristina Kocijan
Department of information
and communication sciences
Faculty of Humanities
and Social Sciences
University of Zagreb
Croatia
krkocijan@ffzg.hr

Krešimir Šojat
Department of linguistics
Faculty of Humanities
and Social Sciences
University of Zagreb
Croatia
ksojat@ffzg.hr

Dario Poljak
Department of information
and communication sciences
Faculty of Humanities
and Social Sciences
University of Zagreb
Croatia
dpoljak@ffzg.hr

Abstract

The paper focuses on derivationally connected verbs in Croatian, i.e. on verbs that share the same lexical morpheme and are derived from other verbs via prefixation, suffixation and/or stem alternations. As in other Slavic languages with rich derivational morphology, each verb is marked for aspect, either perfective or imperfective. Some verbs, mostly of foreign origin, are marked as bi-aspectual verbs. The main objective of this paper is to detect and to describe major derivational processes and affixes used in the derivation of aspectually connected verbs with NooJ. Annotated chains are exported into a format adequate for a web-based system and further used to enhance the aspectual and derivational information for each verb.

1   Introduction

In this paper we deal with the representation of derivational processes in Croatian, a South Slavic language with rich inflectional and derivational morphology. The paper focuses on derivationally connected verbs, i.e. on those verbs which share the same lexical morpheme and which are derived from other verbs mostly via prefixation and suffixation. As in other Slavic languages, each verb is always marked for aspect and classified as perfective, imperfective, or bi-aspectual. Generally, the imperfective aspect is used to describe actions, processes and states as unfinished or ongoing, whereas the imperfective aspect refers to them as finished or completed, e.g.:

- 1a. *Pisao sam* (imperfective) pismo jedan sat.   1b. I *was writing* a letter for an hour.

- 2a. *Napisao* (perfective) *sam* pismo za jedan sat.   2b. I *wrote* a letter in an hour.

Verbs like *pisati* "to write + imperfective" and *napisati* "to write, to finish writing + perfective" are referred to as aspectual pairs. Verbs in aspectual pairs are closely related in meaning, except that one expresses imperfective and the other perfective aspect. Aspect in Croatian is morphologically marked in each verbal form and it affects inflectional properties of verbs (e.g. only perfectives can be used in aorist, and imperfectives in imperfective past tense; gerunds are commonly formed by imperfectives etc). Aspect in Croatian is regarded as a word-formation process and members of aspectual pairs are treated as separate lexical entries in dictionaries. In terms of derivation, perfectives are commonly derived from imperfectives by prefixation, while imperfectives are formed from perfectives by suffixation or stem alternation. The presence of a certain affix indicates whether a verb is a perfective or an imperfective. A relatively small group of bi-aspectual verbs, predominantly of foreign origin, can be used as perfectives and imperfectives in the same morphological form. Various factors can determine whether they will be used as a perfectives or imperfectives (e.g. a context, the type of time adverbial used in a sentence etc.). Although based on the opposition of only two aspects and overtly marked, numerous

---

Proceedings of the First Workshop on Linguistic Resources for Natural Language Processing, pages 28–37
Santa Fe, New Mexico, USA, August 20, 2018.

studies in the area of second language acquisition indicate that aspect is one of the most complicated category for learners of Slavic languages.

In this paper we present preliminary stages in the construction of the database of Croatian aspectually and derivationally connected verbs, i.e. aspectual derivatives. Apart from its potential pedagogical use, the database of aspectual derivatives is one of the first attempts to systematically present this area of Croatian derivational morphology. The paper is structured as follows: In Section 2, we briefly describe major derivational processes in Croatian and focus on the derivation of verbs from other verbs and aspectual changes that take place. Sections 3 and 4 present the processing of aspectual derivatives in Croatian in NooJ and provide an overview of underlying principles. In Section 5, the design and the structure of the database is discussed. The paper concludes with an outline of future work.

2 Derivation of verbs

Major word-formation processes in Croatian are derivation and compounding. Further we discuss only derivation which predominantly consists of affixation. Although there are some other processes like conversion or back formation, they are not as prominent as prefixation or suffixation (Šojat et al, 2013).

Croatian verbs can be thus divided into simple imperfectives (*pisati* "to write + imperfective") and prefixed perfectives (*na-pisati* "to write + perfective") denoting that the action is completed. Other prefixes used for the derivation of perfectives add different semantic features (*pisati* "to write + imperfective" – *pre-pisati* "to copy by writing + perfective" – *pot-pisati* "to sign + perfective") and enable further derivation, either through prefixation, suffixation or simultaneous prefixation and suffixation. These perfectives can be derived into secondary imperfectives denoting iterative actions through suffixation (*potpis-ivati* "to sign several / many times"). Other suffixes are used for the derivation of diminutive verbs (e.g. *pisati– pis-karati* "to scribble + imperfective") or verbs expressing punctual actions (*vikati* "to shout + imperfective" – *viknuti* "to shout once + perfective"). Further, some secondary imperfectives are derived via prefixation into perfectives denoting distributive actions (*is-potpisivati* – "to sign each one + perfective", e.g. each letter, every document etc.). In some cases aspectual distinctions are expressed by vowel variations or suppletive forms (e.g. *doći* "to come + perfective" – *dolaziti* "to come + imperfective"). Detailed account of morpho-semantic relations among Croatian verbal derivatives is found in Šojat et al. (2012).

In the following section we show how existing language resources can benefit from the information about verbal aspect in terms of their extension and enrichment. We demonstrate this on the inflectional dictionary for Croatian verbs in NooJ.

3 Verbs in NooJ Dictionary

The main language resources (LR) for Croatian, as prepared in Vučković (2009) and explained in Vučković et al. (2010), include the dictionary of Croatian verbs. Each verb was originally marked for the main category <V>, reflexive property <V+**Prelaz=pov**> and a paradigm rule **FLX** responsible for describing the rules used to build all the simple verb forms,[1] for example:

```
pisati,V+FLX=PISATI              "to write"
asistirati,V+FLX=SJATI           "to assist"
sjati,V+Prelaz=pov+FLX=SJATI     "to shine".
```

In all cases, a name of a verb is used as a representative of a specific conjugation paradigm. For example, the verb *sjati* "to shine" uses the set of conjugation rules that we refer to as SJATI <FLX=SJATI>. All the other verbs that share the same set of conjugation rules will be associated with this name of the paradigm like the verb *asistirati* "to assist." In addition to these three markers, a small subset of verbs was also marked for valency (Vučković et al., 2010) to improve the performance of the Croatian chunker and some verbs were marked for aspect.

Although each Croatian verb has an aspect by its nature, either perfective, imperfective or bi-aspectual, this information was not originally encoded into the main dictionary entries. This is mainly due to

---

[1] Complex tenses in Croatian such as future I and II, perfect, pluperfect, or conditionals are described within syntax grammars and are beyond the scope of this paper.

the absence of that information in the resources built after the MULTEXT-East specifications prepared by Tadić, as explained in Erjavec (2001), from which NooJ resources have been adopted.

There are 4,168 main verb entries in the NooJ Croatian dictionary. At the beginning of our project, there were only 1,448 verbs that had been marked as either perfective <Aspect=perf>, imperfective <Aspect=imperf> or bi-aspectual <Aspect=bi> regarding the Category of aspect (Table 1). This means that little over 65% of verbs had no marker assigned for this category.

Total	+perf	+imperf	+bi	no marker
4,168	673	534	241	2,720

Table 1: Original distribution of Aspect markers

The importance of information on aspect encoded in the verb, lies, among others, in the list of possible verbal forms. For example, only perfective verbs can have aorist past tense and past adverbial participle forms, while only imperfective verbs can have the imperfect past tense and the present adverbial participle. Before we could add the tag for aspect automatically to the remaining verbs, it was important to check if the existing aspect markers were correctly assigned and what data could be used to correctly mark the remaining 65% of verbs. Since the list of possible tenses is embedded into the conjugation paradigms (FLX), we decided to start our investigation with them.

3.1   Data Analysis of the original dictionary

At the very beginning of our analysis, we found two paradigms that were using both Aorist and Imperfect endings [FLX=POKLONITI and FLX=BIRATIDODATI]. Two does not sound like a large number, but if we take into account that the POKLONITI paradigm is responsible for the conjugation of 106 verbs and the BIRATIDODATI paradigm for 204, we are not talking small numbers any more. We proceeded with the analysis by double-checking each of the 310 verbs. We learned that all the verbs using the POKLONITI paradigm are actually perfective in aspect (as is the paradigm itself), while the other verbs are all dual which makes the presence of aorist and imperfect endings appropriate. Thus, we were able to annotate these verbs with appropriate markers <Aspect=perf> and <Aspect=bi>, respectively. In addition, we revisited the POKLONITI paradigm and removed the endings for Imperfect. At this point, we also decided to recheck the aspect category of all the verbs.

To avoid individual checking each verb, we cross referenced all of the assigned aspects with the aspect of a verb used to mark the conjugation paradigm. From that list (Table 2), after removing all the verbs whose aspect matched the aspect of a paradigm, and all the verbs that had no aspect defined, we were left with only 62 verbs that had been marked as mismatched and that needed to be checked manually.

Since the reason for the mismatched aspect could be due to either an incorrectly marked aspect of a verb or to an incorrectly described paradigm, we checked both, starting with the verbs. Paradigm analysis revealed some missing aorist and/or past participle descriptions in the category of perfective verbs, and missing imperfect and/or present participle descriptions of imperfective verbs. Also, some descriptions of bi-aspectuals were missing, either aorist and past participle descriptions, or imperfect and present participle descriptions. All of these cases were corrected to mirror the related aspect, either by correcting the value of an Aspect attribute or changing the paradigm name.

For the final analysis we wanted to make sure that there are no duplicates among our paradigms, i.e. that we do not have different paradigm names describing the same conjugation occurrences. We detected 16 such occurrences that we have replaced choosing the one paradigm that was used more often in the dictionary.

3.2   The new verb dictionary and paradigms

There are 209 paradigms that describe the conjugation rules for Croatian verbs. Some rules describe only one verb in a dictionary (there are 67 such rules), while others describe more (Figure 1). The largest number of verbs (538) described by the same paradigm BIRATI make up 13% of all the verbs in the dictionary, while the second runner up (SJATI) describes 7% of verbs.

FLX Aspect	FLX	ASPECT			
		perf	bi	imperf	Null
bi	ČUTI	6	1		12
	VIDJETI	2	1		4
perf	DODATI	48		5	164
	BLJESNUTI	17		1	72
	ZASJATI	15	2	1	69
	KAZATI	8	1		23
	DAROVATI	3	3	2	13
	UGASITI	5		1	13
	ZAPAZITI	5		1	11
	UGOSTITI	5		1	10
	PRILEĆI	3		1	5
	OTPUTOVATI	3	1	1	1
imperf	BIRATI	4	5	140	402
	SJATI	1	3	71	236
	POSJEDOVATI		2	13	38
	GUBITI	2		8	19
	SMIJATI	1		10	18
	BRANITI	1		11	17
	CVILITI		1	2	16
	RAZLIKOVATI		6	5	11
	OKRETATI	1		3	9
	KLICATI	1		3	7
	UMJETI	3		2	4
	IZLAGATI	1		7	3
	ODMICATI	1		1	

Table 2. Distribution of different aspects assigned to paradigms

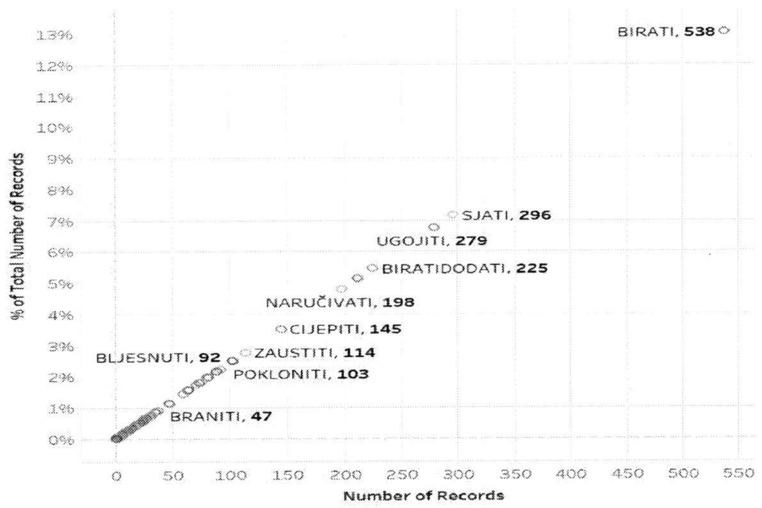

Figure 1. Distribution of paradigms among Croatian verbs

However, a closer look shows us that these descriptions are not as different as they might first appear. We will show this through a detailed analysis of simple verb forms by tense category, starting with present tense.

What makes these paradigms different is the list of tenses they describe, but also how each tense is described. These two categories (list of tenses, form of tenses) are linked by an OR operator, meaning that the difference in either one or both from the existing list of paradigms, results in a new paradigm.

To demonstrate, let us compare the UGOJITI and POKLONITI paradigms. They both have the same list of tenses they can form (present, imperative, PDR - verbal adjective active, PDT - verbal adjective passive, aorist and GPP - past adverbial participle), but the way they make PDT differs [<B3>**en**(:PDT) and <B3>**jen**(:PDT) respectfully] and thus they form different paradigm rules.

However, since NooJ allows multiple usage of its grammars (Silberztein, 2016), each tense rule is described as a separate sub-grammar and then called from a paradigm, where needed. In order to describe derivations of Croatian simple verb forms that are in the NooJ dictionary, we built 280 such sub-grammars whose different combinations build 209 paradigms that describe 4,168 verbs and recognize 377,603 forms, taking into account simple verb tenses (long/short infinitive, present, imperfect, aorist, passive/active verbal adjectives, imperative, present/past adverbial participles), gender (masculine, feminine, neutral), number (singular, plural) and person (1st, 2nd, 3rd).

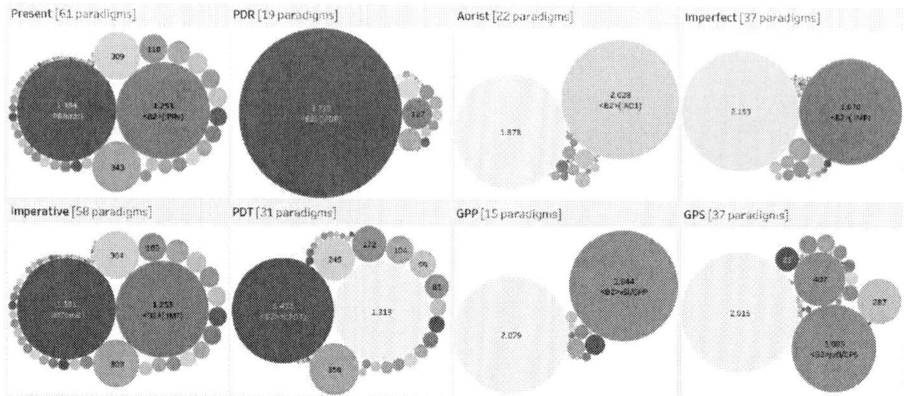

Figure 2. Distribution of sub-grammars per tense

As expected, inside each tense category, some descriptions are more common than others. This distribution (Figure 2) is different for each of the tenses. The same is true for the number of rules which ranges from 15 (*GPP*) to 61 (*Present*). The number of paradigms that do not have rules for a tense are marked in gray (for example: 2,153 paradigms do not have Imperfect, 2,079 do not have GPP, 2,015 do not have GPS etc.). *Present* is the only tense that is found in all paradigms.

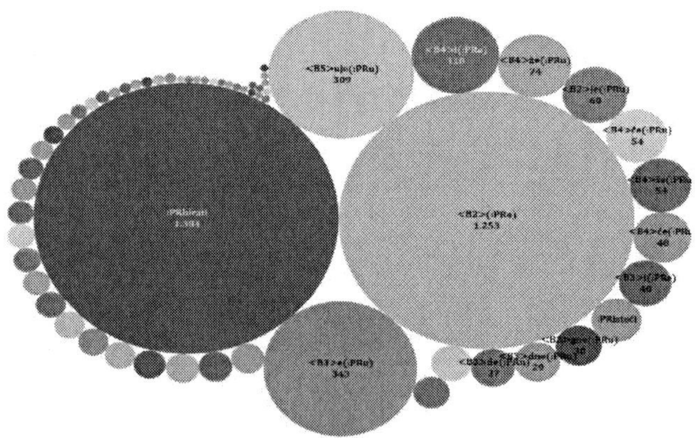

Figure 3. Distribution of Present rules used among existing verbs

Figure 3 shows the distribution of rules[2] used to build the present tense found in the existing 209 paradigms. It may look as if there are 61 different suffixes for the Croatian present, but this is not the case. Throughout the paradigms, the same set of suffixes is used for all three genders (male, female, neutral), for all three persons singular [*-m, -š, -/*], and for the first and second person plural [*-mo, -te*]. The third person plural may have the ending [*-e*] or [*-u*]. So, why are there 61 different present tense descriptions in this figure?

Although the set of suffixes is the same (with two possible alterations for 3rd person plural), changes that occur before the suffix differ. In some cases it is enough to only remove (<B2>) the infinitive ending

___
[2] Each circle represents one rule; the bigger the circle, the more verbs the rule describes.

(*-ti* or *–ći*) and add the suffix, but in some cases more letters need to be removed (<B3>..<B5>) and more letters prior to the suffix need to be added, like in the following examples:

```
isteći -> <B2>če(:PRsingular) => istečem [removes last 2 charac-
ters, inserts 'če' before adding suffix for Present]
izleći -> <B2>že(:PRsingular) => izležem [removes last 2 charac-
ters, inserts 'že' before adding suffix for Present]
otprijeti -> <B5>e(:PRsingular) => otprem [removes last 5 char-
acters, inserts 'e' before adding suffix for Present].
```

After removing duplicate verbs from the dictionary and sorting out the paradigm sets, we were able to automatically add the missing aspect information for all unmarked verbs. Their total now amounts to 4,134. The largest aspect category are perfective verbs, followed by imperfective verbs and bi-aspectual verbs. Their distribution is visualized in Figure 4.

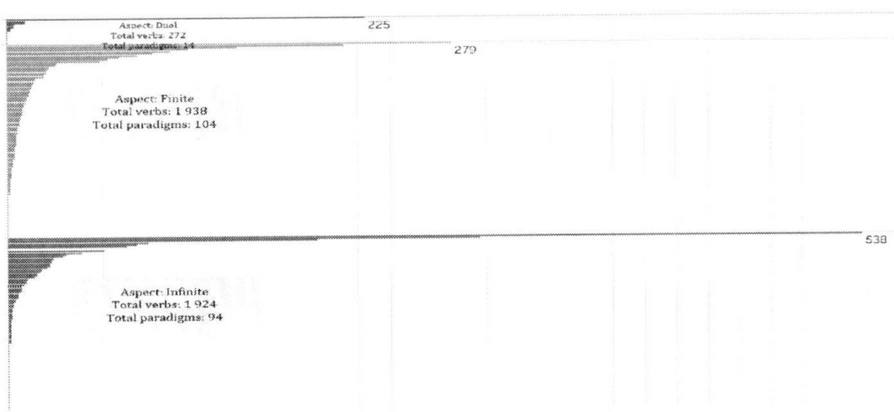

Figure 4. Distribution of verbs per aspect category in the dictionary
and number of paradigms used to describe each category

4   Grammar modeling for aspectual derivatives

Computational derivation is a well-known process when new words need to be created in order to economically enlarge the dictionary (Trost, 2003). NooJ provides two routes to describe derivations.

The first one uses a derivational module that allows a direct link between the dictionary with the list of words that can be derived and a grammar that provides rules for their derivation either graphically in a form of an enhanced recursive transition network (ERTN) or via formal grammar rules as context-free grammar (CFG). This link is defined via an attribute DRV that holds the name of the paradigm responsible for the allowed derivation(s).

The second one uses a morphological grammar module that may simulate the dictionary entries via ERTN. It can recognize a defined set of letters and tag them in the same manner that we would manually do in the dictionary. The difference is that in the grammar can have a few graphs describing multiple dictionary entries (e.g. if we wanted to recognize and tag roman numerals, we can do it by a minimum of five graphs or by 3,999 dictionary entries).

Since our main objective is to produce derivational paths in a format that we can use to populate the web-based database, we have opted for the second approach that left us more room to accommodate the output to the database design (see Figure 5). To avoid recognizing words that start with the same set of letters as prefixes used in derivations, we introduced the constraint that the dictionary check and validate if the primary verb first exists. So, for example, *sufinancirati* "co-finance" will be recognized, since there is a verb '*financirati,V*' in the dictionary. On the other hand, the word *suncobran* "parasol" will not be recognized, since there is no dictionary entry marked as '*ncobran,V*' (nor any such word in Croatian).

For the preliminary grammar model, we used all the derivations for the verb *pisati* "to write" (Table 3a) and the verbs *bacati / baciti* "to throw away" (Table3b). All the pairs have both perfective and imperfective forms. This is not true in only two cases: for the derived form *napisati* that has no aspectual pair, and the aspectual pair *ispotpisati - ispotpisivati* that share the same aspect (perfective).[3] If we put aside these two exceptions, from the remaining pairs we can conclude that if there is a verb in the dictionary to which a prefix is added, then the newly derived verb will be perfective in aspect. If a verb derived in such a manner adds the suffix2 (SUF 2), then the new verb will be imperfective in aspect if the length of suffix2 is 3 or 4 and perfective if its length is 0, 1 or 2.

a) PISATI

| PREF2 | PREF1 | a | SUF 2 |
			iva
0	0	PISATI	
	do	dopisati	dopisivati
	is	ispisati	ispisivati
	na	napisati	
	o	opisati	opisivati
	ot	otpisati	otpisivati
	po	popisati	popisivati
	pot	potpisati	potpisivati
	pre	prepisati	prepisivati
	pri	pripisati	pripisivati
	pro	propisati	propisivati
	ras	raspisati	raspisivati
	u	upisati	upisivati
	za	zapisati	zapisivati
is	pot	ispotpisati	ispotpisivati
na	do	nadopisati	nadopisivati
su	pot	supotpisati	supotpisivati

b) BACATI - BACITI

| PREF2 | PREF1 | a | SUF 2 | |
			i	iva
0	0	BACATI	BACITI	
	do		dobaciti	dobacivati
	iz		izbaciti	izbacivati
	na	nabacati	nabaciti	nabacivati
	od		odbaciti	odbacivati
	po	pobacati	pobaciti	pobacivati
	pod		podbaciti	podbacivati
	pre		prebaciti	prebacivati
	pred		predbaciti	predbacivati
	raz	razbacati		razbacivati
	u		ubaciti	ubacivati
	uz		uzbaciti	uzbacivati
	z		zbaciti	zbacivati
	za		zabaciti	zabacivati
po	raz	porazbacati		porazbacivati

Table 3. Aspectual derivatives of the root verbs
a) *PISATI* "to write" and b) *BACATI / BACITI* "to throw away"

We have applied these rules to the morphological grammar built in NooJ. Figure 5 illustrates how the grammar works, using the verb *ispisivati* "to write out."

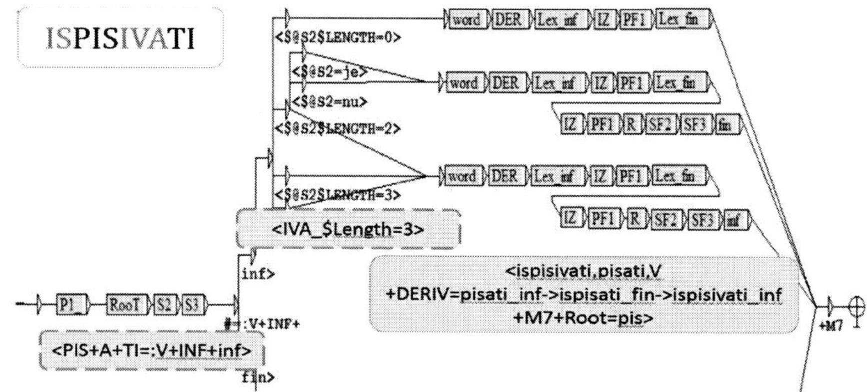

Figure 5. Morphological grammar that recognizes and annotates a verb derived by
a single prefixation and suffixation (example of the verb *ispisivati*)

Possible prefixes in the first position (i.e. the position closest to the root), such as the prefix *is*, are listed in the P1_ node. The following node holds any set of letters which are recognized as the root of the verb used to build the constraints that check if such a root concatenated with *a + ti* exists in the dictionary as a verb in infinitive form whose Aspect is defined as INF <pis+a+ti=:V+INF+inf>. If this constraint is validated, we check against the length of suffix2. Since the length in our example is 3, we proceed with the path where <$@S2$LENGTH=3>. It then leads us to the annotation section that ads

---

[3] This may be due to the fact that the verb *ispotpisivati* is actually derived from *potpisivati*, while the verb *ispotpisati* is redundant in semantical meaning of its prefixes i.e. the prefix *is* does not bring anything new to the meaning of *pot* in this context. In the hrWaC 2.2 web corpus (Ljubešić & Klubička, 2014) it shows up only 7 times, mostly in an informal web setting.

the recognized lemma as the superlemma of the derived verb, and marks the POS, Root and Derivational chain with the aspect marker for each derivation [+DERIV=pisati_inf->ispisati_fin->ispisivati_inf]. This information is then exported from NooJ and added to the *Specifics* table of our web database as discussed in Section 5.

In Table 3b, there is an imperfective verb BACATI "to throw away" from which the perfective verb *nabacati* "to throw onto" is derived by prefixation. Its imperfective pair is the verb *nabacivati* "to throw onto" derived via suffixation. The perfective verb BACITI uses prefixation to produce a perfective form *nabaciti* whose imperfective pair is also *nabacivati*. This means that the imperfective form *nabacivati* should be found in both aspectual derivational chains. But, ambiguity is not a stranger to language.

5   Database and interface design

After extracting data into usable chunks, we wanted to present it in a way usable to others. To reach the widest possible audience with our tool, we focused on bringing it to the web. In that way it will be available to everyone with basic Internet access and can be dynamically updated as new chains are prepared within NooJ. However, to accomplish that, we needed to create a searchable interface backbone in a well-structured database, whose main function is to support our information system as defined in Gunjal (2003).

Due to the nature of our data, we decided to split it into three separate semantic data-groups (Figure 6). The *Main data* set stores all the data at the morphological level that will be searchable through the online tool, with various levels of granularity. The *Specifics* provides derivational data focusing on one model used for the derivation. The *Examples* set unifies all the semantics and should provide a better understanding of the verb's usage.

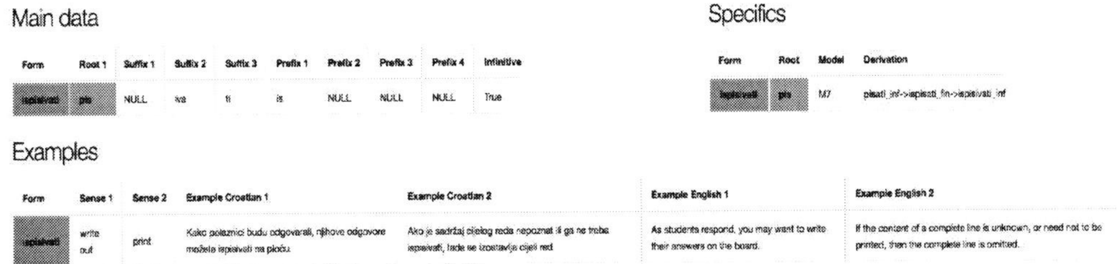

Figure 6. Data structure of three data groups

Since we are using csv to represent our data, it is already in a rather structured state. Thus, our data can be described as a structure in the first normal form. This means that the data itself can fit into tabular format and that it always contains only one value for each cell. The first normal form also assumes the usage of primary keys for the unique representation of every row of data. This can be performed automatically while importing it into the database as described in Gilfillan (2015).

As can be seen, there is still some redundant data (Figure 6) since the *Main Data* file contains both Form and Root components, present in other files as well. The idea behind the interface is to allow users to search either by *Form* or *Root* fields with additional (optional) *Suffix* and *Prefix* information, and then conditionally showing *examples* and *specifics* depending on which *Form* is selected. Thus we can reduce the clutter in the other two files by imposing a foreign key constraint after importing it into our database and removing *Form* and *Root* information from the other two tables (since that data will already be in the search results from querying the *Main Data* file).

We used MySQL (Coulter, 2017) to store the data and created primary keys, as well as foreign key constraints. After importing all the data and imposing foreign key constraints, we are left with 3 tables (Figure 7) with almost identical structure as we had at the beginning (Figure 6). Now the *Form* and *Root* fields are present exclusively in the *Main Data* table. In order to access it from other tables, we use the foreign key named *mainID* constrained to the *ID* field. It also acts as the primary key of our *Main Data* table. The foreign key constraint is set up in a way that easily enables us to update or delete multiple records at once without ever leaving the *Main Data* table.

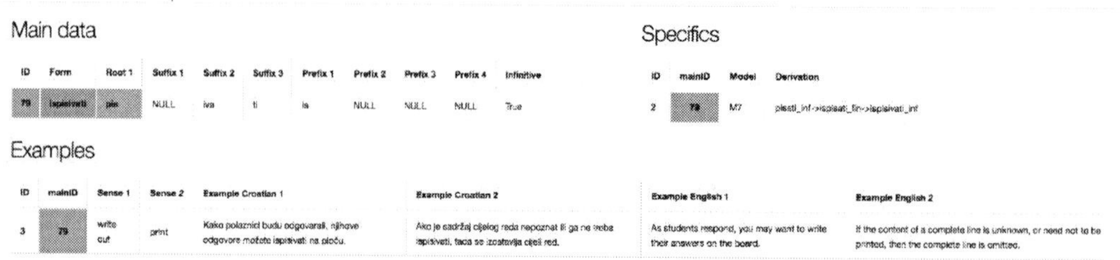

Figure 7. Representation of tables and their data in the database

Furthermore, a search is performed on only one (*Main Data*) table with all the additional information retrieved only upon the user's request. Figure 8 depicts one such instance when the verb form *ispisivati* is selected for search.[4] The derivational chain [Derivacija: *pisati -> ispisati -> ispisivati*] holds additional information on aspect that is color-coded (perfective verbs are marked in red, imperfectives in blue) and available via a hover feature.

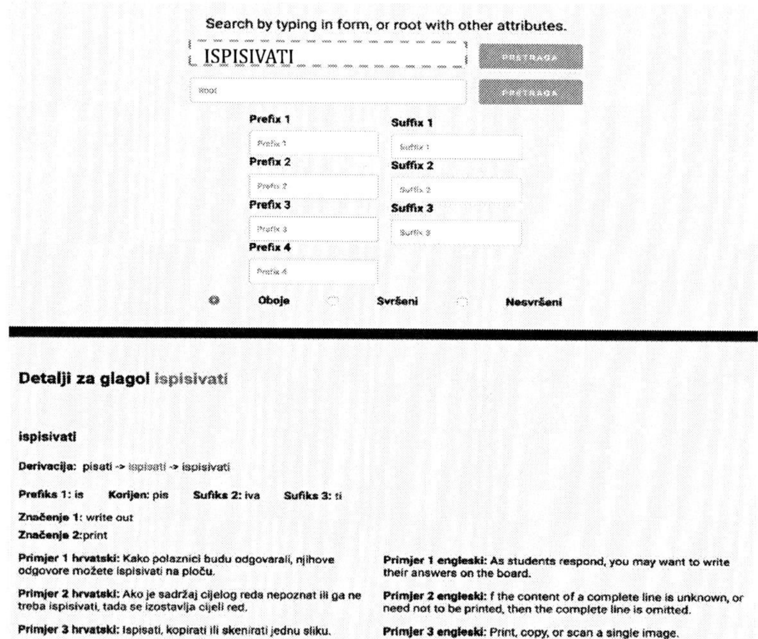

Figure 8. Web interface showing additional information on derivation and examples for the verbs *ispisivati*

6 Conclusion

In this paper we showed some preliminary steps taken in the processing of Croatian aspectual pairs. This phase of the project consists of the extension of the existing verb dictionary and its enrichment with the information on verbal aspect. This preliminary step resulted in the significant expansion and improvement of its coverage. The second step that was taken in the preliminary stage was to design and to build the web-based database of aspectual derivatives. The database will enable various types of queries and provide information about affixes used in a specific derivational process, full derivation chains of verbs, basic meaning definitions, contextual examples, etc. Out next goal is to populate the database with aspectual derivatives from other derivational families. The database will remain free for on-line search.

---

[4] The web interface is deployed on a Heroku server at `https://vidski-parnjaci.herokuapp.com`.

References

Tom Coulter. 14.12.2017. *Why MySQL is still King*, Retrieved 22.06.2018. from `https://www.free-lancer.com/community/articles/why-mysql-is-still-king`

Tomaž Erjavec (ed.). 2001. Specifications and Notation for MULTEXT-East Lexicon Encoding. *MULTEXT-East Report*, Concede Edition D1.1F/Concede, Jožef Stefan Institute, Ljubljana. `http://nl.ijs.si/ME/Vault/V2/msd/msd.pdf`

Ian Gilfillan 13.06.2015. Database Normalization Overview, *MariaDB Docs*, Retrieved 22.06.2018. from `https://mariadb.com/kb/en/library/database-normalization-overview/`

Bhojaraju Gunjal. 2003. Database Management: Concepts and Design, In *Proceedings of 24th IASLIC–SIG-2003*. Dehradun: Survey of India. Retreived 20.06.2018. from `https://www.researchgate.net/publication/257298522_Database_Management_Concepts_and_Design`

Nikola Ljubešić and Filip Klubička. 2014. {bs,hr,sr}WaC – Web corpora of Bosnian, Croatian and Serbian, In *Proceedings of the 9th Web as Corpus Workshop (WaC-9) @ EACL 2014*, (eds.) F. Bildhauer & R. Schäfer, Association for Computational Linguistics, pages 29–35, Gothenburg, Sweden.

Max Silberztein. 2016. *Formalizing Natural Languages: The NooJ Approach*, Cognitive science series, Wiley-ISTE, London, UK.

Krešimir Šojat, Matea Srebačić, and Marko Tadić. 2012. Derivational and Semantic Relations of Croatian Verbs. *Journal of Language Modelling*, 00 (2012), 1: 111-142.

Krešimir Šojat, Matea Srebačić, and Vanja Štefanec. 2013. CroDeriV i morfološka raščlamba hrvatskoga glagola, *Suvremena lingvistika*. 39 (2013), 75: 75-96.

Harald Trost. 2003. Morphology. *The Oxford Handbook of Computational Linguistics* (ed. R. Mitkov), Oxford University Press: 25-47.

Kristina Vučković. 2009. *Model parsera za hrvatski jezik*. PhD dissertation, Faculty of Humanities and Social Sciences, University of Zagreb, Zagreb.

Kristina Vučković, Marko Tadić, and Božo Bekavac. 2010. Croatian Language Resources for NooJ. *CIT: Journal of computing and information technology*, 18(2010):295-301.

Kristina Vučković, Nives Mikelić-Preradović, and Zdravko Dovedan. 2010. Verb Valency Enhanced Croatian Lexicon. In T. Varadi, J. Kuti, M. Silberztein (eds.) *Applications of Finite-State Language Processing*, pages 52-60, Cambridge Scholars Publishing, Newcastle upon Tyne.

A Rule-Based System for Disambiguating French Locative Verbs and Their Translation into Arabic

Safa Boudhina
University of Gabes
safaboudhina1@gmail.com

Héla Fehri
University of Sfax
hela.fehri@gmail.com

Abstract

This paper presents a rule-based system for disambiguating French locative verbs and their translation into Arabic. The disambiguation phase is based on the use of the French Verb dictionary of Dubois and Dubois Charlier (LVF) as a linguistic resource, from which a base of disambiguation rules is extracted. The extracted rules take the form of transducers which are subsequently applied to texts. The translation phase consists in translating the disambiguated locative verbs returned by the disambiguation phase. The translation takes into account the verb tense, as well as the inflected form of that verb. This phase is based on bilingual dictionaries that contain the different French locative verbs and their translation into Arabic. The experimentation and the evaluation are done using the linguistic platform NooJ, both a language resource development environment and a tool for automatic large corpora flow (Fehri, 2012).

1 Introduction

Lexical ambiguity represents an obstacle for the automatic processing of natural language. In fact, the difficulty of automatically dealing with this phenomenon was recognized as early as the first appearance of automatic translation systems (Apidaniaki, 2008). This ambiguity can occur at the level of different grammatical categories of words, including the verb. In its conjugated form, the verb is distinguished by tense, mood, person, number and the syntactic constructions in which this verb appears.

However, the task of solving the problem of ambiguity, known as Word Sense Disambiguation (WSD), is not an easy one. In fact, it's essential to specify the elements that contribute to the selection of the appropriate meaning of the ambiguous word. Gross et al. (1997) state that "any syntactic difference corresponds to an essential semantic difference." This statement emphasizes the importance of syntactic constructions in the choice of the meaning of the verb. In other words, the meaning of the verb strongly depends on the syntactic construction in which it appears. Furthermore, to properly handle this condition, the entire sentence containing the ambiguous verb should be analyzed, and this requires a certain linguistic knowledge.

In this perspective, the dictionary of French Verbs of Jean Dubois and Françoise Dubois-Charlier (LVF) constitutes a relevant and useful resource for the WSD of verbs. Indeed, it proposes a verbal classification that relates the syntactic and semantic characteristics of the verb.

WSD may be seen as an intermediate task for some applications such as machine translation. However, to provide the suitable translation of an ambiguous word, WSD is indispensable in identifying the most appropriate meaning of the word in question. In addition, the quality of the translation does not depend solely on the preservation of the meaning of the translated word in the target language. The consideration of the form of the verb and the tense in which that verb is conjugated is also very useful and influences the quality of the translated word.

The main objective of the present work is to develop a rule-based system for disambiguating French verbs, in particular locative verbs. This system also makes it possible to translate the disambiguated verbs while taking into account the tense of the verb and its inflected form. Our system is based on the LVF dictionary using the NooJ platform.

Proceedings of the First Workshop on Linguistic Resources for Natural Language Processing, pages 38–46
Santa Fe, New Mexico, USA, August 20, 2018.

2   Related work

According to the resources used, WSD approaches can be roughly classified into two main categories. The first one is the corpora-based approach, in which systems are trained to perform the task of word sense disambiguation (Dixit et al., 2015). This type includes supervised and unsupervised methods. The supervised methods are based on a learning corpus grouping examples of disambiguated instances of words, while unsupervised methods exploit the results of automatic meaning-acquisition methods. The second main category is the knowledge-based approach, which exploits knowledge resources to infer the senses of words in context (Dixit et al., 2015).

Supervised WSD methods require annotated corpora to be trained (Nessereddine et al., 2015). However, such corpora are only available for a few languages, which complicates supervised lexical disambiguation. In this perspective, Nassreddine et al. (2015) recently proposed a method for creating a system of lexical disambiguation for the French language. Since this language suffers from a scarcity of annotated corpora, their method consists of constructing an annotated corpus by the transfer of annotations. These annotations are obtained from the automatic translation of an English annotated corpus into French. The Bayesian classifier is then used to build the disambiguation system. The precision obtained is of the order of 52%. The limit of this method is that it strongly depends on the annotations obtained by the translation phase. In addition, the quality of the disambiguation system is restricted by the examples used during the learning phase.

In general, the problem with supervised, corpora-based disambiguation approaches is that getting large amounts of annotated text in one's way is very costly in terms of time and money, which results in a data acquisition bottleneck (Tchechmedjiev, 2012). Moreover, the quality of the disambiguation of these approaches is restricted by the examples used for training.

For unsupervised methods, the notion of meaning is directly induced by the corpus (Audibert, 2003). The method proposed by Schütze (1998), which relies on the use of the vector model can be taken as an example. In this method, a vector is associated with each word m of the corpus. This vector is derived from words that co-occur in the context of m. Subsequently, according to their degree of similarity, these vectors are grouped into clusters. Each cluster refers to a possible meaning of the word m.

The problem with this method, as well as unsupervised approaches in general, is that the senses do not correspond to any well-defined set of meanings. The distinctions of meaning can sometimes be confusing and are, moreover, often difficult to be used by other applications (Audibert, 2003).

In knowledge-based approaches, the information needed for lexical disambiguation is derived from external resources of the studied corpus. These resources are of different natures. Indeed, some studies have tested the adequacy of the definitions provided by the Collins English Dictionary (CED), Merriam-Webster New Pocket Dictionary, and Contemporary English Dictionary (LDOCE) for the automatic processing of disambiguation. Other works have exploited the information provided by Roget's International Thesaurus or by WordNet semantic lexicons explaining the meanings and relations between senses or shades of meaning (Vasilescu, 2003).

The disambiguation system established by Lesk is one of the first systems that relies on a dictionary. The principle of this method is first of all to extract from the dictionary all the possible meanings for each occurrence of the ambiguous word. Each sense corresponds to a particular definition in the dictionary. Subsequently, a score is assigned for each of these senses. This score is equal to the number of words in common between the definition of the word to be disambiguated and the definitions of the words co-occurring in its context (Vasilescu, 2003). The sense selected as being the most appropriate sense is supposed to be the one that maximizes the score. This method correctly disambiguates between 50% and 70% of the cases (Boubekeur-Amirouche, 2008).

The method proposed by Brun et al. (2001) is based on an electronic dictionary. The dictionary used in this method gives an example for each meaning. Each example is analyzed through a specific analyzer, from which rules of disambiguation are elaborated. These rules are then generalized using a semantic network that assigns a semantic class to each existing unit in the rule of origin. Subsequently, to disambiguate a word in any sentence, it is syntactically analyzed and the syntactic relationships are derived from it (Brun et al., 2001). These relationships are then compared with the disambiguation rules. The disambiguation rule whose arguments are the same is then selected and its meaning number is associated with the word in question (Brun et al., 2001).

This method was applied to 850 French sentences for the set of nouns, adjectives and verbs. The precision rate obtained for verbs is of the order of 58%. The problem with this method is that the elaborated rules of disambiguation depend on the words that exist in the examples found in the dictionary. This link has also generated a problem of coherence between the dictionary and the chosen semantic network, due to the semantic classification proposed by the thesaurus. In addition, some lexical entries haven't been disambiguated because of the lack of examples for certain meanings from which the disambiguation rules are extracted.

This method has the disadvantage of being very sensitive to the words that exist in each definition. Indeed, the choice of meanings based on a limited number of common words can be the source of errors.

3 Description of the French Verb Dictionary (LVF)

The LVF is a lexical database of French language, which contains 25,609 entries for 12,310 different verbs. The verbs are classified into 14 classes, which is based on the hypothesis of a correspondence between syntax and meaning (Sénéchal et al., 2007). The class denoted *L* presents the class of locative verbs, the topic of this work. It contains 1524 locative verbs (e.g., *baigner* "to bathe", *apparaître* "to appear"). We note that our choice of the type of verbs is arbitrarily done.

4 The creation of electronic locative verbs dictionary with NooJ

The developed disambiguation system focuses on the use of the LVF dictionary. This dictionary has been built to be used by linguists, and is not directly exploitable by automatic text analysis programs (Silberztein, 2010). For this reason, we opt for the formalization of the LVF dictionary. More precisely, we are interested in the formalization of the locative verbs described in the LVF. This formalization consists in reformulating the information contained in LVF so that it can be exploited by automatic analysis programs, notably NooJ (Silberztein, 2010). The electronic dictionary created in NooJ, called LocativeVerbs.dic contains 1,524 verbal entries. Figure 1 presents an extract from this dictionary.

```
apparaître,V+VA+FLX=CONNAITRE+CONST=A31+sens=paraître+AR=ظَهَرَ
apparaître,V+VA+FLX=CONNAITRE+CONST=A11+sens=se présenter+AR=حَضَرَ
accueillir,V+VT+FLX=CUEILLIR+CONST=T11j0+sens=recevoir+AR=إستَقبَلَ
accueillir,V+VT+FLX=CUEILLIR+CONST=T3100+sens=admettre+AR=قَبِلَ
baigner,V+VP+FLX=AIMER+CONST=P10j0+sens=nager+AR=سَبَحَ
baigner,V+VN+FLX=AIMER+CONST=N1j+sens=immerger+AR=إنغَمَرَ
baigner,V+VT+FLX=AIMER+CONST=T13j0+sens=tremper+AR=غَمَسَ
baigner,V+VP+FLX=AIMER+CONST=P1001++sens=se tremper+AR=إستَحَمَّ
```

Figure 1. Extract of electronic dictionary LocativeVerbs.dic

As can be seen in Figure 1, each locative verbal entry is associated with a set of features: a lemma that corresponds to the verb in the infinitive form; a label indicating the grammatical category (*V*); , the *FLX* property which gives the inflectional model related to the verb; the *CONST*, which shows the syntactic-semantic properties of the verb; the *sens*, which indicates the meaning of the verb; and finally the translation into the target language (*AR*). It's worth-noting that a verb can be associated with more than 10 senses. The verb *baigner* "to bathe" is used as an example. Since this verb has four different meanings described in the LVF dictionary (baigner 01=nager, baigner 02=immeger, baigner 03=tremper, baigner 04=se tremper), it appears four times in the LocativeVerbs dictionary, as shown in Figure 1.

The NooJ implementation of our system involves a two-phase process: (1) disambiguation of French locative verbs and (2) translation into Arabic. Each phase requires the construction of proper transducers.

5 Phase of disambiguation

Each verbal entry described in the LVF dictionary is specified by the different possible meanings that correspond to it. These meanings are illustrated by different uses, semantic indicators, syntactic characteristics, etc. The information related to the given meaning of the ambiguous verb, thus paves the way to extract the necessary disambiguation rules. The extracted rules then make it possible to identify the syntactic patterns that will be transformed into transducers to achieve the task of disambiguating verbs.

5.1 Identification of disambiguation rules

The French verbs described in the LVF are classified into semantic classes defined by syntactic arguments, which make it possible to assign the appropriate meaning to each occurrence of the verb. That is, each use of the verb is described by a particular syntactic construction, and then the meaning of the verb is determined by the construction in which the verb appears. In fact, the verb can have four syntactic constructions: intransitive (A), an indirect transitive (N), direct transitive (T), and pronominal (P). Each construction is composed of a set of components (subject, object, complement), which are also associated with semantic features, such as human, inanimate, animal, etc. For example, the word *apparaître* "to appear" has two different constructions:

A11: Inanimate subject, Human object

A31: Human subject, Complement

To solve these semantic and syntactic ambiguities, we created formal grammars that take into consideration the differences between syntactic constructions and the various types of components (human, inanimate, animal) in each construction. The elaboration of such a grammar is not an easy task because it is necessary to find a representation that considers recursion, as well as the length of the syntactic construction. Since the syntactic construction is formed by other components, its length is not known in advance. The proposed representation is illustrated by syntactic patterns.

5.2 Identification of syntactic patterns

In order to facilitate the identification of the transducers necessary for the disambiguation of verbs, we transformed the definition of each syntactic construction into a syntactic pattern. A major advantage of this method is that if makes it possible to arrange the various constituents of the construction in a linear manner that can be easily transformed into graphs (Fehri, 2012). According to the classification proposed by the LVF, we can construct 56 syntactic patterns that describe the locative verbs. A sample pattern is shown below:

Pattern N1j:=_<human subject><verb><Prepositional complement, PREP = « en, dans »>

This pattern describes the different components of the *N1j* construction. According to this construction, we can distinguish the meaning of the verb when the latter appears in a sentence which has a human subject and a prepositional complement introduced by the preposition (PREP) *en* "in, to" or *dans* "in, inside". We notice that the identified patterns have been refined.

5.3 Creation of transducers for locative verbs

For a reliable disambiguation system of locative verbs, we transformed each syntactic pattern into a transducer, which is manually built in NooJ. The meaning of the verb is related to the type of the construction and its constituents. The created transducer is represented in Figure 2.

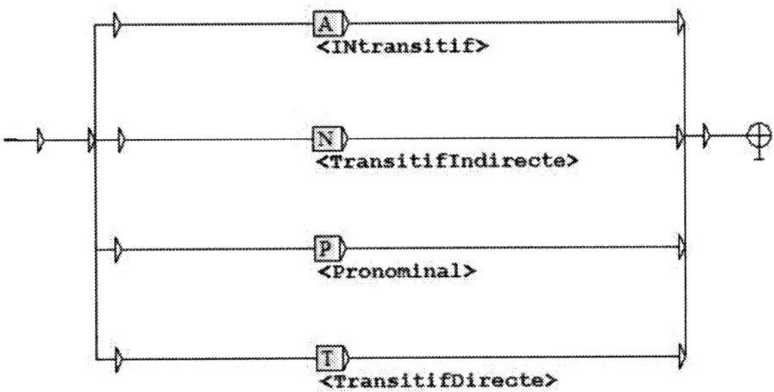

Figure 2. Main transducer of verb disambiguation

The transducer illustrated in Figure 2 contains four sub-graphs. Each sub-graph represents a category of syntactic construction -- intransitive (A), an indirect transitive (N), a pronominal (P), and a direct transitive (T),

6   Phase of Translation

Understanding a word sense is an inherent part of correct translation of words whose meanings depend on the context (Turdakov, 2010). For this reason, the proposed method of translation takes as input the disambiguated verbs returned by the phase of disambiguation. In addition, the quality of the translation of the verb does not depend only on the preservation of the meaning of the translated verb in the target language but also on the consideration of the tense in which the verb is conjugated and the inflected form of that verb. It also influences the quality of the translated verb. In this context, we built a syntactic grammar allowing the translation of each disambiguated locative verb by taking into account the tense of the verb and its inflected form.

However, the creation of such a grammar is not an easy task because this study deals with two very different languages: French, an Indo-European language, and Arabic, a Semitic language. We now examine some cases of translation of French locative verbs into Arabic. For example, unlike the French verb, the Arabic verb is not based on tense but on the aspect. In fact, the Arabic verbal system, is essentially represented by three aspects: accomplished, unaccomplished and imperative. Consider the following dictionary entry and French sentence:

accueillir 02: meaning = recevoir (to welcome) + AR= اِسْتَقْبَلَ istaqbala "welcomed"

La fille accueillait une amie dans sa maison.

The tense of the verb *accueillir* is in the imperfect. In Arabic, the imperfect is translated by كان يَفْعَلُ Kāna yafaalu "has done" and the verb *accueillait* will be translated by كَانت تَسْتَقْبِلُ Kānat tastaqbilu "have welcomed."

Another difference between the two language can be seen in the case of gender. In French, the verb is conjugated with the same form for both the third person singular subject masculine pronoun *il* "he' and the feminine pronoun *elle* "she " – *il écrit* "he writes", *elle écrit* "she writes". In Arabic, however, the conjugation of the verb differs for the two subject pronouns. Indeed, *il écrit* is translated into Arabic as كَتَبَ kataba "he writes", while *elle écrit* is translated by كَتَبَتْ katabat "she writes".

Finally, the Arabic language specifically notes when there are two of something, called المَثَّى al-mutaná "dual". This form does not exist in French, which has only singular and plural. In Arabic, the dual number has its own suffixes, which totally differ from those of the plural.

After, this level of analysis, we move to the practice of automatic translation using the NooJ platform. In this step, we will integrate locative verbs into a bilingual dictionary. We also create a formal grammar, seen in Figure 3.

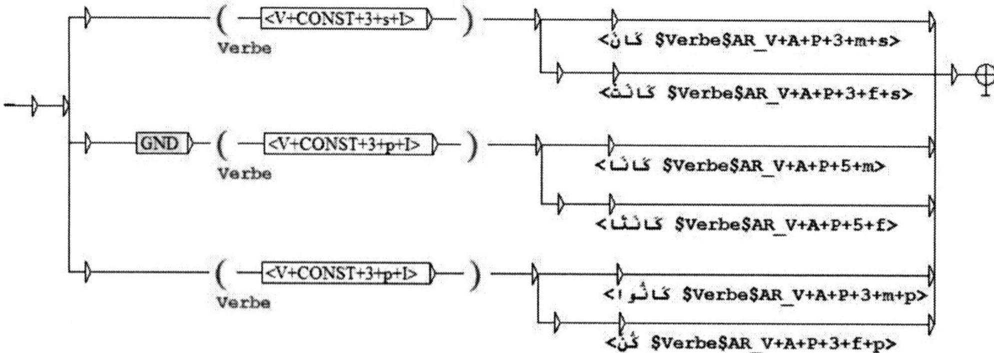

Figure 3. Transducer for the translation of conjugated verbs in imperfect

Figure 3 represents an extract of the transducer relating the translation of a verb when it is conjugated in the imperfect. The node that exists between brackets called *Verbe*, represents the form of the French verb to translate. For example, <V+CONST+3+s+I> indicates that the verb is conjugated in the imperfect (I) with the third person singular (3+s).

7 Experimentation and evaluations

WE tested the developed system is done with NooJ. As mentioned above, this platform uses already built syntactic local grammars (Fehri et al., 2011). Table 1 gives an idea about the dictionaries which we added to the resources in NooJ.

Dictionaries	Number of inputs	Annotation in the dictionary
Human nouns	250	N+Hum
Inanimate nouns	305	N+Chose
Animal nouns	480	N+Anl

Table 1. Added dictionaries

In addition to the dictionaries mentioned in Table 1, other NooJ dictionaries -- adjectives, determinants and verbs -- are used (Fehri et al., 2016).

7.1 Experimentation of disambiguation phase

To evaluate the disambiguation phase, we applied our resources to a corpus of journalistic articles published in *Le Monde Diplomatique* newspaper. The various topics that are covered deal with current world politics, economics, culture, sports, etc. The purpose of using a wide variety of subject areas is to have a broad coverage of the complex structures of sentences that constitute the context of the verbs to be disambiguated. This corpus contains 1,009 articles giving a total of 2,006,631 graphic words including 1,544 occurrences of locative verbs. These verbs are manually identified using NooJ queries.

Before	Seq.	After
ent que	les ouvriers baignaient dans une atmosphère/<V+N1j> Verbe= baignaient sens=immerger	saturé
allées à	l'hôtel Président de Yamoussoukro, qui abritait des militaires/<V+T3100> Verbe= abritait sens=loger	des fo
iriennes	Les autorités sanitaires avaient fondé leur décision sur l'absense/<V+T13g0> Verbe= avaient fondé sens=baser	de ris(
imission	Plusieurs étudiantes assistaient à mes cours/<V+N1a> Verbe= assistaient sens=se présenter	chaqu
onomie	, Jason, 22 ans, habitait chez ses parents/<V+A11> Verbe= habitait sens=demeurer	à Bor(
rdeaux	Son nom avait figuré dans des agendas de personnes/<V+A31> Verbe= avait figuré sens=se trouver	impliq
ait que	le bateau ne finira pas en Méditerrané./<V+A31> Verbe= ne finira pas sens=aboutir	La sol(
terrané.	La soldate, qui figurait sur bon nombre des photographies/<V+A11> Verbe= figurait sens=se trouver	de sé\
Nord.'	Trois milliards de gens vivaient dans les régions/<V+A11> Verbe= vivaient sens=habiter	côtièr(
angères	, Laila Freivalds, assistait tranquillement à une pièce de théâtre/<V+N1a> Verbe= assistait sens=se présenter	à Stoc
Jacob.	Beaucoup de réfugiés gravèrent des histoires d'une lourdeur infinie dans leurs mémoires./<V+T13j0> Verbe= gravèrent sens=imprimer	Les fe\
imoires.	Les femmes jetaient un voile sur leur tête,/<V+T13g0> Verbe= jetaient sens=placer	une ét
voisins	Sa petite maison se trouvait à une trentaine de mètres du bord de l'eau/<V+P3001> Verbe= se trouvait sens=se situer	L'anci
de l'eau	L'ancien chef de la délégation palestinienne à la conférence de Madrid apparaissait sur d'innombrables affiches,/<V+A11> Verbe= apparaissait sens=se présenter	aux c(
Depuis	, les frères Finaly vivaient en Israël./<V+A11> Verbe= vivaient sens=habiter	Il s'agi
ndiale (	500 soldats japonais se trouvaient actuellement dans le sud de l'Irak,/<V+P1001> Verbe= se trouvaient sens=se tenir	une ini
out de	ce camp, qui abritait quelque 3 000 réfugiés/<V+T3100> Verbe= abritait sens=loger	sur les
e.Mais	Tony Blair, qui cachait sa passion sous ses bonnes manières/<V+T1308> Verbe= cachait sens=masquer	et sa l
l'adage	Les quelque 190 familles qui campaient dans les bois sous des toiles de plastique/<V+A11> Verbe= campaient sens=bivouaquer	ont tou
toutes	les personnes qui se trouvaient dans le village/<V+P1001> Verbe= se trouvaient sens=se tenir	à ce n

Figure 4. Concordance table of locative verb disambiguation

Each line of the concordance table shown in Figure 4 displays the sequence identified by the disambiguation transducer. For example, in the first line of Figure 4, the verb is assigned the meaning of the construction <N1j>. Consequently, the context of the verb *baignaient* (< *baigner* "to bathe") takes on the meaning of *immerger* "immerse" in this particular context. To measure the performance of our tool, the following evaluation metrics are used: precision, recall and F-measure. The results obtained are described in Table 2.

	Nb. of occurrences (locative verbs)	Precision	Recall	F-measure
Newspaper *Le Monde diplomatqiue* (1009 texts)	1544	0.75	0.85	0.79

Table 2. Obtained results

The results shown in Table 2 reflect the existence of some issues that have not been resolved by our tool. These problems lie in the inability to disambiguate the verbs that appear in sentences whose subject is implicitly defined and so it is not possible to identify its nature. Take the example of the following phrase: *most being located near the islands*. In this example, the subject is represented by the noun *most*. This noun is not followed by anything that specifies the subject, such as *most people*. As a result, we cannot decide on the nature of the subject (human, animal or thing) and subsequently the verb *to locate* cannot be disambiguated.

In addition, the LVF construction codes describe the semantic traits of the arguments (subject, object, etc.) of each verbal use, as human, thing, animal, etc. For example, to distinguish the use *shelter 3* in *The embassy shelters the refugees* from *shelter 2* used in *The ambassador shelters refugees at home*, one must take into account that the noun *embassy* is a thing, while *ambassador* and *refugee* are human nouns. But such a purely lexical characterization of the arguments of a verb does not allow researchers to analyze many sentences that include semantic mechanisms, such as metaphor or metonymy, or to modify the function of nominal groups. Thus, for example, the noun *embassy*, principally lexicalized as a thing, can play the role of a human by metonymy: the phrase *The embassy shelters the refugees* must then be considered as ambiguous, depending on whether *embassy* designates the building itself or the embassy staff.

7.2 Disambiguation phase

The translation phase is applied to the disambiguated locative verbs returned by the disambiguation phase. Thus, as pointed out before, this verb translation from French into Arabic takes into account the verbal tense used and the inflected form of the verb. The results obtained are illustrated in Figure 5.

Figure 5. Concordance table of locative verb translation

Figure 5 shows the Arabic equivalent assigned to the ambiguous verbs shown in Figure 4 of the previous section. As a result, we have translated the verb according to the context in which it appears. Take

44

the example of the verb *baignaient* (< *baigner* "to bathe") on the first line of the concordance table. This verb can have four different meanings, corresponding to four separate translations. Here, in this particular context, the verb *baigner* "to bathe" has been disambiguated with the meaning *immerger* "immerse" which is then translated into Arabic by اِنْغَمَرَ enghamara "immersed," thus eliminating the other three translations.

Our translation tool gives satisfactory results, with a precision of 87%, which is comparable to well-known translators such as Google and Babylon that support the translation from French to Arabic.

French Locative Verbs	Obtained result (Our tool)	Obtained result (Google)	Obtained result (Babylon)
Les ouvriers **baignaient** dans une atmosphère	كَانُوا يَنْغَمِرونَ	و استحم العمال في جو	في جو **baignaient** العمال
Les autorités sanitaires **avaient fondé** leur décision sur des preuves	كُنَّ قَد بَنَيْنَ	و استندت السلطات الصحية الى قراراتها بشأن الأدلة	السلطات الصحية التي **تقوم** على قرار بشأن الأدلة
Son nom **figurait** dans des agendas	وَرَدَ	و كان اسمه في يوميات	اسمه وارد في مذكرات
Le bateau **finira** en Méditerrané	سَيَنْتَهِي	فإن القارب **ينتهي** في البحر الأبيض المتوسط	مركب **ستنجز** بالفعل في Méditerrané

Table3. Experimental results

As shown in Table 3, it is noted that Google did not use the correct sense of the verb. Moreover, the tense and the form of the verb have not been respected, such as for the verb *baigner* which appears in the sentence *Les ouvriers baignaient dans une atmosphère* "the workers were immersed in an atmosphere." Our tool gives as result كانوا ينغمرون Kânû yanghamirûna "have immersed." This translation corresponds to the meaning of the verb *baigner* in this particular context. Also, the translated verb respects the tense and the form of the source verb. However, Google translates the verb *baignaient* into استحم estahama "has bathed" where the verbal tense and the inflected form of the verb have not been respected. Babylon does not even produce any translation of the verb *baigner.*

Note also that there are verbs that are not recognized by either Google or Babylon and therefore no translation is provided for the verb *appear* in the sentence *His name appeared in diaries*. The results obtained reflect the effectiveness of our translation tool. Indeed, a specific treatment for the locative verbs allows us to understand the meaning of the verb according to the statements produced in the source language and thus to propose a satisfactory translated version that takes into account the characteristics of the verb.

8   Conclusion and future perspectives

In the present work, we have developed a rule-based system for disambiguating French locative verbs and their translation into Arabic. The proposed disambiguation approach is based on the LVF dictionary. We have shown the effectiveness of this dictionary as a relevant resource for the task of disambiguation. As for the translation, it consists in translating the already disambiguated French locative verbs into Arabic. This translation takes into account the verbal time used as well as the inflected form of the verb. The experimentation and the evaluation were done using the linguistic platform NooJ, with satisfactory results.

In the future, we intend to study the syntactic and semantic phenomena in more detail. We also plan to generalize our phase of disambiguation to all the verbs. As for translation, we plan to take into account the linguistic context of the verb in order to specify the most appropriate verbal tense with the syntax of the Arabic sentence.

References

Marianna Apidaniaki. 2008. *Acquisition automatique de sens pour la désambiguïsation et la sélection lexicale en traduction*. PhD thesis, PARIS University. DIDEROT (Paris 7).

Laurent Audibert. 2003. *Outils d'exploration de corpus et désambiguïsation lexicale automatique*. Autre [cs.OH]. University of Provence - Aix-Marseille I, French.

Fatiha Boubekeur-Amirouche. 2008. *Contribution à la définition de modèles de recherche d'information flexibles basés sur les CP-Nets*. PhD thesis in computer science, University of Toulouse.

Caroline Brun. Bernard Jacquemin, and Frédérique Segond. 2001. *Exploitation de dictionnaires électroniques pour la désambiguïsation sémantique lexicale*. Automatic Language Processing, ATALA, 42 (3): 677-691.

Vimal Dixit, Kamlesh Dutta and Pardeep Singh. 2015. *Word Sense Disambiguation and Its Approaches*. CPUH-Research Journal: 2015, 1(2): 54-58.

Héla Fehri. 2012. *Reconnaissance automatique des entités nommées arabes et leurs traductions vers le français*. PhD thesis in computer science, University of Sfax.

Héla Fehri, Kais Haddar, and Abdelmajid Ben Hamadou. 2011. *Recognition and Translation of Arabic Named Entities with NooJ Using a New Representation Model*. Proceedings of the 9th International Workshop on Finite State Methods and Natural Language Processing, Blois, France, pages 134–142.

Héla Fehri, Mohamed Zaidi, and Kamel Boudhina. 2016. *Création d'un dictionnaire des verbes NooJ open source pour la langue Arabe*. Report of the end of studies project. Higher Institute of Management of Gabes.

Gaston Gross and André Clas. 1997. *Synonymie, polysémie et classes d'objets. Meta* 421 (1997.DOI: 10.7202/002977ar): 147–154.

Mohammad Nessereddine, Andon Tchechmedjiev, Hervé Blanchon, and Didier Schwab. 2015. *Création rapide et efficace d'un système de désambiguïsation lexicale pour une langue peu dotée*. 22nd Automatic Processing of Natural Languages, Caen. `http://talnarchives.atala.org/TALN/TALN-2015/taln-2015-long-008.pdf`.

Hinrich Schütze. 1998. Automatic word sense discrimination. *Computational Linguistics: Special Issue on Word Sense Disambiguation*, 24 (1): 97–123.

Morgane Sénéchal and Dominique Willems. 2007. Classes verbales et régularités polysémiques : le cas des verbes trivalenciels locatifs. *French language* (no. 153): 92-110.

Max Silberztein. 2010. La formalisation du dictionnaire LVF avec NooJ et ses applications pour l'analyse automatique de corpus. *Languages* (No. 179-180), DOI 10.3917 / lang.179.0221: 221-241.

Andon Tchechmedjiev. 2012. État de l'art : mesures de similarité sémantique locales & algorithmes globaux pour la désambiguïsation lexicale à base de connaissances. *Proceedings of the joint JEP-TALN-RECITAL conference volume 3: RECITAL*, Grenoble, pages 295–308.

D.Yu Turdakov. 2010. Word Sense Disambiguation Methods. *Programming and Computer Software*. Vol. 36, No. 6: 309–326.

Florentina Vasilescu. 2003. *Désambiguïsation de corpus monolingues par des approches de type Lesk*. Master of Science in Computer Science, University of Montréal.

A Pedagogical Application of NooJ in Language Teaching: the Adjective in Spanish and Italian

Andrea Rodrigo
Universidad Nacional de Rosario
Entre Ríos 758
S2000CRN Rosario, Argentina
andreafrodrigo@yahoo.com.ar

Mario Monteleone
Universitá di Salerno
Via Giovanni Paolo II, 132
84084 Fisciano SA, Italy
mmonteleone@unisa.it

Silvia Reyes
Universidad Nacional de Rosario
Entre Ríos 758
S2000CRN Rosario, Argentina
sisureyes@gmail.com

Abstract

This paper relies on the work developed by the research team IES_UNR (Argentina) and presents a pedagogical application of NooJ for the teaching and learning of Spanish as a foreign language. However, as this proposal specifically addresses learners of Spanish whose mother tongue is Italian, it also entailed vital collaboration with Mario Monteleone from the University of Salerno, Italy. The adjective was chosen on account of its lower frequency of occurrence in texts written in Spanish, and particularly in the Argentine Rioplatense variety, and with the aim of developing strategies to increase its use. The features that the adjective shares with other grammatical categories render it extremely productive and provide elements that enrich the learner's proficiency. The reference corpus contains the front pages of the Argentinian newspaper *Clarín* related to an emblematic historical moment, whose starting point is March 24, 1976, when a military coup began, and covers a thirty year period until March 24, 2006. The use of the linguistic resources created in NooJ for the automatic processing of texts written in Spanish accounts for the adjective in a relevant historical context for Argentina.

1 Introduction

1.1 Research Subject

Our subject matter deals with the pedagogical application of NooJ in the teaching and learning of Spanish as a foreign language, which relies on the research project carried out by the IES_UNR group since 2015 (Rodrigo et al. 2018). An antecedent of this work can be observed in Frigière and Fuentes (2015), which examines the pedagogical application of NooJ for learners of French as a foreign language. In this paper, we focus on a specific group: native speakers of Italian learning Spanish as a foreign language. Our interest lies in a main grammatical category: the adjective. And our work entails the following steps: (1) selection of a reference corpus in Spanish; (2) presentation of the adjective in relation to other categories and inserted in real texts; (3) use of NooJ for automatic text processing (Silberztein 2015); and (4) presentation of a pedagogical proposal specifically directed to learners of Spanish whose mother tongue is Italian (see Appendix B).

1.2 Reference corpus

Our approach to Spanish takes the Argentine Rioplatense variety[1] and centres on journalistic texts produced during thirty years in Argentina. These written texts represent an important historical moment since they are concerned with the last dictatorship and the democratic period immediately following it.

---

[1] Although our conclusions may also apply to other Spanish dialects, whether European or American varieties.

Proceedings of the First Workshop on Linguistic Resources for Natural Language Processing, pages 47–56
Santa Fe, New Mexico, USA, August 20, 2018.

Our reference corpus, the *Clarín*_corpus,[2] spans the years 1976 to 2006, and includes the same date each year, March 24, which was the day the Armed Forces took power by force in 1976 and overthrew the democratic Argentine government in charge of President María Estela Martínez de Perón. This repressive de facto regime known as *la Junta Militar* "the Military Junta" seized power and ruled until December 1983, when a democratic government was again elected by the Argentinian people. The first front page that was published by *Clarín* when the coup d'état began is displayed in Figure 1.

Figure 1. Front page published on March 24, 1976.

The phrase *Nuevo Gobierno* "New Government" is a distant and neutral expression, whereas at the bottom right corner of the last front page of the corpus, which corresponds to March 24, 2006 (see Appendix A), the word *noche* "night," in the expression *A 30 años de la noche más larga* "30 years after the longest night," overtly condemns the beginning of the military regime.

The corpus comprises 2,898 words and always deals with the front pages of the daily newspaper *Clarín*, assuming the front page to be a focus of journalistic and ideological attention.

1.3 The adjective

At a first stage, the adjective is presented in relation to the noun, the verb and the adverb; then, the frequency of adjectives in the *Clarín*_corpus is detected, in contrast to other categories. At a second stage, our intention is to observe what types of adjectives appear there. For instance, if the term *desaparecido* "disappeared" – which from a historical viewpoint has so many connotations in Argentina – is used, we observe what prefixes and suffixes are allowed with derivations, and in what types of constructions it is included. It is important to recall that the word *desaparecido* is also listed in English dictionaries. The *Oxford Dictionary of English*[3] defines it as, "(especially in South America) a person who has disappeared, presumed killed by members of the armed services or the police." And the *Merriam-Webster's Dictionary*[4] offers the following definition: "an Argentine citizen who has been abducted and usually murdered by right-wing terrorists."

---

[2] *Clarín* Corpus available at `http://tapas.clarin.com/tapa.html#19780324`
[3] *Oxford Dictionary of English* available at `https://en.oxforddictionaries.com`
[4] *Merriam-Webster's Dictionary* available at `https://www.merriam-webster.com`

1.4 Use of NooJ

We have been working with the linguistic resources created for the Spanish Module Argentina,[5] specifically built by the IES_UNR research team to be used with NooJ,[6] a computational tool designed by Max Silberztein. Our linguistic resources include dictionaries and grammars that are now in full development. In this paper we will particularly deal with the dictionary of adjectives and some specific grammars, leaving aside the dictionaries of other grammatical categories, which we use to recognise different types of entries such as nouns, verbs and adverbs.

Similarly, the linguistic resources created for the Italian Module[7] provide an anchor to the Italian learners of Spanish as a foreign language. Notice however that the Italian Module is not our main purpose, for it is only tangentially addressed as a starting point for those learners.

The choice of NooJ entails, above all, a methodological decision, which assumes that it is possible to create language teaching and learning situations by taking into account natural language processing. Then, it is understood that in a given environment and with a given input, learners formulate linguistic hypotheses that may be checked with a computational tool. The NooJ platform provides a favourable means to create this type of situations since: (1) it articulates different levels of analysis (orthography, morphology, syntax, etc.); (2) its connected dictionaries and grammars involve an integral knowledge of language; and (3) a single platform allows a comparison of Italian and Spanish using a common language.

We will try to formulate possible language teaching and learning strategies for learners of Spanish as a foreign language, whose mother tongue is Italian.

2 Development

2.1 Comparison between the adjective and other categories in Spanish

From a morphological viewpoint, Spanish nouns and adjectives share the same diminutive suffix *-ito* (e.g., *mesa* "table" - *mesita* "little table" and *claro* "clear"- *clarito* "very clear"). Many adjectives derive from nouns as in: *cultura* "culture" - *cultural* "cultural" and *trabajo* "work" - *trabajador* "worker". From a syntactic viewpoint, an adjective may become the head of a noun phrase, as in the sentence *el militar abrió fuego* "the military (man) opened fire," where the adjective *militar* "military" functions as a noun.

From a morphological viewpoint, it is possible to create adjectives out of certain verbs (e.g., *tonificar* "to tone" - *tonificante* "toning" and *desear* "to desire" - *deseable* "desirable"). From a syntactic viewpoint, past participles and adjectives occur in common environments, as in: *un traje combinado* "a combined suit" and *un traje azul* "a blue suit."

From a morphological viewpoint, adjectives and adverbs admit the same diminutive and superlative suffixes *-ito* and *-ísimo* respectively (e.g., *buenito* "very good" - *tempranito* "very early" and *buenísimo* "great" - *tempranísimo* "very early"). Moreover, adverbs in *-mente* derive from adjectives as in: *lento* "slow" - *lentamente* "slowly." From a syntactic and semantic viewpoint, adjectival adverbs constitute an intersection of adjectives and adverbs, as in the sentence *llovió fuerte* "it rained hard," where *fuerte* "hard" functions as an adjectival adverb modifying the verb *llovió*; whereas in the phrase *un fuerte viento* "a strong wind," *fuerte* "strong" is simply an adjective modifying a noun.

2.2 Comparison between the adjective and other categories in Italian

In Italian, adjectives have a high percentage of categorical ambiguity with two other grammatical categories, specifically those of the noun and the past participle (Monteleone 2016). A typical example of this ambiguity is the word *anguished*. In the sentence *Giovanni è angosciato* "Giovanni is anguished," *angosciato* is an adjective. And in the sentence *Paolo è un angosciato* "Paul is an anguished man," *angosciato* functions as a noun. However, in the sentence *Paolo è angosciato da Giovanna* "Paolo is anguished because of Giovanna," *angosciato* is a past participle.

---

[5]Spanish Module (Argentina) available at `http://www.nooj-association.org/index.php?option=com_k2&view=item&id=6:spanish-module-argentina&Itemid=611)`

[6] Software NooJ available at `http://nooj-association.org`

[7]Italian Module available at `http://www.nooj-association.org/index.php?option=com_k2&view=item&task=download&id=80_cf86247a0b995f68b04b2d484130c7f4&Itemid=611)`

However, through specific automatic parsing tools (grammars, automata and finite-state transducers in NooJ), it is possible to solve this ambiguity and automatically tag syntactic sequences containing only adjectives. For reasons of space, those tools will not be discussed here, but developed in a future paper.

3 Analysis of the *Clarín*_corpus

3.1 Category frequency

Within NooJ, we apply the command "Linguistic Analysis" in order to obtain the frequency of the categories contained in the corpus: nouns, verbs, adjectives and adverbs. Then, by applying Locate for each category in turn: <N>, <V>, <ADJ> and <ADV>, the following piece of information is obtained: Nouns: 1,200; Verbs: 658; Adjectives: 353; Adverbs: 137; Other categories: 550 (conjunctions, prepositions, pronouns).

The graph in Figure 2 shows that adjectives and adverbs are the least frequent out of the five categories. This data provides a first conclusion. The low frequency of adjectives points out that, due to its low proportion in the text input, this category is susceptible to be reinforced by the foreign language teacher's intervention.

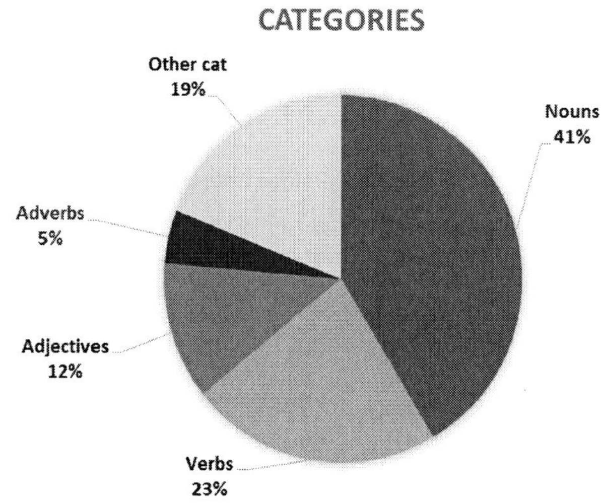

Figure 2. Frequency of grammatical categories in the *Clarín*_corpus.

3.2 Adjectives

As frequency is our working criterion, those adjectives recording more frequency in the corpus represent the starting point. It is then specified which categories precede these adjectives, which morphological suffixes and prefixes they admit, and which adjectival structures are more recurrent.

In Figure 3, after applying the commands "Locate" and "Statistical Analysis," it is possible to recognise the twenty most frequent adjectives in the corpus: *militar* "military," *político* "political," *política* "political," *desaparecidos* "disappeared," *general* "general," *muertos* "dead," *derechos* "right," *Militar* "Military," *Argentina* "Argentinian, *listas* "ready," *heridos* "injured," *humanos* "human," *Armadas* "Armed, *solo* "alone," *fuerte* "strong," *primer* "first," *exclusivo* "exclusive," *argentino* "Argentine," *central* "central" and *especial* "special."

Some of the adjectives of the above list are selected in order to specify their inflectional and derivational paradigms, their context of occurrence and their syntactic structure.

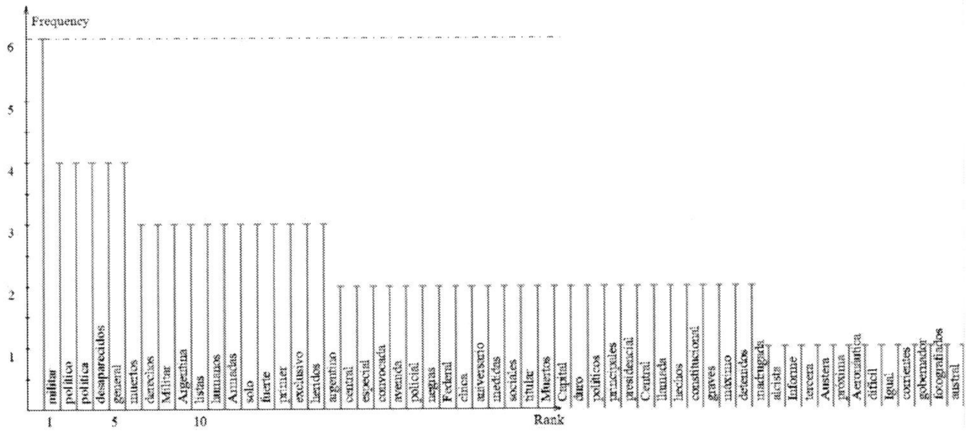

Figure 3. Frequency of adjectives in the *Clarín*_corpus.

3.3 Morphological Inflection and Derivation

Next, the inflectional paradigms of some of the most frequent adjectives are shown, as they are recorded in the inflectional grammars (Rodrigo et al. 2018) and in the dictionary of adjectives created in NooJ for the Spanish Module Argentina.

The adjective *militar* "military" inflects like ÁGIL: *militar, militares*. The following words are part of its derivational paradigm as recorded in the dictionary of adjectives: *antimilitar* "anti-military," *antimilitarista* "anti-militarist," *paramilitar* "paramilitary," *desmilitarizado* "demilitarised," *militarizado* "militarised."

The adjective *político* "political" belongs to the paradigm FLACO: *político, política, políticos, políticas*. The words *apolítico* "apolitical," *geopolítico* "geopolitical" and *impolítico* "non-political" are part of its derivational paradigm in the dictionary of adjectives.

The adjective *desaparecido* "disappeared" also follows the paradigm FLACO: *desaparecido, desaparecida, desaparecidos, desaparecidas*. It is important to note that there are no words derived from *desaparecido*.

The adjective *general* "general" inflects like ÁGIL: *general, generales*. The words *generalista* "generalist," *generalizable* "generalisable" and *generalizado* "generalised" are part of its derivational paradigm as it is recorded in the dictionary of adjectives.

3.4 Context of occurrence

The context of occurrence allows us to know which categories can accompany the adjective. The adjective *militar* "military" is preceded by nouns, as in the phrases *reacción militar* "military reaction," *autocrítica militar* "military self-criticism," *caudillo militar* "military leader," *uniforme militar* "military uniform," *golpe militar* "military coup," *colegio militar* "military college."

The adjectives *político, política* "political" are preceded by nouns, as in: *sector político* "political sector," *Reforma política* "political Reform," *favoritismo político* "political favouritism," *enemigo político*" political enemy" and *terror político* "political terror." However, they may also be preceded by determiners: *su política* "his/her/their/your politics," *la política* "(the) politics."

The adjective *desaparecidos* "disappeared" is preceded by verbs (e.g., *son desaparecidos* "(they) are disappeared"), by the construction adjective+preposition (e.g., *miles de desaparecidos* "thousands of disappeared"), by numeral adjectives (e.g., *catorce desaparecidos* "fourteen disappeared"), and by nouns (e.g., *alumnos desaparecidos* "disappeared students").

3.5 Syntactic structure

The analysis of two expressions containing adjectives and selected from the *Clarín*_corpus, *Hubo miles de desaparecidos* "There were thousands of disappeared" and *último golpe militar* "last military coup" will be shown. The first example is an impersonal sentence and the second one is a noun phrase.

51

The basis of our analysis are the concepts developed by Bès (1999) and our approach is related to context-sensitive grammars. Our NooJ grammars take into account two types of constructions: nucleus phrases, such as a nucleus verb phrase (SVN), a nucleus adjective phrase (SADJN), a nucleus preposition phrase (SPN), a nucleus noun phrase (SNN), and larger phrases, such as the noun phrase (SINNOM), which contain nucleus phrases. These expressions will be analysed with the different syntactic grammars available in the Spanish Module Argentina.

In Spanish, the expression *Hubo miles de desaparecidos* "There were thousands of disappeared" is an impersonal sentence, i.e., without a subject. In the above example, we distinguish a nucleus adjective phrase (SADJN), *miles* "thousands" and a nucleus preposition phrase (SPN), *de desaparecidos* "of disappeared," both inside the noun phrase (SINNOM). On the other hand, the verb *hubo* "were," which is the past indicative of *haber* "to be," constitutes a nucleus verb phrase (SVN). These two structures make up the impersonal sentence, as it can be seen in Figure 4.

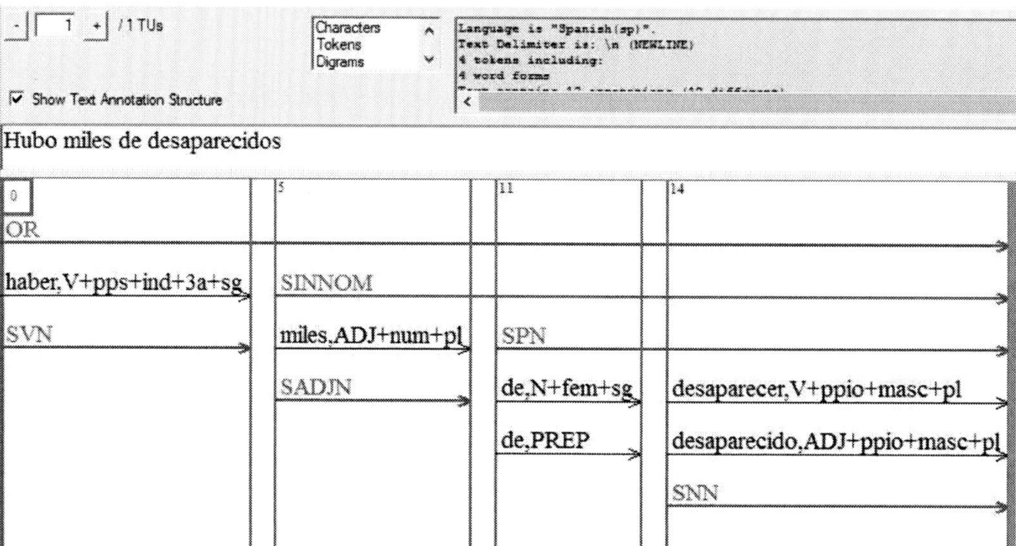

Figure 4. Analysis of *Hubo miles de desaparecidos*.

The corresponding main grammar for impersonal sentences is displayed in Figure 5.

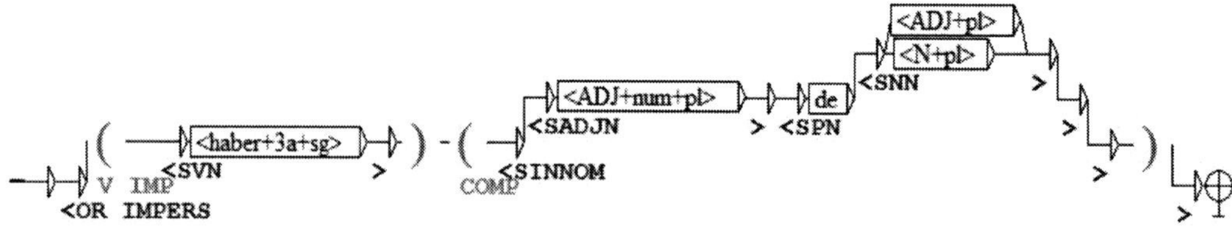

Figure 5. Grammar for impersonal sentences.

As regards the second expression, the noun phrase *último golpe militar* "last military coup", instead of analysing it with the "Linguistic Analysis" command, we use the NooJ "Show Debug" feature instead. By using "Show Debug," it is possible to analyse whether the phrase entered can be considered acceptable, when the noun phrase grammar is applied. As can be seen in Figure 6, the result is a Perfect Match.

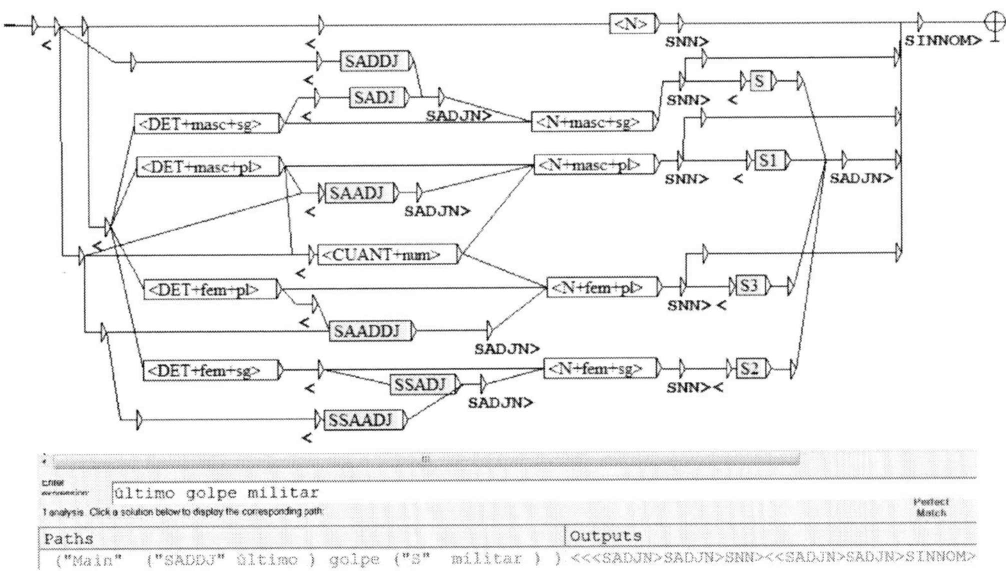

Figure 6. Noun Phrase Grammar.

"Show Debug" checks to see if the grammar designed for the noun phrase identifies that *último* "last" and *militar* "military" are two nucleus adjective phrases (SADJN), inside a larger unit, the noun phrase (SINNOM). The intermediate unit is the nucleus noun phrase (SNN), *último golpe* "last coup."

The analyses of both expressions, *Hubo miles de desaparecidos* "There were thousands of disappeared" and *último golpe militar* "last military coup," show the adjective in two different syntactic constructions. In the first example, the adjective *miles* "thousands" is the nucleus of the noun phrase (SINNOM) *miles de desaparecidos* "thousands of disappeared" and is part of an impersonal sentence; in the second example, two adjectives occur in different positions: *último* "last" is a nucleus adjective phrase (SADJN) inside the nucleus noun phrase (SNN) *último golpe* "last coup," and, at the same time, *último* "last" is part of the noun phrase (SINNOM) *último golpe militar* "last military coup," and *militar* "military" is a nucleus adjective phrase (SADJN) inside a noun phrase (SINNOM), peripheral to the nucleus noun phrase (SNN).

The syntactic structure shows how the adjective can integrate noun phrases and even become the nucleus of a noun phrase.

4   Conclusions

In this paper, we have proposed a pedagogical application of the NooJ approach to a specific situation by choosing a significant corpus (the *Clarín*_corpus), which can provide an idea of the use of the Spanish language in a particular historical and cultural context. Our intention has been to identify adjectives and to do a global reading of them within the corpus. Our focus was mainly placed on the adjective *desaparecido* "disappeared," because of its ideological importance. As we have already stated in the Introduction, our subject matter deals with the pedagogical application of NooJ in the teaching-learning of Spanish as a foreign language. And we have concentrated on a specific group: native speakers of Italian learning Spanish as a foreign language. Our strategy has been to make explicit some contact points between Spanish and Italian by using NooJ as a common platform. Our purpose was not to compare the Italian and Spanish resources, but to highlight that both languages can be formalised using a common platform, since the structure of dictionaries and grammars is the same. This provides unity and coherence to our pedagogical proposal, which is the goal of the research project carried out by the IES_UNR team, since both languages can be analysed with NooJ (Appendix B).

References

Gabriel G. Bès, 1999. La phrase verbale noyau en français. *Recherches sur le français parlé*, volume 15: 273–358. Université de Provence.

Andrea Rodrigo, Silvia Reyes and Rodolfo Bonino. 2018. Some Aspects Concerning the Automatic Treatment of Adjectives and Adverbs in Spanish: A Pedagogical Application of the NooJ Platform. In: Mbarki S., Mourchid M., Silberztein M. (eds) Formalizing Natural Languages with NooJ and Its Natural Language Processing Applications. NooJ 2017. Springer, Cham. https://doi.org/10.1007/978-3-319-73420-0_11. *Communications in Computer and Information Science*, volume 811: 130-140.

Julia Frigière and Sandrine Fuentes. 2015. Pedagogical Use of NooJ dealing with French as a Foreign Language. In J. Monti, M. Silberztein, M. Monteleone, and M. P. di Buono (eds.) *Formalizing Natural Languages with NooJ*, Cambridge Scholars Publishing, London, 186-197.

Mario Monteleone. 2016. Local Grammars and Formal Semantics: Past Participles vs. Adjectives in Italian. In T. Okrut, Y. Hetsevich,M. Silberztein, and H. Stanislavenka, (eds) Automatic Processing of Natural-Language Electronic Texts with NooJ. *Communications in Computer and Information Science*, volume 607:83-95, Springer, Cham.

Max Silberztein, 2015. *La formalization des langues, l´approche de NooJ*. Iste Ediciones, London.

Appendices

A. Last front page of the *Clarín*_corpus.

The last front page that was published by Clarín (2006) is displayed in Figure 7.

Figure 7. Last front page published on March 24, 2006.

B. A pedagogical proposal.

Our work will be carried out in parallel to the NooJ Italian module, since the starting point is the same platform and our proposal includes the activities detailed below.

- Open the text in the Italian Module: Ringraziamenti (Dan Brown, The Da Vinci Code, 2003)[8].

- Apply Locate <A> in order to extract all adjectes, as stated in the properties_definiton file (Figure 8):

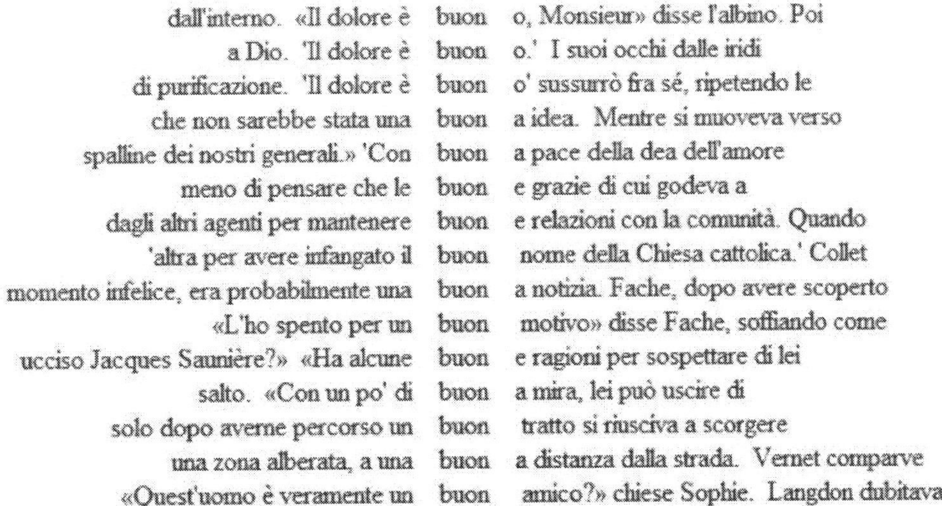

Figure 8. Locate <A> in the Italian text.

- Apply Locate and search a string of characters for the adjective *buon* "good." Note how concordance is done. Figure 9 presents a sample of some of the sequences.

dall'interno. «Il dolore è	buon	o, Monsieur» disse l'albino. Poi
a Dio. 'Il dolore è	buon	o.' I suoi occhi dalle iridi
di purificazione. 'Il dolore è	buon	o' sussurrò fra sé, ripetendo le
che non sarebbe stata una	buon	a idea. Mentre si muoveva verso
spalline dei nostri generali.» 'Con	buon	a pace della dea dell'amore
meno di pensare che le	buon	e grazie di cui godeva a
dagli altri agenti per mantenere	buon	e relazioni con la comunità. Quando
'altra per avere infangato il	buon	nome della Chiesa cattolica.' Collet
momento infelice, era probabilmente una	buon	a notizia. Fache, dopo avere scoperto
«L'ho spento per un	buon	motivo» disse Fache, soffiando come
ucciso Jacques Saunière?» «Ha alcune	buon	e ragioni per sospettare di lei
salto. «Con un po' di	buon	a mira, lei può uscire di
solo dopo averne percorso un	buon	tratto si riusciva a scorgere
una zona alberata, a una	buon	a distanza dalla strada. Vernet comparve
«Quest'uomo è veramente un	buon	amico?» chiese Sophie. Langdon dubitava

Figure 9. Locate *buon* "good" in the Italian text.

---

[8]Ringraziamenti (Dan Brown The Da Vinci Code, 2003) available at
`https://archive.org/stream/IlCodiceDaVinciDanBrown/Il%20codice%20Da%20Vinci%20-%20Dan%20Brown_djvu.txt`

- Identify the inflectional features of some of the nouns following the previous adjective: e.g., *il buon nome* "the good name," *un buon amico* "a good friend," etc.

- Return to the Spanish Module Argentina, and perform Linguistic Analysis on the following sequence: *un hombre bueno* "a good man" (Figure 10).

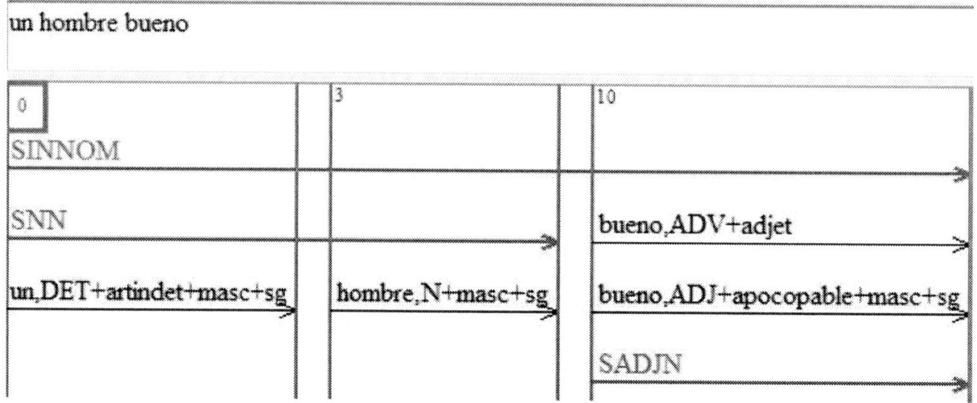

Figure 10. Linguistic Analysis of an adjectival sequence

- Detect concordance features in the sequence: masculine (masc) and singular (sg).

- State which variations this adjective may adopt, since according to the corresponding lexical grammar, *bueno* "good" inflects like FLACO (FLACO = <E>/masc+sg | s/masc+pl | <B> a/fem+sg | <B> as/fem+pl;).

- Look up, in the dictionary of adjectives, another adjective inflecting like *desaparecido* and complete the following expressions:

```
Un    hombre… .. "A man…"
Unos  hombres… .. "Some men…"
Mi libro…     .."My book…"
La    señora… .. "The lady…"
```

- Check through Linguistic Analysis how it is possible, by virtue of concordance, to build noun phrases.

- Do an online search to complete the analysis with its historical implications of the term *desaparecido* in expressions such *desaparecidos Argentina* and *disappeared Argentina*[9].

---

[9]The searches 'desaparecidos Argentina' and 'disappeared Argentina' are available at https://es.wikipedia.org/wiki/Desaparecidos_durante_el_terrorismo_de_Estado_en_Argentina and https://en.wikipedia.org/wiki/Dirty_War.

STYLUS: A Resource for Systematically Derived Language Usage

Bonnie Dorr
Institute for Human and Machine Cognition
15 SE Osceola Ave, Ocala, FL 34471
bdorr@ihmc.us

Clare Voss
U.S. Army Research Laboratory
Adelphi, MD 20783
clare.r.voss.civ@mail.mil

Abstract

Starting from an existing lexical-conceptual structure (LCS) Verb Database of 500 verb classes (containing a total of 9525 verb entries), we automatically derived a resource that supports argument identification for language understanding and argument realization for language generation. The extended resource, called STYLUS (SysTematicallY Derived Language USage), supports constraints at the syntax-semantics interface through the inclusion of components of meaning and collocations. We show that the resulting resource covers three cases of language usage patterns both for *spatially* oriented applications such as dialogue management for robot navigation and for *non-spatial* applications such as generation of cyber-related notifications.

1 Introduction

This paper presents a derivative resource, called STYLUS (SysTematicallY Derived Language USage), produced through extraction of a set of argument realizations from lexical-semantic representations for a range of different verb classes (Appendix A). Prior work (Jackendoff, 1996; Levin, 1993; Olsen, 1994; Kipper et al., 2008; Palmer et al., 2017) has suggested a close relation between underlying lexicalsemantic structures of predicates and their syntactic argument structure. Subsequent work (Dorr and Voss, 2018) argued that regular patterns of language usage can be systematically derived from lexicalsemantic representations and used in applications such as dialogue management for robot navigation. The latter investigation focused on the *spatial* dimension, e.g., motion and direction.

We adopt the view that this systematicity also holds for verbs in the *non-spatial* dimension, including those that have been metaphorically related to the spatial dimension by a range of corpus-based techniques (Dorr and Olsen, 2018). We consider one example of a non-spatial application: generation of cyber-related textual notifications. We argue that this application requires knowledge at the syntaxsemantics interface that is analogous to spatial knowledge for robot navigation. A recent survey of narrative generation techniques (Kybartas and Bidarra, 2017) highlights several important components of narrative generation (including a story, plot, space, and discourse for telling the story), leaving open the means for surface-realization of arguments from an underlying lexical-semantic structure. STYLUS is designed to accommodate mechanisms for filling this gap.

STYLUS extends an existing Lexical-Conceptual Structure Verb Database (LVD) (Dorr et al., 2001) that includes 500 verb classes (9525 verb entries) with structurally-specified information about realization of arguments for both spatial and non-spatial verbs. STYLUS was produced through systematic derivation of regular patterns of language usage (Block, Overlap, Fill) without requiring manual annotation. The next section reviews related work, starting with the spatial underpinnings of the original LVD. Following this, we describe our extensions and present examples for two applications: natural language processing for robot navigation and generation of cyber-related notifications.

2 Background

2.1 Spatial Language Understanding

Spatial language understanding has made great strides in recent years, with the emergence of language resources and standards for capturing spatial information, e.g., (ISO-24617-7, 2014), which provide guidelines for annotating spatial information in English language texts (Pustejovsky and Lee, 2017;

Proceedings of the First Workshop on Linguistic Resources for Natural Language Processing, pages 57–64
Santa Fe, New Mexico, USA, August 20, 2018.

Pustejovsky and Yocum, 2014). This work differs from the perspective adopted for STYLUS in that it provides annotation guidelines for training systems for spatial information extraction, and so it does not focus on generalized mappings at the syntax-semantics interface.

The Semantic Annotation Framework (semAF) identifies places, paths, spatial entities, and spatial relations that can be used to associate sequences of processes and events in news articles (Pustejovsky et al., 2011). Prepositions and particles (*near, off*) and verbs of position and movement (*lean, swim*) have corresponding components of meanings and collocations adopted in this paper.

Spatial role labeling using holistic spatial semantics (i.e., analysis at the level of the full utterance) has been used for identifying spatial relations between objects (Kordjamshidi et al., 2011). The association between thematic roles and their corresponding surface realizations has been investigated previously, including in the LCS formalism (described next), but Kordjamshidi et al's approach also ties into deeper notions such as *region of space* and *frame of reference*.

2.2 Lexical-Conceptual Structure Verb Database (LVD)

Lexical Conceptual Structure (LCS) (Jackendoff, 1983; Jackendoff, 1990; Dorr, 1993; Dowty, 1979; Guerssel et al., 1985) has been used for wide-ranging applications, including interlingual machine translation (Voss and Dorr, 1995; Habash and Dorr, 2002), lexical acquisition (Habash et al., 2006), crosslanguage information retrieval (Levow et al., 2000), language generation (Traum and Habash, 2000), and intelligent language tutoring (Dorr, 1997).

LCS incorporates primitives whose combination captures syntactic generalities, i.e., actions and entities must be systematically related to a syntactic structure: GO, STAY, BE, GO-EXT, ORIENT, and also an ACT primitive developed by Dorr and Olsen (1997). LCS is grounded in the spatial domain and is naturally extended to non-spatial domains, as specified by *fields*. For example, the spatial dimension of the LCS representation corresponds to the (*Loc*)*ational* field, which underlies the meaning of *John traveled from Chicago to Boston* in the LCS [John GO$_{Loc}$ [From Chicago] [To Boston]]. This is straightforwardly extended to the (*Temp*)*oral* field to represent analogous meanings such as *The meeting went from 7pm to 9pm* in the LCS [Meeting GO$_{Temp}$ [From 7pm] [To 9pm]].

The LVD developed in prior work (Dorr et al., 2001) includes a set of LCS templates classified according to an extension of Levin (1993)'s 192 classes to a total of 500 classes covering 9525 verb entries (an additional 5500+ verb entries beyond the original 4000+ verb entries). The first 44 classes were added beyond the original set of semantic classes (Dorr and Jones, 1996). The remaining classes were derived through aspectual distinctions to yield a set of LCS *classes* that were finer-grained than the original Levin classes (Olsen et al., 1997). Each LCS class consists of a set of verbs and, in several cases, the classes included *non-Levin words* (those not in Levin (1993)), derived semi-automatically (Dorr, 1997).

The original LVD provides a mapping of lexical-semantic structures to their surface realization. This mapping serves as a foundation for the enrichments that yield STYLUS. The new resource benefits from decades of prior study that led to the LVD. Specifically, Levin's classes are based on significant corpus analysis and have been validated in numerous within-language studies (Levin and Rappaport Hovav, 1995; Rappaport Hovav and Levin, 1998) and cross-language studies (Guerssel et al., 1985; Levin, 2015). Thus, STYLUS is expected to have an important downstream impact, in both depth and breadth, for future linguistic investigations and computational applications.

2.3 Syntax-Semantics Interface

Prior work (Jackendoff, 1996; Levin, 1993; Dorr and Voss, 1993; Voss and Dorr, 1995; Kipper et al., 2004; Kipper et al., 2008; Palmer et al., 2017) suggests that there is a close relation between underlying lexical-semantic structures of verbs and nominal predicates and their syntactic argument structure. VerbNet (Kipper et al., 2004) reinforces the view in this resource paper, that prepositions and their relation with verb classes serve as significant predictors of semantic content, but does not leverage an inner structure of events for compositional derivation of argument realizations.

FrameNet also sits at the syntax-semantics interface (Fillmore, 2002), with linking generalizations based on valency to map semantic frames (events and participants) to their corresponding surface structure. Osswald and Van Valin (2014) point out that such generalizations are hindered by bottom-up/datadriven frames and they argue for a richer frame representation with an inner structure of an event. This notion of "inner structure" is seen in the work of Voss et al. (1998) and Dorr and Voss

(2018), which suggests that the generation of a preposition (in English) is dependent on both the internal semantics of the predicate and structural idiosyncracies at the syntax-semantics interface. As such, the following two definitions are fundamental to the syntax-semantics mappings adopted in STYLUS[1]:

- **Component of meaning**: Implicit semantic unit, such as UPWARD for the verb *elevate*

- **Collocation**: Explicit juxtaposition of a particular word, such as *up* for the verb *lift* in "*lift up*"

Leveraging these definitions, Section 3 describes the enrichments necessary to produce STYLUS without requiring training on annotated data.

3   Addition of Components of Meaning and Collocations to LVD Classes

We investigate the systematic derivation of language usage patterns for both understanding and generation of language and leverage this investigation to simplify and enrich the LVD presented in Section 2. The resulting resource, STYLUS (downloadable as described in Appendix 5), relies on lexically implicit *components of meaning* and lexically explicit *collocations* (as defined above) to cover three cases of language usage patterns applicable to language understanding and generation:

- **Block** refers to components of meaning that do not co-occur with their collocational counterparts, e.g., *elevate* and *ascend* include the UPWARD component and thus do not co-occur with the collocation *up*;

- **Overlap** refers to components of meaning that optionally co-occur with their collocational counterparts, e.g., *lift* and *raise* include the UPWARD component but optionally co-occur with the collocation *up*;

- **Fill** refers to underspecified components of meaning that fall into one of two cases:

    – Oblig: *obligatory* co-occurrence with collocations, e.g., the verb *put* does not specify a direction and thus always co-occurs with a collocation such as *up*;
    – Opt: *optional* co-occurrence with collocations, e.g., the motion verb *move* does not specify a direction but optionally co-occurs with a collocation such as *up*.

STYLUS contains simplified verb classes from the LVD, omitting the full LCS structures and thematic roles while adding prepositional *collocations* and *components of meaning*. For example, in the LVD *Verbs of inherently directed motion* (Class 51.1.a in (Levin, 1993)), the verb *leave* need not co-occur with a prepositional collocate (e.g., *leave the room*) whereas the verb *depart* can co-occur with *from* (e.g., *departed from the room*). For either case, the component of meaning is uniformly "GO TO (outside the room) FROM (inside of the room)," and the collocation *from* is optional:

```
LVD Class Entry:
(:NUMBER "51.1.a"
 :NAME "Verbs Inherently Directed Motion / -from/to"
 :WORDS (advance arrive ascend climb come depart descend enter escape
         exit fall flee go leave plunge recede return rise tumble)
 :NON_LEVIN_WORDS (approach come! defect head)
 :LCS (go loc (* thing 2)
          ((* from 3) loc (thing 2) (at loc (thing 2) (thing 4)))
          ((* to 5) loc (thing 2) ([at] loc (thing 2) (thing 6)))
          (!!+ingly 26))
 :THETA_ROLES ((1 "_th,src(from),goal(towards)")
               (1 "_th,goal,src(from)")
               (1 "_th,src(from),goal(to)")))
```

Derivation of components of meaning and collocations, along with their obligatoriness or optionality, was achieved by a simple automated procedure, without manual annotation. Components of mean-

---

[1] Teletype font is used for components of meaning such as UPWARD. Several examples throughout this paper were purposely selected to illustrate the full range of syntactic realizations for the concept of "upwardness." Other verbs and collocations could easily have been selected (e.g., *lower* with the collocation *down*), but a varied selection of lexical distinctions would confound the illustration of more general distinctions at the syntax-semantics interface.

ing were derived either from the LCS structure or from verb-prepositions pairs in a "Categorial Variation" database (Habash and Dorr, 2003). For example, the LCS above (from the `:LCS` slot) includes a sublexical component of meaning, ((*$from$ 3) loc ($thing$ 2) ($at loc$ ($thing$ 2) ($thing$ 4))), that maps optionally to a preposition *from* in the surface form (as in *exit* (*from*) *the room*). Prepositional collocations (such as *from*) were derived from the thematic roles (in the `:THETA ROLES` slot) of the original LVD. These prepositions are specified in parentheses, and are preceded either by a comma (`,`) for optional collocations or by underscore (`_`) for obligatory collocations. In the example above, the theme is obligatory (`_th`), whereas the source (`,src`) and goal (`,goal`) are optional. Verbs are thus paired with their corresponding prepositions by virtue of their class membership in the final STYLUS resource[2]:

```
STYLUS Class Entry:
(:NUMBER "51.1.a"
 :NAME "Verbs Inherently Directed Motion / -from/to"
 :WORDS (advance arrive ascend climb come depart descend enter escape
         exit fall flee go leave plunge recede return rise tumble)
 :NON_LEVIN_WORDS (approach come! defect head)
 :COLLOCATIONS ("from" "to" "towards")
 :COMPONENT_OF_MEANING (FROM, AWAY_FROM, OUT_OF, OR, UP_TO, UP,
  BEFORE, INTO, TO)) ;; Fill-Opt <<SPATIAL>>
```

The derivative collocations and components of meaning obviate the need for spelling out the full LCS, thus ensuring a more compact representation of the original LVD. In addition, the Block, Overlap, Fill-Oblig, and Fill-Opt designations were easily derived automatically from the `:COLLOCATIONS` and `:COMPONENT OF MEANING` slots according to the four rules below:

(1) Tag **Block** if `:COMPONENT OF MEANING` filled and `:COLLOCATIONS` not filled, e.g., *Face the doorway*;
(2) Tag **Overlap** if `:COMPONENT OF MEANING` and `:COLLOCATIONS` both filled, and use of comma (`,`) in front of the corresponding thematic role, e.g., "`,src(behind)`" for *Follow (behind) the car*;
(3) Tag **Fill-Oblig** if `:COMPONENT OF MEANING` and `:COLLOCATIONS` both filled, and use of underscore (`_`) in front of the corresponding thematic role, e.g., "`_goal(to)`" for *Put the box onto the table*;
(4) Tag **Fill-Opt** if `:COMPONENT OF MEANING` not filled and either `:COLLOCATIONS` not filled or use of comma (`,`) in front of a modifier role, as in *Move the box (to the table)*.

Finally, each entry was automatically tagged <<SPATIAL>> if the LCS indicated a Loc(ational) or Poss(essional) field in association with the underlying primitive (GO, BE, etc.). All non-spatial entries were automatically tagged <<NON-SPATIAL>>.

4   STYLUS: Spatial and Non-Spatial Subset of LVD Classes

The number of classes associated with the language usage patterns introduced above is in the table below, with tallies for the full set of LVD classes, the spatial subset, and non-spatial subset.[3] Representative examples of verbs in both the spatial subset (e.g., for robot navigation) and the non-spatial subset (e.g., cyber-notification generation) are provided in Table 1.

Interestingly, the Spatial Subset of classes is sizeable (44% of the entire set). However, STYLUS development has yielded generalizations beyond prior LCS-inspired work that focused strictly on spatial verbs (Voss et al., 1998). Most notably, the Block, Overlap and Fill patterns are generalizable to a high number of LCS classes that are non-spatial as well. The obvious cases are those with non-zero values in Table 1 (Overlap and Fill): e.g., *tread on* (Overlap), *cram for* (Fill-Oblig), and *blend together* (Fill-Opt). However, although the number of non-spatial Block cases appears to be 0, the corresponding 7 spatial usages also extend to metaphorical extensions, e.g., in the phrase *elevated her spirits*, the use of "up" is blocked. Although STYLUS encodes *elevate* as a spatial verb, this same lexico-semantic

---

[2] In the original LVD, the `:SPATIAL COMPONENT OF MEANING` field name was used. More recently, such components have been determined to be useful for non-spatial verbs as well. For example, *admire* (in class 31.2.c) has a `toward` component of meaning, whereas *abhor* has an `away-from` component of meaning. Thus, the more general `:COMPONENT OF MEANING` field name has been subsequently adopted.

[3] N/A refers to verb classes whose members take bare NP or S arguments. Intrans refers to Intransitive verbs.

property applies for its non-spatial (metaphorical) usage. Analogously, STYLUS encodes the contrasting verb *lift* as a spatial verb, designated as Overlap, to enable *lifted up her hand*. A metaphorical (non-spatial) usage would be *lift up her spirits*. Such cases indicate that Block, Overlap, and Fill apply even more broadly than was conceived in the original LVD—which means that the numbers in the Non-Spatial Subset column above are understated and would benefit from additional analysis of metaphorical extensions.

Lexical Ops	LVD Classes	Spatial Subset	Spatial Examples	Non-Spatial Subset	Non-Spatial Examples
Block	7	7	elevate, face, pocket	0	infect, archive
Overlap	17	10	advance, lower, lift	7	follow, precede
Fill-Oblig	310	128	drive, rotate, put	182	mount, install
Fill-Opt	87	49	remove, slide	38	move, add
Intrans	6	3	float, part, squirm	3	choke, drown, snap
N/A	73	12	—	61	—
Tot. Classes	500	219		281	
Tot. Verbs	9525	4640		4885	

Table 1: Language Usage Patterns for Spatial and Non-Spatial Verbs with Representative Examples

To explore the broader applicability of the Block, Overlap, and Fill patterns, we first examined verbs in the Spatial Subset and determined that many of them are among those relevant to robot navigation, e.g., *move, go, advance, drive, return, rotate*, and *turn*. Others are easily accommodated by extending classes—without modification to the spatial language usage patterns described above. For example, *back up* matches the class template containing *advance*, and *pivot* matches the class template containing *rotate*. We then considered the Non-Spatial Subset for generation of cyber-related notifications, a sub-task of an ongoing cyber-attack prediction project (Dalton et al., 2017). We determined that the Fill, Overlap, and Block patterns apply to members of the same classes that were relevant to robot navigation. Specifically, we examined the four classes shown in Table 2.

Class [Pattern]	Robot Navigation		Cyber Notification (Generation Only)
	Understanding	**Generation**	
9.8-Fill [Block]	*Face* the doorway / *Face* to the doorway	Where do I *face*? / *Where do I *face* to?	Risk that trojan horse virus will *infect* (*to) System A increased 5%
47.8.1-Contig [Overlap]	*Follow* the car / Follow behind the car	Which car do I *follow* (behind)?	Risk increased 25% that VPN failure will *follow* (behind) malware attack
9.1-Put [FillOblig]	*Put* it on the table / *Put the box	Where do I *put* it? / *Do I *put* the box?	Risk of malware increases 5% if disk A *mounted* on file server B
11.2-Slide [FillOpt]	*Move* it to the table / *Move* it	Where do I *move* it? / Do I *move* it?	10% increased malware risk if System A files are *moved* (to System B)

Table 2: Class-Based Patterns for Robot Navigation and Cyber Notification

Note that Block, Overlap, and Fill can be applied as validity constraints on language usage patterns in the *spatial* domain of human-robot commands (for understanding and generation).4 Correspondingly, for the *non-spatial* domain of cyber notification generation, these same four classes included other class members (e.g., for 9.8 and 9.1) or meaning extensions of the same class members (e.g., for 47.8.1 and 11.2) that exhibited the same language usage patterns as their robot navigation counterparts.

5   Conclusion and Future Work

STYLUS provides the basis for both understanding and generation in the spatial robot navigation domain and for generation in the *non-spatial* cyber notification domain. A larger scale application and evaluation of the effectiveness of STYLUS for understanding and generation in these two domains is a

---

4 An asterisk at the start of a sentence indicates an invalid generated form. Verbs in the designated class are italicized.

future area of study. A starting point is an ongoing Bot Language project (Marge et al., 2017) that has heretofore focused on dialogue annotation (Traum et al., 2018) and has not yet incorporated lexicon-based knowledge necessary for automatically detecting incomplete, vague, or implicit navigation commands.

Another avenue for exploration is the enhancement of cyber notifications through systematic derivation of mappings to surface realizations for other parts of speech. This work will involve access to a "Categorial Variation" database (CatVar) (Habash and Dorr, 2003) to map verbs in the LCS classes to their nominalized and adjectivalized forms. For example, the CatVar entry for *infect* includes the nominalized form *infection*, which provides additional options that may be more fluent in cyber-related notifications, e.g., *viral infection of system* might be considered less stilted than *virus will infect system*.

Although STYLUS is strictly for English, the lexical-semantic foundation from which it is derived has been investigated for a range of multilingual applications (Habash et al., 2006; Cabezas et al., 2001; Levow et al., 2000). Future work will examine the derivation of this resource for non-English languages.

Acknowledgements

This research is supported, in part by the Institute for Human and Machine Cognition, in part by the U.S. Army Research Laboratory, and in part by the Office of the Director of National Intelligence (ODNI) and the Intelligence Advanced Research Projects Activity (IARPA) via the Air Force Research Laboratory (AFRL) contract number FA875016C0114. The U.S. Government is authorized to reproduce and distribute reprints for Governmental purposes notwithstanding any copyright annotation thereon.
Disclaimer: The views and conclusions contained herein are those of the authors and should not be interpreted as necessarily representing the official policies or endorsements, either expressed or implied, of ODNI, IARPA, AFRL, ARL, or the U.S. Government.

References

Clara Cabezas, Bonnie J. Dorr, and Philip Resnik. 2001. Spanish Language Processing at University of Maryland: Building Infrastructure for Multilingual Applications. In *Proceedings of the Second International Workshop on Spanish Language Processing and Language Technologies (SLPLT-2)*, Jaen, Spain, http://www.umiacs.umd.edu/users/bonnie/Publications/slplt-01.htm.

Adam Dalton, Bonnie Dorr, Leon Liang, and Kristy Hollingshead. 2017. Improving cyber-attack predictions via unconventional sensors discovered through information foraging. In *Proceedings of the 2017 International Workshop on Big Data Analytics for Cyber Intelligence and Defense*, BDA4CID '17, pages 4560–4565. IEEE.

Bonnie Dorr and Doug Jones. 1996. Acquisition of Semantic Lexicons: Using Word Sense Disambiguation to Improve Precision. In In *Proceedings of theWorkshop on Breadth and Depth of Semantic Lexicons, 34th Annual Conference of the Association for Computational Linguistics*, pages 42–50. Kluwer Academic Publishers.

Bonnie J. Dorr and Mari Broman Olsen. 1997. Deriving Verbal and Compositional Lexical Aspect for NLP Application. In *Proceedings of the 35th Annual Meeting of the Association for Computational Linguistics and Eighth Conference of the European Chapter of the Association for Computational Linguistics*, pages 151–158.

Bonnie J. Dorr and Mari Broman Olsen. 2018. Lexical Conceptual Structure of Literal and Metaphorical Spatial Language: A Case Study of Push. In *Proceedings of the NAACLWorkshop on Spatial Language Understanding*, pages 31–40.

Bonnie J. Dorr and Clare R. Voss. 1993. Machine Translation of Spatial Expressions: Defining the Relation between an Interlingua and a Knowledge Representation System. In *Proceedings of the Twelfth Conference of the American Association for Artificial Intelligence*, pages 374–379.

Bonnie J. Dorr and Clare Voss. 2018. The Case for Systematically Derived Spatial Language Usage. In *Proceedings of the NAACL Workshop on Spatial Language Understanding*, pages 63–70.

Bonnie J. Dorr, Mari Olsen, Nizar Habash, and Scott Thomas. 2001. LCS Verb Database Documentation. http://www.umiacs.umd.edu/~bonnie/Demos/LCS_Database_Documentation.html.

Bonnie J. Dorr. 1993. *Machine Translation: A View from the Lexicon*. MIT Press, Cambridge, MA.

Bonnie J. Dorr. 1997. Large-Scale Dictionary Construction for Foreign Language Tutoring and Interlingual Machine Translation. *Machine Translation*, 12:271–322.

David Dowty. 1979. *Word Meaning and Montague Grammar*. Reidel, Dordrecht.

Charles J. Fillmore. 2002. Linking sense to syntax in FrameNet (keynote speech). In *19th International Conference on Computational Linguistics*, Taipei. COLING, http://www.lirmm.fr/~lafourca/ML-enseign/DEA/DEA03-TALN-articles/fillmore.pdf.

M. Masten Guerssel, Kenneth Hale, Mary Laughren, Beth Levin, and Josie White Eagle. 1985. A Cross-linguistic Study of Transitivity Alternations. In W. H. Eilfort and P. D. Kroeber nad K. L. Peterson, editor, *Papers from the Parasession in Causatives and Agentivity at the Twenty-first Regional meeting of the Chicago Linguistic Society*, pages 48–63.

Nizar Habash and Bonnie J. Dorr. 2002. Handling Translation Divergences: Combining Statistical and Symbolic Techniques in Generation-Heavy Machine Translation. In *Proceedings of the Fifth Conference of the Association for Machine Translation in the Americas*, pages 84–93, Tiburon, CA.

Nizar Habash and Bonnie Dorr. 2003. A categorial variation database for English. In *NAACL/HLT 2003, Proceedings of the Human Language Technology and North American Association for Computational Linguistics Conference*, pages 96–102.

Nizar Habash, Bonnie J. Dorr, and Christof Monz. 2006. Challenges in Building an Arabic GHMT system with SMT Components. In *Proceedings of the 7th Conference of the Association for Machine Translation in the Americas*, pages 56–65, Boston, MA, August.

ISO-24617-7. 2014. Language Resource management Semantic Annotation Framework Part 7: Spatial information (ISOspace), http://www.iso.org/standard/60779.html.

Ray Jackendoff. 1983. *Semantics and Cognition*. MIT Press, Cambridge, MA.

Ray Jackendoff. 1990. *Semantic Structures*. MIT Press, Cambridge, MA.

Ray Jackendoff. 1996. The Proper Treatment of Measuring Out, Telicity, and Perhaps Even Quantification in English. *Natural Language and Linguistic Theory*, 14:305–354.

Karin Kipper, Benjamin Snyder, and Martha Palmer. 2004. Using Prepositions to Extend a Verb Lexicon. In *Proceedings of the HLT/NAACL Workshop on Computational Lexical Semantics*, pages 23–29.

Karin Kipper, Anna Korhonen, Neville Ryant, and Martha Palmer. 2008. A Large-scale Classification of English Verbs. *Language Resources and Evaluation*, 42(1):21–40.

Parisa Kordjamshidi, Martijn Van Otterlo, and Marie-Francine Moens. 2011. Spatial Role Labeling: Task Definition and Annotation Scheme. In *Proceedings of the Seventh Conference on International Language Resources and Evaluation*, pages 413–420.

Ben Kybartas and Rafael Bidarra. 2017. A survey on story generation techniques for authoring computational narratives. *IEEE Transactions on Computational Intelligence and AI in Games*, 9(3):239–253.

Beth Levin and Malka Rappaport Hovav. 1995. *Unaccusativity: At the Syntax-Lexical Semantics Interface, Linguistic Inquiry Monograph 26*. MIT Press, Cambridge, MA.

Beth Levin. 1993. *English Verb Classes and Alternations: A Preliminary Investigation*. The University of Chicago Press.

Beth Levin. 2015. Verb Classes Within and Across Languages. In B. Comrie and A. Malchukov, editors, *Valency Classes: A Comparative Handbook*, pages 1627–1670. De Gruyter, Berlin.

Gina-Anne Levow, Bonnie J. Dorr, and Dekang Lin. 2000. Construction of Chinese-English Semantic Hierarchy for Cross-Language Retrieval. In *Workshop on English-Chinese Cross Language Information Retrieval, International Conference on Chinese Language Computing*, pages 187–194, Chicago, IL.

Matthew Marge, Claire Bonial, Ashley Foots, Cassidy Henry Cory Hayes, Kimberly Pollard, Ron Artstein, Clare Voss, and David Traum. 2017. Exploring Variation of Natural Human Commands to a Robot in a Collaborative Navigation Task. In *ACL2017 RoboNLP workshop*, pages 58–66.

Malka Rappaport Hovav and Beth Levin. 1998. Building Verb Meanings. In M. Butt and W. Geuder, editors, *The Projection of Arguments: Lexical and Compositional Factors*, pages 97–134. CSLI Publications, Stanford, CA.

Mari Broman Olsen, Bonnie J. Dorr, and Scott Thomas. 1997. Toward Compact Monotonically Compositional Interlingua Using Lexical Aspect. In *Proceedings of the Workshop on Interlinguas in MT*, pages 33–44, San Diego, CA, October.

Mari Broman Olsen. 1994. The Semantics and Pragmatics of Lexical and Grammatical Aspect. *Studies in the Linguistic Sciences*, 24(1–2):361–375.

Rainer Osswald and Robert D. Van Valin. 2014. Framenet, Frame Structure, and the Syntax-semantics Interface. In T. Gamerschlag, D. Gerland, R. Osswald, andW. Petersen, editors, *Frames and Concept Types: Applications in language and philosophy (Studies in Linguistics and Philosophy 94)*, pages 125–56. Heidelberg: Springer.

Martha Palmer, Claire Bonial, and Jena D. Hwang. 2017. VerbNet: Capturing English Verb behavior, Meaning and Usage. In Susan Chipman, editor, *The Oxford Handbook of Cognitive Science*. Oxford University Press.

James Pustejovsky and Kiyong Lee. 2017. Enriching the Notion of Path in ISOspace. In *Proceedings of the 13th Joint ISO-ACL Workshop on Interoperable Semantic Annotation (ISA-13)*, `http://aclweb.org/anthology/W17-7415`.

James Pustejovsky and Zachary Yocum. 2014. Image annotation with iso-space: Distinguishing content from structure. In *Proceedings of the Ninth International Conference on Language Resources and Evaluation (LREC'14)*, pages 426–431.

James Pustejovsky, Jessica Moszkowicz, and Marc Verhagen. 2011. Using ISO-Space for Annotating Spatial Information, `http://www2.denizyuret.com/bib/pustejovsky/pustejovsky2011cosit/COSIT-ISO-Space.final.pdf`.

David Traum and Nizar Habash. 2000. Generation from Lexical Conceptual Structures. In *Proceedings of the Workshop on Applied Interlinguas, North American Association for Computational Linguistics / Applied NLP Conference*, pages 34–41.

David Traum, Cassidy Henry, Stephanie Lukin, Ron Artstein, Felix Gervits, Kimberly Pollard, Claire Bonial, Su Lei, Clare Voss, Matthew Marge, Cory Hayes, and Susan Hill. 2018. Dialogue Structure Annotation for Multi-Floor Interaction. In Nicoletta Calzolari (Conference chair), Khalid Choukri, Christopher Cieri, Thierry Declerck, Sara Goggi, Koiti Hasida, Hitoshi Isahara, Bente Maegaard, Joseph Mariani, Hlne Mazo, Asuncion Moreno, Jan Odijk, Stelios Piperidis, and Takenobu Tokunaga, editors, *Proceedings of the Eleventh International Conference on Language Resources and Evaluation (LREC 2018)*, Miyazaki, Japan, May 7-12, 2018. European Language Resources Association (ELRA).

Clare R. Voss and Bonnie J. Dorr. 1995. Toward a Lexicalized Grammar for Interlinguas. *J. of Machine Translation*, 10:143–184.

Clare R. Voss, Bonnie J. Dorr, and M. U. Şencan. 1998. Lexical Allocation in Interlingua-based Machine Translation of Spatial Expressions. In Patrick Oliver and Klaus-Peter Gapp, editor, *Representation and Processing of Spatial Expressions*, pages 133–148. L. Erlbaum Associates Inc., Hillsdale, NJ, USA.

Appendices

Appendix A. Supplemental Material: STYLUS

STYLUS (SysTematicallY Derived Language USage) is a simplified and extended version of Lexical Conceptual Structure Verb Database (LVD) (Dorr et al., 2001) with 500 classes of verbs that incorporate components of meaning and prepositional collocations (in ascii .txt format). The classes include over 9500 verb entries—about 5500 entries beyond the original 4000+ entries in Levin 1993. This resource can be downloaded from the link below:

`https://www.dropbox.com/s/3fwzlg1wrirjhv1/LCS-Bare-Verb-Classes-Final.txt?dl=0`

Contemporary Amharic Corpus: Automatically Morpho-Syntactically Tagged Amharic Corpus

Andargachew Mekonnen Gezmu
Otto-von-Guericke-Universität
andargachew.gezmu@ovgu.de

Binyam Ephrem Seyoum
Addis Ababa University
binyam.ephrem@aau.edu.et

Michael Gasser
Indiana University
gasser@cs.indiana.edu

Andreas Nürnberger
Otto-von-Guericke-Universität
andreas.nuernberger@ovgu.de

Abstract

We introduce the contemporary Amharic corpus, which is automatically tagged for morpho-syntactic information. Texts are collected from 25,199 documents from different domains and about 24 million orthographic words are tokenized. Since it is partly a web corpus, we made some automatic spelling error corrections. We have also modified the existing morphological analyzer, HornMorpho, to use it for automatic tagging.

1 Introduction

Amharic is a Semitic language that serves as the working language of the Federal Government of Ethiopia. Next to Arabic, it is the most spoken Semitic language. Though it plays several roles, it is considered one of the less-resourced languages. This is because it lacks basic tools and resources for carrying out natural language processing research and applications.

One of the main hurdles in natural language processing of Amharic is the absence of sizable, clean and properly tagged corpora. Since Amharic is morphologically rich and the boundary of the syntactic word in an orthographic word is unclear in most cases. Even if it is possible to use some techniques of collecting a big corpus from the web, the basic natural language tasks like POS tagging or parsing would be challenging if we base our analysis on orthographic words. In Amharic, orthographic words represent different linguistic units. It is possible for an orthographic word to represent a phrase, a clause, or a sentence. This is because some syntactic words like prepositions, conjunctions, axillaries, etc. can be attached to other lexical categories. Thus, for proper tagging and syntactic analysis, these morphemes should be separated from their phonological host. In this project, we made an effort to collect, segment, and tag text documents from various sources.

2 Related Works

Even though Amharic is a less-resourced language, there are some corpus collections by different initiatives. Since the introduction of the notion of considering the web as a corpus, which is motivated for practical reasons of getting larger data with open access and low cost, there have been corpora of different sizes for Amharic. In this section, we describe three corpora: the Walta Information Center (WIC), the HaBit (amWaC17), and the An Crúbadán.

The WIC corpus is a medium-sized corpus of 210,000 tokens collected from 1,065 Amharic news documents (Demeke and Getachew, 2006). The corpus is manually annotated for POS tags. The number of tag-sets, which is proposed based on the orthographic word, is 31. They use compound tag-sets for those words with prepositions and conjunctions. Even though they distinguish some subclasses of a given category (like noun and verb), the distinction no longer exists when these forms attach prepositions and/or conjunctions. However, they propose independent tags for both prepositions and conjunctions without favoring segmentation of these clitics. In the annotation process, annotators were given training

Proceedings of the First Workshop on Linguistic Resources for Natural Language Processing, pages 65–70
Santa Fe, New Mexico, USA, August 20, 2018.

and guidelines. Each annotator was given a different news article. They were asked to write the tags by hand and the annotation was given to a typist to insert the handwritten tag into the document. In such a process, there may be some loss of information which could be attributed to the inconsistencies of the annotation (Gambäck et al., 2009; Tachbelie and Menzel, 2009; Yimam et al., 2014). In the WIC report, they did not provide the annotation consistencies measurement and method of keeping consistency during the process of the annotation. According to the recent report of Rychlý and Suchomel (2016), the efficiency of an automatic tagger developed or trained on this corpus is 87.4%. Since this corpus can be accessible to most NLP researchers on Amharic, it is used to train a stemmer (Argaw and Asker, 2007), Named Entity recognition (Alemu, 2013) and a chunker (Ibrahim and Assabie, 2014).

The HaBit corpus, called amWaC17 (Amharic 'Web as Corpus', the year 2017) is another web corpus, which was developed by crawling using SpiderLing (Rychlý and Suchomel, 2016). Most of the crawling was done in August 2013, October 2015, and January 2016. The current version includes a web corpus crawled from May to September 2017 and consists of 30.5 million tokens collected from 75,509 documents. The corpus is cleaned and tagged for POS using a TreeTagger trained on WIC. They have used the same tag-sets used in WIC and followed the same principles as WIC in tagging tokens.

The An Crúbadán corpus was developed under the project called corpus building for under-resourced languages. The initiative aimed at the creation of text corpora for a large number of under-resourced languages by crawling the web (Scannell, 2007). The project collected written corpora for more than 2,000 languages. Amharic was one of the languages to be included in this project. The Amharic corpus consists of 16,970,855 words crawled from 9,999 documents. The major sources used are Amharic Wikipedia, Universal Declaration of Human Right, and JW.org. This corpus is a list of words with their frequencies.

In the three corpora mentioned above, the written or orthographic form is considered as a word. Syntactic words like prepositions, conjunctions, and articles are not separately treated. In other words, clitics were not segmented from their host. In addition, though it is possible to collect authentic data entry from the web, such sources are inaccurate. As Amharic is not standardized, in these sources one may face lots of variation and expect to find misspellings, typographical errors, and grammatical errors. This calls for manual or automatic editing.

3   Data Collection and Preprocessing

3.1   Data Collection

The Contemporary Amharic Corpus (CACO) is collected from archives of various sources which are edited and made available for the public. All of the documents are written in modern or contemporary Amharic. Table 1 summarizes documents used in the corpus.

Type of Documents	Titles
Newspapers	አዲስ አድማስ, አዲስ ዘመን, ሪፖርተር, ነጋሪት ጋዜጣ
News articles	Ethiopian News Agency, Global Voices
Magazines	ንቁ, መጠበቂያ ግንብ
Fictions	የልምገት, ግርዶሽ, ልጅነት ተመልሶ አይመጣም, የአመጽ ኑዛዜ, የቅናት ዛር, አገዐዚ
Historic novel	አሉላ አባነጋ, ማዕበል የአብዮቱ ማግሥት, የማይጨወው ቄስለኛ, የታንጉት ሚስጢር
Short stories	የዓለም መስታወት, የቡና ቤት ስዕሎችና ሌሎችም ወጎች
History books	አጭር የኢትዮጵያ ታሪክ, ዳግማዊ አጤ ምኔልክ, ዳግማዊ ምኔልክ,
	የአቴጌ ጣይቱ ብጡል (፲፯፻፵፪ - ፲፱፻፲) አጭር የሕይወት ታሪክ, ከወልወል እስከ ማይጨው
Politics book	ማርክሲዝምና የቋንቋ ችግሮች, መሬት የማን ነው
Children's book	ፒኖኪዮ, ውድድር
Amharic Bible[1]	አዲስ ዓለም ትርጉም መጽሐፍ ቅዱስ

Table 1: Data sources for CACO.

In total 25,199 documents from these sources are preprocessed and tagged. The preprocessing and tagging tasks are discussed in the subsequent sections.

---

[1] We used the New World Translation of the Bible which is translated into contemporary (not archaic) Amharic.

3.2 Preprocessing

The preprocessing of the documents involves spelling correction, normalization of punctuation marks, and sentence extraction from paragraphs. In the documents, different types of misspellings are observed. Misspellings result from missed out spaces (e.g., አንዳንድየህክምናተቋጣትናሳለሙ·ያዎቻቸው·), replacing letters with visually similar characters (e.g., ቃብረ for ቃብረ), and typographical errors. In addition, four Amharic phonemes have one or more homophonic character representations. The homophonic characters are commonly observed to be used interchangeably, which can be considered real-word misspellings. To correct the misspellings, we used the spelling corrector developed by Gezmu et al. (2018). Mainly the spelling corrector is employed to correct the first two types of spelling errors. As intensive manual intervention is needed to select the correct spelling from the plausible suggestions for typographical errors, in the current version of the corpus we have not corrected the typographical errors. To deal with the problems of real-word spelling errors resulting from homophonic letters, we adhere to the Ethiopian Languages Academy (ELA) spelling reform (ELA, 1970; Aklilu, 2004). Following their reform, homophonic characters are replaced with their common forms; ሐ and ኀ are replaced with ሀ, ሠ with ሰ, ዐ with አ, and ጸ with ፀ.

The other issue that needs attention is normalization of punctuation marks. Different styles of punctuation marks have been used in the documents. For instance, for double quotation mark two single quotation marks, ", ", «, », `, ", « or » are used. Thus, normalization of punctuation marks is a non-trivial matter. We normalized all types of double quotes by ", all single quotes by ', question marks (e.g., ? and ፧) by ?, word separators (e.g., ፥ and ፡) by plain space, full stops (e.g., ∷ and ።) by ።, exclamation marks (e.g., ! and !) by !, hyphens (e.g., :-, and ፦) by ፦, and commas (e.g., ፣ and ÷) by ፣.

From the collected documents, sentences are identified and extracted by their boundaries—either double colon-like symbols (።) or question marks (?)—and are tokenized based on the orthographic-word boundary, a white space.

About 1.6 million sentences are collected from the documents. When the sentences are tokenized by plain space as a word boundary, around 24 million orthographic words are found. We build a 3-gram language model using the corpus. The corpus statistics are given in Table 2.

Elements	Numbers
Sentences	1,605,452
Tokens	24,049,484
Unigrams	919,407
Bigrams	9,170,309
Trigrams	16,033,318

Table 2: Statistical information for CACO corpus.

4 Segmentation and Tagging

4.1 Amharic Orthography

The Amharic script is known as Ge'ez or Ethiopic. The system allows representing a consonant and a vowel together as a symbol. Each symbol represents a CV syllable. However, a syllable in Amharic may have a CVC structure. It is worth taking into account that the writing system does not mark gemination. Gemination is phonemic; it can bring meaning distinctions and in some cases can also convey grammatical information.

As in other languages, Amharic texts show variation in writing compound words. They can be written in three ways: with a space between the compound words (e.g., ሆደ ሰፊ /hodə səffi/ "patient", ምግብ ቤት /migib bet/ "restaurant"), separated by a hyphen (e.g., ስነ-ልሳን /sinə-lisan/ "linguistics", ስነ-ምግባር /sinə-migibar/ "behavior") or written as a single word (e.g., ቤተሰብ /betəsəb/ "family", ምድረበዳ /midrəbəda/ "desert").

Orthographic words, which are separated by whitespace (semicolon in old documents), may be coupled with function words like a preposition, a conjunction or auxiliaries. In most cases, an orthographic word may function as a phrase (e.g., ከቤትዋ /kəbətwa/ "from her house"), a clause (e.g., የመጣው· /jəmmət't'aw/ "the one who came"), or even a sentence (e.g., አልበላችም /ʔalbəllaʧʧɨm/ "She did not eat.").

In addition, the writing system allows people to write in a phonemic form (the abstract form or what one intends to say) or in a phonetic form (what is actually uttered). As a result, we have different forms for a given word.

All the above features need to be addressed in processing Amharic texts. Some of the above problems call for standardization efforts to be made, whereas others are due to the decision to write what is in mind and what is actually produced. Furthermore, for proper syntactic analyses, clitics could be segmented. We used an existing morphological analyzer with some improvements to perform the possible segmentation and tagging.

4.2 Proposed Tag-sets

As we have indicated in Section 2, most works on POS tags in Amharic are based on orthographic words. In such approach, they proposed compound tagsets for words with other syntactic words. Tagged corpora following this approach may not be used for syntactic analyses. For syntactic analysis, we need information about the structure within a phrase, a clause and a sentence. Tagging with a bundle of tagset will hide such syntactic information.

Since one of the main objectives of the tagging task is to provide lexical information that can be employed for syntactic analysis like parsing, we suggest that syntactic words should be the unit of analysis for tagging rather than orthographic words. In light of this, we can follow what is proposed by Seyoum et al. (2018). In this work, a syntactic word is used for the analysis in favor of a lexicalist syntactic view. They suggested that clitics should be segmented as a pre-processing step. Since manual segmentation is very costly and time taking, we opted for doing morphological segmentation using an existing tool that could be closer to our intention. For this purpose, we have found HornMorpho to be a possible candidate with some improvement. Although this tagset has not yet been fully integrated into HornMorpho, we use it for analysis since no other analyzer has comparable coverage.

4.3 HornMorpho Analysis and Limitations

HornMorpho (Gasser, 2011) is a rule-based system for morphological analysis and generation. As in many other modern computational morphological systems, it takes the form of a cascade of composed finite-state transducers (FSTs) that implement a lexicon of roots and morphemes, morphotactics, and alternation rules governing phonological or orthographic changes at morpheme boundaries (Beesley and Karttunen, 2003). To handle the complex long-distance dependencies between morphemes that characterize the morphology of Amharic, the transducers in HornMorpho are weighted with feature structures, an approach originally introduced by Amtrup (2003). During transduction, the feature structure weights on arcs that are traversed are unified, resulting in transducer output that includes an accumulated feature structure as well as a character string. In this way, the transducers retain a memory of where they have been, allowing the system to implement agreement and co-occurrence constraints and to output characters based on morphemes encountered earlier in the word.

As an example, consider the imperfective forms of Amharic verbs, which, as in other Semitic languages, include subject person/gender/number agreement prefixes as well as suffixes. The prefix *t-* encodes either third person singular feminine or second person singular masculine, singular feminine or plural. The suffix following an imperfective stem, or absence thereof, may disambiguate the prefix. Once it has seen the prefix, the HornMorpho transducer "remembers" the set of possible subject person, gender, and number features that are consistent with the input so far. When it reaches the suffix (or finds none), it can reduce the set of possible features (or reject the word if an inconsistent suffix is found). So in the word ትፈልጊያለሽ */tifəlligijalləʃ/* "you (sing. fem.) want," where we have *t - fəllig - i - alləʃ*, the presence of the suffix *-i* following the stem *-fəllig-* tells HornMorpho to constrain the subject person and number to second person singular feminine; without the proper prefix, HornMorpho would reject the word at this point.

The major focus in the development of HornMorpho was on lexical words not on function words. More specifically, it analyzes nouns and verbs. Since Amharic adjectives behave like nouns, HornMorpho does not distinguish between adjectives and nouns. In addition, compound words and light verb constructions (in version 2.5) are not handled. It also gives wrong results when it gets words with more than two clitics attached to a word. For instance, ባቧላፏው */bəbbəkkulaʧʧəw/* "from his/her side or perspective" (this word occurs 4,293 times in the amWaC17). For this word, the system guessed fifteen analyses. Furthermore, since clitics are not considered as separate words, the system does not give any analysis for clitics. Therefore, in order to use this tool for tagging a big corpus, we need to improve the coverage of the tool.

4.4 Improvement to HornMorpho

For the purposes of this paper, we modified HornMorpho in several ways. Since the major focus of HornMorpho is to give analysis for nouns and verbs, it does not give morphological analysis for syntactic words. However, as a result of the improvement, it distinguishes more parts-of-speech (verbs, nouns, adjectives, adverbs, conjunctions, and adpositions). Morphological analysis for constructions like light verbs, compound nouns and verbs, are now included in the improved version. As a rule-based system, it has limited lexicon. The improved version, however, recognizes personal and place names. For our purpose, we have enhanced the coverage of the lexicon.

```
<s>
  <w pos="PRON" morphemes="be(prep)-{yh}" latin="bezihu">በዚህ </w>
  <w pos="NM_PRS" morphemes="ye(gen)-{dereja}" lain="yedereja">
     የደረጃ </w>
  <w pos="N" morphemes="{zrzr}" latin="zrzr">ዝርዝር </w>
  <w pos="NADJ" morphemes="{'and}-m(cnj)" latin="'andm">አንድም </w>
  <w pos="N" morphemes="{'ityoP_yawi}" latin="'ityoPyawi">ኢትዮጵያዊ </w>
  <w pos="V" morphemes="al(neg1)-{ktt+te1a2_e3}(prf,recip,pas)-
     e(sb=3sm)-m(neg2)" latin="'altekatetem">አልተካተተም </w>
  <w pos="PUN">። </w>
</s>
```

Figure 1. An example sentence that is tagged with HornMorpho.

Figure 1 shows an example sentence from our corpus that is tagged by HornMorpho, *በዚህ የደረጃ ዝርዝር አንድም ኢትዮጵያዊ አልተካተተም ።* /bəzihu jədərədʒa zirzir ʔandɨmm ʔitjop'ijawi ʔaltəkatətəm./ "No Ethiopian has been included in the ranking list," transliterated as *bezihu yedereja zrzr 'andm 'ityoPyawi 'altekatetem ::*. The HornMorpho segmenter puts the stem between {}, gives a POS label for the lexical word, and labels grammatical morphemes, which are mostly function words, that are separated by hyphens, with features/tags. For verbs, the stem is represented as a sequence of root consonants and a template consisting of root consonant positions, vowels and gemination characters. The root consonants and template are separated by a "+", the root consonant positions in the template are represented by numbers, and underscore indicates gemination. During analysis by HornMorpho, the Amharic text is transliterated to Latin script using the System for Ethiopic Representation in ASCII (Firdyiwek and Yaqob, 1997).

5 Conclusion and Future Works

In this paper, we have introduced a new resource, CACO, a partly web corpus of Amharic. The corpus has been collected from different sources with different domains including newspapers, fiction, historical books, political books, short stories, children books and the Bible. These sources are believed to be well edited but still need automatic editing. The corpus consists of 24 million tokens from 25,199 documents. It is automatically tagged for POS using HornMorpho. We made some modifications to HornMorpho for the tagging. In doing so, we noticed that Amharic orthographic words should be properly segmented in a preprocessing stage. Currently, we have more words with unclassified tags because of the limitation of HornMorpho. Therefore, as future work, we plan to enhance HornMorpho for automatic tagging. In addition, we plan to increase the size of the data and apply our method to other existing corpora.

Acknowledgments

We would like to extend our sincere gratitude to the anonymous reviewers for their valuable feedback. We would also like to thank the University of Oslo for the partial support under a project called Linguistic Capacity Building-Tools for inclusive development of Ethiopia.

References

Amsalu Aklilu. 2004. Sabean and Ge'ez symbols as a guideline for Amharic spelling reform. In *Proceedings of the first international symposium on Ethiopian philology*, pages 18-26.

Besufikad Alemu. 2013. *A Named Entity Recognition for Amharic*. Master's thesis at Addis Ababa University. Addis Ababa, Ethiopia.

Jan W. Amtrup. 2003. Morphology in machine translation systems: Efficient integration of finite state transducers and feature structure descriptions. *Machine Translation*, 18(3): 217–238.

Atelach Alemu Argaw and Lars Asker. 2007. An Amharic stemmer: Reducing words to their citation forms. In *Proceedings of the 2007 workshop on computational approaches to Semitic languages: Common issues and resources*, pages 104-110. Association for Computational Linguistics.

Kenneth R. Beesley and Lauri Karttunen. 2003. *Finite-state morphology: Xerox tools and techniques*. CSLI, Stanford.

Girma A. Demeke and Mesfin Getachew. 2006. Manual annotation of Amharic news items with part-of-speech tags and its challenges. *Ethiopian Languages Research Center Working Papers*, 2, 1-16.

ELA. 1970. የአማርኛ ፡ ፊደል ፡ ሕግን ፡ አንዲጠብቅ ፡ ለማድረግ ፡ የተዘጋጀ ፡ ራፖር ፡ ማስታወሻ, (engl. A memorandum for standardization of Amharic spelling) *Journal of Ethiopian Studies*, 8(1): 119–134.

Yitna Firdyiwek and Daniel Yaqob. 1997. *The system for Ethiopic representation in ASCII*. https://www.researchgate.net/publication/2682324_The_System_for_Ethiopic_Representation_in_ASCII.

Björn Gambäck, Fredrik Olsson, Atelach Alemu Argaw, and Lars Asker. 2009. Methods for Amharic part-of-speech tagging. In *Proceedings of the First Workshop on Language Technologies for African Languages*, pages 104-111. Association for Computational Linguistics.

Michael Gasser. 2011. HornMorpho: a system for morphological processing of Amharic, Oromo, and Tigrinya. In *Conference on Human Language Technology for Development*, pages 94-99, Alexandria, Egypt.

Andargachew Mekonnen Gezmu, Andreas Nürnberger and Binyam Ephrem Seyoum. 2018. Portable Spelling Corrector for a Less-Resourced Language: Amharic. In *Proceedings of the Eleventh International Conference on Language Resources and Evaluation*, pages 4127– 4132. Miyazaki, Japan: European Language Resources Association (ELRA).

Abeba Ibrahim and Yaregal Assabie. 2014. Amharic Sentence Parsing Using Base Phrase Chunking. In *International Conference on Intelligent Text Processing and Computational Linguistics*, pages 297-306. Springer, Berlin, Heidelberg.

Pavel Rychlý and Vít Suchomel. 2016. Annotated Amharic Corpora. In *International Conference on Text, Speech, and Dialogue*, pages 295-302. Springer, Cham.

Kevin P. Scannell. 2007. The Crúbadán Project: Corpus building for under-resourced languages. In *Building and Exploring Web Corpora: Proceedings of the 3rd Web as Corpus Workshop*, Vol. 4, pages 5-15.

Binyam Ephrem Seyoum, Yusuke Miyao and Baye Yimam Mekonnen. 2018. Universal Dependencies for Amharic. In *Proceedings of the Eleventh International Conference on Language Resources and Evaluation*, pages 2216–2222. Miyazaki, Japan: European Language Resources Association (ELRA).

Martha Yifiru Tachbelie and Wolfgang Menzel. 2009. Amharic Part-of-Speech Tagger for Factored Language Modeling. In *Proceedings of the International Conference RANLP-2009*, pages 428-433.

Seid Muhie Yimam. 2014. Automatic annotation suggestions and custom annotation layers in WebAnno. In *Proceedings of 52nd Annual Meeting of the Association for Computational Linguistics: System Demonstrations*, pages 91-96.

Gold Corpus for Telegraphic Summarization

Chanakya Malireddy
LTRC, IIIT Hyderabad
`chanakya.malireddy`
`@research.iiit.ac.in`

Srivenkata N M Somisetty
IIIT Hyderabad
`mounikas@gmail.com`

Manish Shrivastava
LTRC, IIIT Hyderabad
`m.shrivastava@iiit.ac.in`

Abstract

Most extractive summarization techniques operate by ranking all the source sentences and then select the top-ranked sentences as the summary. Such methods are known to produce good summaries, especially when applied to news articles and scientific texts. However, they do not fare so well when applied to texts such as fictional narratives, which do not have a single central or recurrent theme. This is because usually the information or plot of the story is spread across several sentences. In this paper, we discuss a different summarization technique called Telegraphic Summarization. Here, we do not select whole sentences, rather pick short segments of text spread across sentences, as the summary. We have tailored a set of guidelines to create such summaries and, using the same, annotate a gold corpus of 200 English short stories.

1 Introduction

The purpose of summarization is to capture all the useful information from the source text in as few words as possible. Extractive summarization involves identifying parts of the text which are important. Such summaries are usually generated by ranking all the source sentences, according to some heuristic or metric, and then selecting the top sentences as the summary. Most extractive summarization systems have been developed for domains such as newswire articles (Lee et al., 2005), encyclopedic and scientific texts (Teufel and Moens, 2002). They work well in such domains because these texts revolve around a central theme and the information is often enforced by reiteration across several sentences. However, fictional narratives do not talk about a single topic. They describe a sequence of events and often contain dialogue. Information is not repeated and each sentence contributes to developing the plot further. Hence, selecting a subset of such sentences does not accurately capture the story.

In this paper, we focus on telegraphic summarization. Telegraphic summary does not contain whole sentences, instead, shorter segments are selected across sentences, and reads like a telegram. We have described a set of guidelines to create such summaries. These guidelines were used to annotate a gold corpus of 200 English short stories. The dataset can be very useful to gain an insight into story structures. No such corpus already exists, to the best of our knowledge. Formally, the paper makes the following contributions:

1. Discusses drawbacks of applying traditional extractive summarization methods to narrative texts.

2. Describes a set of guidelines to generate telegraphic summaries.

3. Provides a gold corpus of 200 short stories and their telegraphic summaries annotated using these guidelines.

4. Provides abstractive summaries for 50 stories and a set of 45 multiple-choice questions (MCQs) for evaluation purposes.

Proceedings of the First Workshop on Linguistic Resources for Natural Language Processing, pages 71–77
Santa Fe, New Mexico, USA, August 20, 2018.

The paper is organized as follows. Section 2 discusses existing and related work. Section 3 describes the data collection and summarization process. Section 4 discusses the analysis performed on the dataset. Section 5 discusses conclusions and future work.

2 Related Work

Automatic text summarization was first attempted in the middle of the 20th century (Luhn, 1958). Since then it has been applied to several domains and corpora, such as news articles (Lee et al., 2005), scientific articles (Teufel and Moens, 2002), and blogs (Hu et al., 2007).

News articles have been the focus of summarization systems for a long time because of the vast practical applications. In fact, most datasets available today are built from news corpora. However, a comparative study has shown that a single summarization technique does not perform equally well across all domains (Ceylan et al., 2010). Therefore, separate systems have to be built to deal with the domain of fiction and its nuances, and news corpora based datasets are not sufficient to train and evaluate the same.

There has been research on short fiction summarization (Kazantseva and Szpakowicz, 2010), fairy tales (Lloret and Palomar, 2009) and whole books (Mihalcea and Ceylan, 2007). But the aforementioned work in short fiction summarization had a different objective - helping a reader decide whether one would be interested in reading the complete story. Hence it contains just enough information to help the reader decide but does not reveal the entire plot. However, our dataset aims to summarize the entire plot. This is useful to learn plot structures and story organization.

Turney (2000) and the KEA algorithm by Witten et al. (1999) have attacked the problem of key-phrase extraction. But the key-phrases extracted by them do not form a cohesive summary and just try to list the major themes discussed in the article and therefore cannot be applied to the domain of fiction.

Grefenstette (1998) proposed the use of sentence shortening to generate telegraphic texts that would help a blind reader skim a page (using text-to-speech). He provided eight levels of telegraphic reduction. The first (and the most drastic) generated a stream of all the proper nouns in the text. The second generated all nouns present in the subject or object position. The third, in addition, included the head verbs. The least drastic reduction generated all subjects, head verbs, objects, subclauses, prepositions and dependent noun heads. Since then Jing (2000), Riezler et al. (2003) and Knight and Marcu (2000) have explored statistical models for sentence shortening that, in addition, aim at ensuring grammaticality of the shortened sentences. Intuitively it appears that sentence-shortening can allow more important information to be included in a summary. However, Lin (2003) showed that statistical sentence-shortening approaches like Knight and Marcu (2000) resulted in significantly worse content selection. He concluded that pure syntax-based compression does not improve overall summarizer performance, even though it performs well at the sentence level. Which is why there is a need for semantically aware techniques. Our dataset provides the tools to evaluate and, in the future, maybe even train such algorithms.

3 Data Construction

3.1 Collection and Preprocessing

We collected English short stories containing 300 to 1100 words, available in the public domain[1]. 200 stories were then randomly picked, after ensuring that works from at least 20 different authors had been selected to keep the dataset diverse in terms of genre and writing style. As a result, the dataset spans 39 authors. These stories were then manually processed to remove any spelling, grammatical and encoding errors that might have crept in.

3.2 Summarization

The summarization was performed by 5 annotators. The annotators are not native English speakers but are fluent in the language. They summarized 40 stories and cross-annotated 4 stories each (1 from each remaining annotator), to help calculate inter-annotator agreement. Each annotator also performed

---

[1] https://americanliterature.com/short-story-library

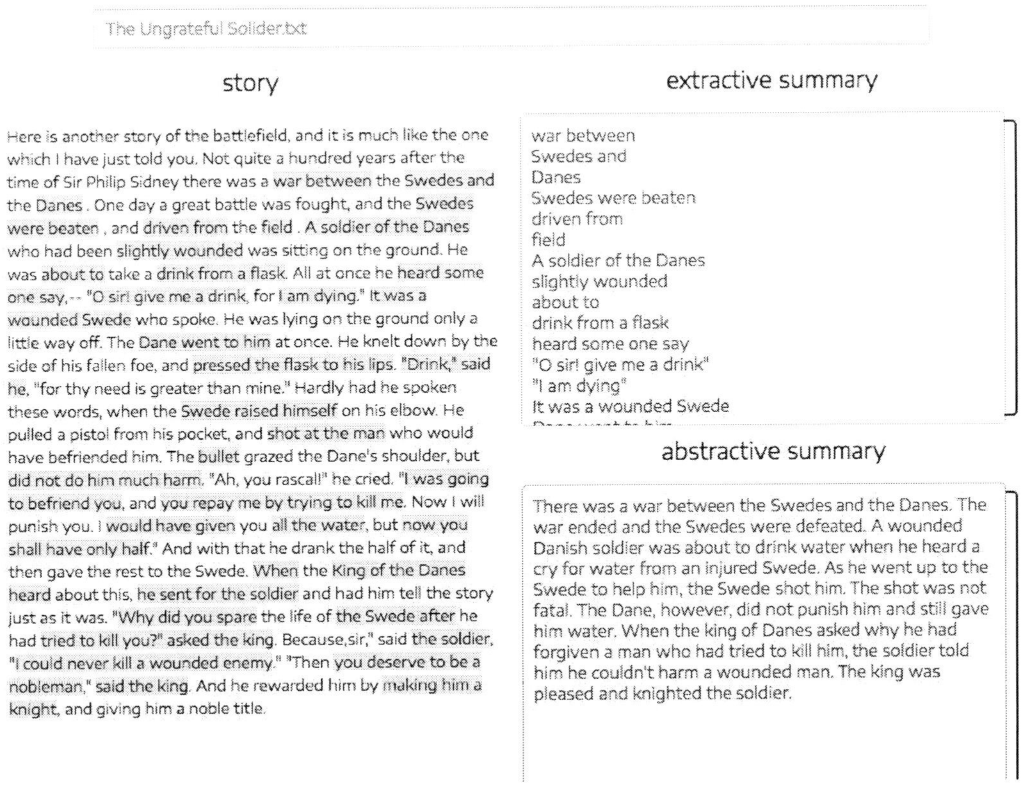

story

extractive summary

abstractive summary

Figure 1: An example of telegraphic and abstractive summaries created according to the guidelines. The story is displayed in the left panel, the telegraphic summary is highlighted and also listed in the box titled 'extractive summary' and the abstractive summary is shown below it.

abstractive summarization on 10 stories. Unlike extractive summarization, abstractive summaries need not contain the same words as used in the source and are instead written by the annotator in their "own words" based on their understanding of the text. Abstractive summary for a story was not provided by the same annotator who generated its telegraphic summary. An example is shown in Figure 1.

Guidelines followed for telegraphic summarization:

1. A segment is defined as a continuous span of words in the source, chosen as a part of the summary.

2. A word should not be fragmented e.g., if the word "breaking" appears in the source, it should not be broken into fragments like "break".

3. Each segment should be relevant to the plot, try to advance the story and have some continuity with the preceding and the following segment.

4. Segments extracted from dialogues or parentheses should be enclosed in quotes or parentheses respectively.

5. Segments should be arranged in the same order as they appear in the story.

6. The summary should be minimal. If multiple segments mean the same thing, pick the shortest. Adjectives, adverbs, and modifiers are not to be included if they are not relevant to the plot.

7. When the segments are read in sequence the plot should be apparent and unambiguous.

Guidelines followed for abstractive summarization:

1. Summaries should be written from a third party perspective e.g., "This story is about a girl..."

2. Summaries should only discuss the plot and try to avoid inferences and opinions not immediately apparent from the story.

3. Summaries should maintain the same order of events as they occur in the source text.

4 Data Analysis and Evaluation

The length of the stories varies from 300 to 1100 words, with the average length being 650. The average summarization factor (length of summary/length of the story) is 0.37 and 0.36 for telegraphic and abstractive summaries respectively.

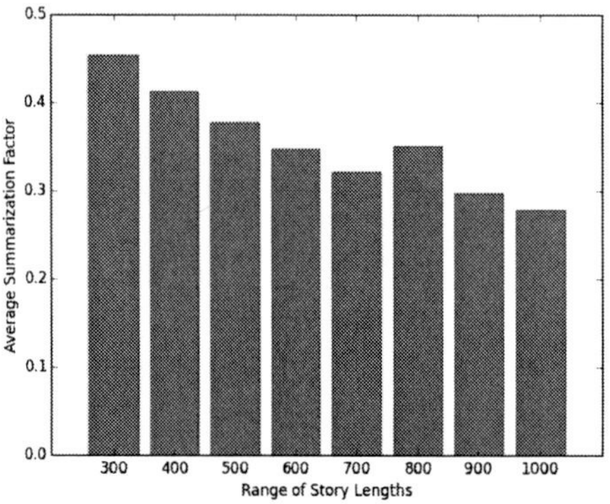

Figure 2: Summarization Factor vs Story Length

From Figure 2 we can see that the summarization factor tends to be high for very short stories since nearly every word is important. It reduces gradually as the length of the story increases because longer stories tend to be more descriptive and contain extraneous information not relevant to the central plot.

4.1 Quantitative Evaluation

We used the Alpha metric proposed in Krippendorff (1980) to measure the inter-annotator agreement. Alpha was computed based on 20 cross-annotated stories and found to be 0.73.

We generated 50 summaries using popular online extractive summarization tools, Smmry[2] and Resoomer[3], which generate summaries by ranking and selecting the top sentences (after the selection step the sentences are re-arranged according to the source order). These summaries have the same summarization factor as the corresponding telegraphic summaries.

$$Rouge_N = \frac{\sum_{s\epsilon\{ReferenceSummaries\}} \sum_{gram_n \epsilon S} Count_{match}(gram_n)}{\sum_{s\epsilon\{ReferenceSummaries\}} \sum_{gram_n \epsilon S} Count(gram_n)} \quad (1)$$

ROUGE-N score (Lin, 2004) is a popular metric used to evaluate summaries produced by a system. ROUGE-N recall is computed as shown in Eq. 1, where N stands for the length of the n-gram, $gram_n$ and $Count_{match}(gram_n)$ is the maximum number of n-grams co-occurring in a candidate summary and a set of reference summaries. ROGUE-N precision can be calculated by replacing the denominator in Eq. 1 by the total number of n-grams present in all the reference summaries instead of system summaries. The F1 score is defined as the Harmonic Mean of precision and recall.

---

[2]https://smmry.com/
[3]https://resoomer.com/en/

In our case, there was only one reference (the abstractive summary) and one summary from each system - Telegraphic, Smmry, and Resoomer. We report the average F1 score, after removing stop words and stemming, for N = 1,2,3,4 in Table 1.

	N=1	N=2	N=3	N=4
Telegraphic	0.582	0.258	0.108	0.051
Smmry	0.498	0.184	0.092	0.056
Resoomer	0.483	0.179	0.093	0.057

Table 1: ROUGE-N F1 score

The higher F1 score for N = 1,2,3 telegraphic summaries indicates that they are more adequate in terms of capturing relevant content. Since telegraphic summaries select shorter segments of text, they can retain more information while maintaining the same summarization factor as their sentence-level counterparts. The ROUGE-4 score for Smmry and Resoomer summaries is slightly higher because they select entire source sentences and are therefore likely to have more 4-gram overlaps.

4.2 Qualitative Evaluation

High-order n-gram ROUGE measures try to judge fluency to some degree but since ROUGE is based only on the content overlap, it can only measure adequacy and not coherence. In order to gain an insight into the coherence of the summaries, we made a set of 45 MCQs from 15 stories in the dataset. Questions were not set by the same annotator who generated the corresponding telegraphic summary. The test was administered to three groups of two participants each. Each group was allotted the summaries produced by a single system - Telegraphic, Smmry or Resoomer.

```
{
    "id": 154,
    "questions": [
        "Why couldn't the little girl go home?",
        "What did the girl think when one of the stars fell down?",
        "Why did the girl burn the whole bundle of matches?"
    ],
    "options": [
        ["She was lost", "She didn't have a home", "Her father would beat her for not selling any matches"],
        ["She should make a wish", "Someone is just dead", "Her grandmother has come back for her"],
        ["To keep warm", "To make it brighter", "To make her grandmother stay longer"]
    ],
    "answers": [3, 2, 3]
},
```

Figure 3: An example set of questions for the story 'The Little Match Girl'.

An example set of questions for the story 'The Little Match Girl' is shown in Figure 3. The 'id' field refers to the unique id we assign to each story in the dataset. For each story, we made a set of 3 multiple-choice questions with 3 options each. The answers refer to the index of the correct option in the list. Apart from the given options, the participants were allowed to choose option 4, "Can't say", if they could not answer a question based on the summary. Average scores are reported in Table 2.

	Correct	Incorrect	Can't say
Telegraphic	88.9%	2.2%	8.9%
Smmry	62.2%	4.4%	33.4%
Resoomer	60.0%	2.2%	37.8%

Table 2: Questionnaire Results

Higher scores on the questionnaire indicate that the telegraphic summaries were more coherent and allowed the reader to understand the story better. Participants who read the Smmry and Resoomer summaries were unable to understand the story and chose "Can't say" as the answer for nearly a third of the questions.

5 Conclusion and Future Work

In this paper, we highlight the shortcomings of applying traditional extractive summarization techniques to narrative texts and show how telegraphic summarization can be used to overcome these shortcomings.

We defined a set of guidelines to help generate telegraphic summaries. Using the same, we then construct a corpus of 200 English short stories and their telegraphic summaries. 50 abstractive summaries and 45 MCQs are also provided for evaluation purposes. This corpus has been made public [4] and can be used as a gold standard to evaluate such summarization tasks. The MCQs can also be used to evaluate QA systems.

In future, we intend to extend this corpus by adding more stories. We plan on developing algorithms to automatically generate high-quality telegraphic summaries and an extended corpus could be used as training data for supervised techniques.

References

Hakan Ceylan, Rada Mihalcea, Umut Özertem, Elena Lloret, and Manuel Palomar. 2010. Quantifying the limits and success of extractive summarization systems across domains. In *Human language technologies: The 2010 annual conference of the North American chapter of the Association for Computational Linguistics*, pages 903–911. Association for Computational Linguistics.

Gregory Grefenstette. 1998. Producing intelligent telegraphic text reduction to provide an audio scanning service for the blind. In *Working notes of the AAAI Spring Symposium on Intelligent Text summarization*, pages 111–118. The AAAI Press Menlo Park, CA.

Meishan Hu, Aixin Sun, and Ee-Peng Lim. 2007. Comments-oriented blog summarization by sentence extraction. In *Proceedings of the Sixteenth ACM Conference on Conference on Information and Knowledge Management*, CIKM '07, pages 901–904, New York, NY, USA. ACM.

Hongyan Jing. 2000. Sentence reduction for automatic text summarization. In *Proceedings of the Sixth Conference on Applied Natural Language Processing*, ANLC '00, pages 310–315, Stroudsburg, PA, USA. Association for Computational Linguistics.

Anna Kazantseva and Stan Szpakowicz. 2010. Summarizing short stories. *Comput. Linguist.*, 36(1):71–109.

Kevin Knight and Daniel Marcu. 2000. Statistics-based summarization-step one: Sentence compression. *AAAI/IAAI*, 2000:703–710.

Klaus Krippendorff. 1980. *Content analysis: an introduction to its methodology.* Sage commtext series. Sage Publications.

Chang-Shing Lee, Zhi-Wei Jian, and Lin-Kai Huang. 2005. A fuzzy ontology and its application to news summarization. *IEEE Transactions on Systems, Man, and Cybernetics, Part B (Cybernetics)*, 35(5):859–880.

Chin-Yew Lin. 2003. Improving summarization performance by sentence compression: a pilot study. In *Proceedings of the sixth international workshop on Information retrieval with Asian languages-Volume 11*, pages 1–8. Association for Computational Linguistics.

Chin-Yew Lin. 2004. Rouge: A package for automatic evaluation of summaries. *Text Summarization Branches Out*.

Elena Lloret and Manuel Palomar, 2009. *A Gradual Combination of Features for Building Automatic Summarisation Systems*, pages 16–23. Springer Berlin Heidelberg, Berlin, Heidelberg.

Hans Peter Luhn. 1958. The automatic creation of literature abstracts. *IBM J. Res. Dev.*, 2(2):159–165.

Rada Mihalcea and Hakan Ceylan. 2007. Explorations in automatic book summarization. In *Proceedings of the 2007 joint conference on empirical methods in natural language processing and computational natural language learning (EMNLP-CoNLL)*, pages 380–389.

---

[4]https://github.com/m-chanakya/shortstories

Stefan Riezler, Tracy H King, Richard Crouch, and Annie Zaenen. 2003. Statistical sentence condensation using ambiguity packing and stochastic disambiguation methods for lexical-functional grammar. In *Proceedings of the 2003 Conference of the North American Chapter of the Association for Computational Linguistics on Human Language Technology-Volume 1*, pages 118–125. Association for Computational Linguistics.

Simone Teufel and Marc Moens. 2002. Summarizing scientific articles: experiments with relevance and rhetorical status. *Computational linguistics*, 28(4):409–445.

Peter D Turney. 2000. Learning algorithms for keyphrase extraction. *Information retrieval*, 2(4):303–336.

Ian H. Witten, Gordon W. Paynter, Eibe Frank, Carl Gutwin, and Craig G. Nevill-Manning. 1999. KEA: practical automatic keyphrase extraction. *CoRR*, cs.DL/9902007.

Design of a Tigrinya Language Speech Corpus
for Speech Recognition

Hafte Abera
Addis Ababa University
Addis Ababa, Ethiopia
hafte.abera@ aau.edu.et

Sebsibe H/Mariam
Addis Ababa University
Addis Ababa, Ethiopia
sebsibe2004@gmail.com

Abstract

In this paper, we describe the first Tigrinya Language speech corpus designed and developed for speech recognition purposes. Tigrinya, often written as Tigrigna (ትግርኛ) /tɪˈgrinjə/ belongs to the Semitic branch of the Afro-Asiatic languages and shows characteristic features of a Semitic language. It is spoken by ethnic Tigray-Tigrigna people in the Horn of Africa. This paper outlines different corpus designing processes and related work on the creation of speech corpora for different languages. The authors also provide procedures that were used for the creation of a speech recognition corpus for Tigrinya, an under-resourced language. One hundred and thirty native Tigrinya speakers were recorded for the training and test datasets. Each speaker read 100 texts, which consisted of syllabically rich and balanced sentences. Ten thousand sets of sentences were used, which contained all of the contextual syllables and phones of Tigrinya.

1 Introduction

Speech corpus is defined as a collection of speech signals that is accessible in computer readable form, and has an annotation, metadata and documents to allow re-use of the data in house or by scientists (Gibbonet et al., 1997). Speech corpus is one of the fundamental requirements for developing speech recognition and synthesis systems and to analyze the characteristics of speech signals. Moreover, for phonetic research, speech corpus can also provide diverse and accurate data to help researchers find the rules of languages. The main reason for preparing a Tigrinya speech corpus is, as a first step, to explore the possibility of developing a Tigrinya speech recognition system (Li & Zu, 2006). Tigrinya, often written as Tigrigna (ትግርኛ) /tɪˈgriːnjə/belongs to the Semitic branch of the Afro-Asiatic languages and shows characteristic features of a Semitic language (Tewolde, 2002; Berhane, 1991). It is spoken by ethnic Tigray-Tigrigna people in the Horn of Africa.

Speech corpora design is one of the key issues in building high quality text to speech recognition systems (mostly read speech). Radová (1998) pointed out that most speech corpora contain read speech, either for practical reasons because annotating non-read speech is more difficult, or simply because the intended application or investigation requires read speech. Due to the first reason a read speech corpus is prepared and used for this work.

The preparation of any type of speech corpus is normally a project on its own and handled on the basis of an agreement between corpus producers and corpus users. However, in cases like this study, where the required corpus is not available, speech recognition experiments are conducted on the newly produced corpus. The advantage in the latter case is that the corpus is produced with full and specific knowledge of its intended use.

According to Li & Yin (2006), the development of speech corpus has created new problems: (1) many corpora have been established, and much money and time have been put into their technology; and (2) these corpora are difficult to share among different affiliations. The foremost cause of this problem is the lack of general specifications for corpus collection, annotation, and distribution. In order to solve this problem, standardization research on speech corpora is necessary and specifications should be stipulated (Li &Yin, 2012).

Proceedings of the First Workshop on Linguistic Resources for Natural Language Processing, pages 78–82
Santa Fe, New Mexico, USA, August 20, 2018.

2 Benchmarks and procedure for speech corpus construction

The Tigrinya Speech Recognition Corpus has been designed to satisfy a set of guidelines, which specify the required quality of speech data and the proportional distribution of data with different speaker characteristics. In this paper the authors provide a brief overview of the criteria defined for the speech corpus from Li & Zu (2006). The criteria are explained in the following sub-sections.

2.1 Specification of speakers

Any speech corpus should be representative of speakers of both genders in equal proportions and contain speech from speakers of different ages. In this work, the speakers were grouped into six age groups, as seen in Table 1: from 18 to 22 (up to 19%), from 23 to 27 (at least 25%), from 28 to 32 (at least 25%), from 33 to 37 (at least 15%), from 38 to 42 (at least 13%), and from 43-70 (at least 4%). The upper boundary is relatively small, since we did not have enough speakers to cover that age group. The researchers excluded the speech of children and people older than 70, because the speech characteristics in these groups are quite different and require training of separate acoustic models.

Age Range	Training set		Test Set		Adaptive data set		Total
	Male	Female	Male	Female	Male	Female	
18-22	10	9	1	1	3	1	25
23-27	12	10	1	2	4	3	32
28-32	14	12	1	2	1	2	32
33-37	8	8	1	1	1	1	20
38-42	9	6	0	0	1	1	17
43- 70	1	1	0	0	1	1	4
Total	54	46	4	6	11	9	130

Table 1: Age and Sex Distribution of the Readers

2.2 Specification of corpus design

After having the text corpus, the next important step in preparing a read speech corpus is recording the speech. In the recording of selected sentences, each speaker is asked to read exactly what is presented to him or her. The text to be read is presented on a mobile phone. In the read speech recording, the degree of control is very high. For example during the recording, each utterance of the speaker can be checked directly for errors, and if an error is found, the speaker is asked to re-read the text.

The recordings of the Tigrigna speech corpus were done in an office environment, as well as outside the office. The text was read by 130 native Tigrigna speakers. For recording purposes, the mobile application Lig-Akuma, which displays one sentence at a time for the speaker to read, was used. The entire recording was done in the presence of a researcher. The speaker was first explained the purpose of the project and instructed what to do. The recording session was controlled by the researcher, which included running the recording program, starting and stopping the recording session, playing back the recorded speech, re-recording the sentences (if required), and moving to the next sentence. Every speaker was instructed to start the recording when he or she was ready. After each reader's session was finished, all the utterances were listened to both by the reader and the researcher for possible corrections.

The Tigrigna speech corpus was designed according to best practice guidelines established for other languages. Standard speech corpora, such as the Amharic speech corpus (Abate et al., 2005), consist of a training set, a speaker adaptation set, and test sets. To make it comparable with commonly used standard corpora, the Tigrinya corpus was designed to contain the same components.

The recording training set consists of a total of ten thousand different sentences. The training set was read by 100 speakers of the different Tigrai dialects. As already mentioned, Table 1 shows the age and sex distribution of all speakers. Due to time constraints, it was difficult to keep the age and sex balance in the speaker sample.

Each test and speaker adaptation set was read by 10 and 20 speakers, respectively, from different dialects. For the test sets, different sentences were selected for each speaker. Table 2 shows the number of sentences that have been automatically selected from the text database and read for the collection of speech data for the corpus.

Data-Set	Number of selected sentences	Number of recorded sentences	Duration (hours)
Training set	10,000	10,000	17:57
Speaker Adaptation set	69	69	2:30
Development test set	1,000	600	2:10
Evaluation test set	1,000	400	1:20

Table 2: Elements of Tigrinya Speech Corpus

2.3 Specification of recording

Data collection was carried out using an improved version of the Android application Lig-Aikuma, developed by Steven Bird and colleagues (Blachon et al., 2016). The resulting app, called Lig-Aikuma, runs on various mobile phones and tablets and proposes a range of different speech collection modes (recording, re-speaking, translation and elicitation). Lig-Aikuma's improved features include a smart generation and handling of speaker metadata as well as re-speaking and parallel audio data mapping.

For every mode, a metadata file was saved with the recording file. Metadata forms are filled in before any recording. In addition, metadata have been enriched with new details about the languages (language of the recording, mother tongue of the speaker, other languages spoken) and about the speaker (name, age, gender, region of origin). Moreover, in order to save time, a feature saves the latest metadata as a session and uses it to preload the form the next time it is necessary. The files are now named using the specific following format: DATE-TIMEDEVICE-NAME LANG. As an example 2016-02-07-01-32-18_HUAWEI-HUAWEI Y625-U32_tir is the name of a recording made on February, 07, 2016, at 1pm (01:32:18), in Tigrinya, on a HUAWEI device.

Similarly to the general trend of speech recognition system development (e.g., Abate et al., 2005; Blachon et al., 2016; De Vries et al., 2011), all speech data were sampled in 16 KHz and 16 bits allocated per sample. In order to be able to develop speech recognition systems that can be executed in different environments and that can be used for wide purposes, we should be able to build speech acoustic models that are robust, as well as noise representative to different environments (Li &Zu, 2006). Therefore, the Tigrinya speech recognition corpus has been developed to include speech data with different types of background noise (office, street, in-car, etc. noise) and with different signal-to-noise ratios (SNR). The majority of the data, however, contain a relatively low level of noise (the SNR being between 20-85dB). Overlapping speech segments (with two or more simultaneous speakers) are not included in the corpus. The Tigrigna Speech Corpus consists of utterances from Tigrinya literary (formal) language, however, pronounced by a variety of speakers, including speakers with different dialect from both the Southern and Northern Tigrinya dialects (Berhane, 1991).

2.4 Specification of annotation

Following recent research on other language speech recognition corpora (Abushariah et al., 2012; Radová, 1999; Arora et al., 2004) the corpus has been designed to be phonetically balanced in order to be representative of natural speech and phonetically rich so that the trained acoustic models would efficiently generalize over different speakers with different characteristics. Abera et al. (2016) previously showed how to analyze and create corpora with respect to syllabic richness and balance. An example of an orthographically annotated utterance is given in Figure 1.

2.5 Availability

Thus far the corpus has been used for our research in developing an automatic speech recognizer for Tigrinya. As our research is at its last phase, we have the intention of making the corpus available for researchers and developers by means of a third party.

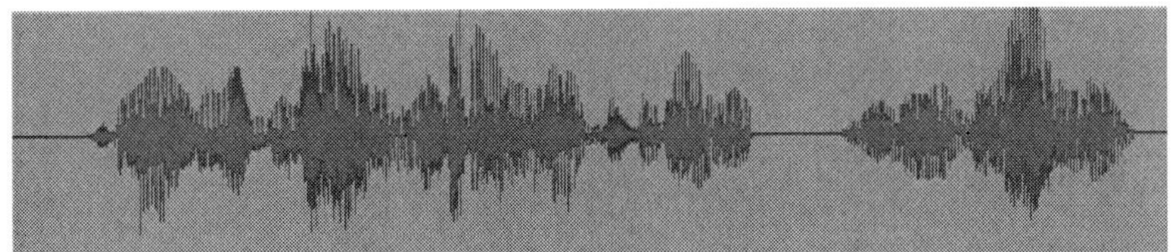

Figure 1: Example of the Phonologically Annotated Utterance ፀሪ ግብፅን ንግድ ኢትዮጵያን እቶም ነዊሕ ዝቋሜቶም ሰብ ሳባን ናባኻ ኺሓልፉ ናትካውን ኪኹኑ እዮም "Tsaeri gbtsn ngd etyopyan etom newih zquametom seb saban nabaKa KiHalf Natkawn kiKuinu eyom"

3 Conclusion and future work

In this paper the authors presented the overall design of the Tigrinya Speech Recognition Corpus. The corpus is the first database available to train and test an Automatic Speech Recognition system, which takes into account dialectal variation in Tigrinya. The corpus consists of 17.57 hours of speech audio data set for training and 3.3 hours of phonetically annotated speech audio data for development and evaluation. The corpus is both phonetically rich and balanced. This paper also described the reasoning behind different choices made during the development of the corpus. We believe that this paper can serve as a guideline for other researchers, who are developing, or want to develop speech recognition corpora for under-resourced languages.

The Tigrinya Speech Recognition Corpus in the years to come will be an asset for further research in speech recognition in general, as well as speech synthesis of Tigrinya – a language that did not have a dedicated speech recognition corpus before. In addition, the speech corpus should be able to play a crucial role in linguistic research, such as comparing the differences in pronunciation made by men and women. Additional experiments with this corpus are anticipated to improve the performance of our speech recognition system.

References

Solomon Teferra Abate. 2006. *Automatic speech recognition for Amharic*. Ph.D. Thesis. University of Hamburg. Hamburg.

Solomn Teferra Abate, Wolfgang Menzel, and Bairu Tafila. 2005. An Amharic speech corpus for large vocabulary continuous speech recognition. In Eurospeech, 9th *European Conference on Speech Communication and Technology*, pages 1601-1604, Lisbon, Portugal.

Hafte Abera, Climent Nadeu, and Sebsibe H. Mariam. 2016. Extraction of syllabically rich and balanced sentences for Tigrigna language. In *2016 International Conference on Advances in Computing, Communications and Informatics (ICACCI)*, IEEE, pages 2094-2097, Jaipur, India.

Mohammad AM Abushariah, Raja N. Ainon, Roziati Zainuddin, Moustafa Elshafei, and Othman O. Khalifa. 2012. Phonetically rich and balanced text and speech corpora for Arabic language. *Language resources and evaluation*, 46(4), 601-634.

Karunesh Arora, Sunita Arora, Kapil Verma, and Shyam Sunder Agrawal. 2004. Automatic extraction of phonetically rich sentences from large text corpus of Indian languages. In *Proceedings of the 8th International Conference on Spoken Language Processing (ICSLP)*, pages 2885-2888, Jeju, Korea.

David Blachon, Elodie Gauthier, Laurent Besacier, Guy-Noël Kouarata, Martine Adda-Decker, and Annie Rialland. 2016. Parallel speech collection for under-resourced language studies using the Lig-Aikuma mobile device app. *Procedia Computer Science*, 81, 61-66.

Nic De Vries, Jaco Badenhorst, Marelie H. Davel, Etienne Barnard, and Alta De Waal. 2011. Woefzela-an open-source platform for ASR data collection in the developing world. In *Proceedings of INTERSPEECH 2011, 12th Annual Conference of the International Speech Communication Association*, pages 3177-3180, Florence, Italy.

Dafydd Gibbon, Roger Moore, and Richard Winski. 1997. *Handbook of Standards and Resources for Spoken Language Systems*. Mouton de Gruyter, Berlin New York.

Ai-jun Li and Zhi-gang Yin. 2007. Standardization of speech corpus. *Data Science Journal*, 6,: S806-S812.

Ai-jun Li and Zu, Yiqing. 2006. Corpus design and annotation for speech synthesis and recognition. *Advances in Chinese spoken language processing*: 243-268.

Vlasta Radová. 1998. Design of the Czech Speech Corpus for Speech Recognition Applications with a Large Vocabulary. In *Text, Speech, Dialogue. Proc. of the First Workshop on Text, Speech, Dialogue*. Brno, Czech Republic, pages 299-304.

Vlasta Radová, Petr Vopálka, and P. Ircing. 1999. Methods of Phonetically Balanced Sentences Selection. In *Proceedings of the 3rd Multiconference on Systemics, Cybernetics and Informatics*, pages 334-339, Orlando, USA.

Parallel Corpora for bi-Directional Statistical Machine Translation for Seven Ethiopian Language Pairs

Solomon Teferra Abate
Addis Ababa University,
Addis Ababa, Ethiopia
solomon.teferra@aau.edu.et

Michael Melese Woldeyohannis
Addis Ababa University,
Addis Ababa, Ethiopia
michael.melese@aau.edu.et

Martha Yifiru Tachbelie
Addis Ababa University,
Addis Ababa, Ethiopia
martha.yifiru@aau.edu.et

Million Meshesha
Addis Ababa University,
Addis Ababa, Ethiopia
million.meshesha@aau.edu.et

Solomon Atinafu
Addis Ababa University,
Addis Ababa, Ethiopia
solomon.atnafu@aau.edu.et

Wondwossen Mulugeta
Addis Ababa University,
Addis Ababa, Ethiopia
wondwossen.mulugeta@aau.edu.et

Yaregal Assabie
Addis Ababa University,
Addis Ababa, Ethiopia
yaregal.assabie@aau.edu.et

Hafte Abera
Addis Ababa University,
Addis Ababa, Ethiopia
hafte.abera@aau.edu.et

Biniyam Ephrem
Addis Ababa University,
Addis Ababa, Ethiopia
binyam.ephrem@aau.edu.et

Tewodros Abebe
Addis Ababa University,
Addis Ababa, Ethiopia
tewodros.abebe@aau.edu.et

Wondimagegnhue Tsegaye
Bahir Dar University,
Bahir Dar, Ethiopia
wendeal@gmail.com

Amanuel Lemma
Aksum University,
Axum, Ethiopia
amanu.infosys@gmail.com

Tsegaye Andargie
Wolkite University,
Wolkite, Ethiopia
adtsegaye@gmail.com

Seifedin Shifaw
Wolkite University,
Wolkite, Ethiopia
seifedin28@gmail.com

Abstract

In this paper, we describe the development of parallel corpora for Ethiopian Languages: Amharic, Tigrigna, Afan-Oromo, Wolaytta and Ge'ez. To check the usability of all the corpora we conducted baseline bi-directional statistical machine translation (SMT) experiments for seven language pairs. The performance of the bi-directional SMT systems shows that all the corpora can be used for further investigations. We have also shown that the morphological complexity of the Ethio-Semitic languages has a negative impact on the performance of the SMT especially when they are target languages. Based on the results we obtained, we are currently working towards handling the morphological complexities to improve the performance of statistical machine translation among the Ethiopian languages.

Proceedings of the First Workshop on Linguistic Resources for Natural Language Processing, pages 83–90
Santa Fe, New Mexico, USA, August 20, 2018.

1 Introduction

The advancement of technology and the rise of the internet as a means of communication led to an ever-increasing demand for Natural Language Processing (NLP) Applications. NLP applications are useful in facilitating human-human communication via computing systems. One of the NLP applications which facilitate human-human communication is Machine Translation. Machine Translation (MT) refers to a process by which computer software is used to translate a text from one language to another (Koehn, 2009). In the presence of high volume digital text, the ideal aim of machine translation systems is to produce the best possible translation with minimal human intervention (Hutchins, 2005).

The translation of natural language by machine becomes a reality, for technologically favored languages, in the late 20th century although it is dreamt since the seventieth century (Hutchins, 1995). Various approaches to MT have been and are being used in the research community. These approaches are broadly classified into rule based and corpus-based MT (Koehn, 2009). The rule-based machine translation demands various kinds of linguistic re- sources such as morphological analyzer and synthesizer, syntactic parsers, semantic analyzers and so on. On the other hand, corpus-based approaches (as the name implies) require parallel and monolingual corpora. Since corpus-based approaches do not require deep linguistic analysis of the source and target languages, it is the preferred approach for under-resourced languages of the world, including Ethiopian languages.

1.1 Machine Translation for Ethiopian Languages

Research in the development of MT has been conducted for technologically favored and economically as well as politically important languages of the world since the 17th century. As a result, notable progress towards the development and use of MT systems has been made for these languages. However, research in the area of MT for Ethiopian languages, which are under-resourced as well as economically and technologically disadvantaged, has started very recently. Most of the researches on MT for Ethiopian languages are conducted by graduate students (Tariku, 2004; Sisay, 2009; Eleni, 2013; Jabesa, 2013; Akubazgi, 2017), including two PhD works: one that tried to integrate Amharic into a unification-based machine translation system (Sisay, 2004) and the other that investigated English-Amharic Statistical Machine translation (Mulu, 2017). Beside this, Michael and Million (Michael and Million, 2017) experimented a bi-directional Amharic-Tigrigna SMT system using word and morpheme as a unit.

Due to unavailability of linguistic resources and since the most widely used MT approach is statistical, most of these researches have been conducted using statistical machine translation (SMT), which requires large bilingual and monolingual corpora. However, as there were no such corpora for SMT experiments for Ethiopian languages, the researchers had to prepare their own small size corpora for their experiment. This in turn, affects the results that they obtain.

In addition, since there are no standard corpora for conducting replicable and consistent experiments for performance evaluation, it is difficult to know the progress made in the area for local languages. Moreover, since the researchers had to spend their time on corpora preparation, they usually have limited time for experimentation, exploration and development of MT systems.

1.2 Motivation of this Paper

African languages, which contribute around 30% (2139) of the world language highly suffer from the lack of sufficient language resources (Simons and Fennig, 2017). This is true for Ethiopian languages. On the other hand, Ethiopia being a multilingual and multi-ethnic country, its constitution decrees that each citizen has the right to speak, write and develop in his/her own language. However, there is still a need to share information among citizens who speak different languages. For example, Amharic is the regional language of the Amhara and Southern Nations and Nationalities regions, Afan-Oromo is that of the Oromia region while the Tigray region uses Tigrigna. All these regions produce a lot of information that need to be shared among the other regions of the nation. There is, therefore, a lot of translation demands among the different language communities of the federal government of Ethiopia.

In order to enable the citizens of the country to use the documents and the information produced in other Ethiopian languages, the documents need to be translated to the languages they understand most. Since manual translation is expensive, a promising alternative is the use of machine translation, particularly SMT as Ethiopian languages suffer from lack of basic linguistic resources such as morphological analyser, syntactic analyser, morphological synthesizer, etc. The major and basic resource required for SMT is parallel corpora, which are not available for Ethiopian languages. The collection and preparation of parallel corpora for Ethiopian languages is, therefore, an important endeavour to facilitate future MT research and development.

We have, therefore, collected and prepared parallel corpora for seven Ethiopian Language pairs taking representatives from the Semitic, Cushitic and Omotic language families. We have considered Amharic, Tigrigna and Ge'ez from the Semitic, Afan-Oromo from the Cushitic and Wolaytta from Omotic language families. This paper, therefore, describes the parallel corpora we collected and prepared for these Ethiopian languages and the SMT experiments conducted using the corpora as a way of verifying their usability.

2 Nature of the Language Pairs

The language pairs in the corpora belong to Semitic (Ge'ez, Amharic and Tigrigna), Cushitic (Afan-Oromo) and Omotic (Wolaytta) language families. Except Ge'ez, these languages have native speakers. Ge'ez serves as a liturgical language of Ethiopian Orthodox Church. It is thought as a second language in the traditional schools of the church and given as a course in different Universities. There is a rich body of literature in Ge'ez, including philosophical, medical and astrological writings. Because of this, there is a big initiative in translating the documents written in Ge'ez to other widely used languages. On the other hand, Amharic is spoken by more than 27 million people which makes it the second most spoken Semitic language in the world. Tigrigna is spoken by 9 million people. Afan-Oromo and Wolaytta are spoken by more than 34 million and 2 million speakers, respectively (Simons and Fennig, 2017).

The writing systems of these language pairs are Ge'ez or Ethiopic script and Latin alphabet. Ge'ez, Amharic and Tigrigna are written in Ge'ez script whereas both Afan-Oromo and Wolaytta are written in Latin alphabet. It is believed that the earliest known writing in the Ge'ez script date back to the 5th century BC. The Ge'ez script is syllabary in which each character represents a consonant and a vowel. Each character gets its basic shape from the consonant of the syllable, and the vowel is represented through systematic modifications of the basic shape. The script is also used to write other languages like Argobba, Harari, Gurage, etc.

The language pairs have got different functions in the country. Amharic for instance is the working language of the Federal Government of Ethiopia. It also serves as regional working language of some other regional states. It facilitates inter-regional communication. Tigrigna and Afan-Oromo are working languages in Tigray and Oromia regional administrations, respectively. Apart from this, they serve as medium of instructions in primary and secondary schools. These languages are also used widely in the electronic media like news, blogs and social media. Some of the governmental websites are available in Amharic, Tigrigna and Afan-Oromo. Currently, Google offers a searching capability using these Ethiopian languages. Further, Google also included Amharic in its translation service recently.

2.1 Morphological Features

Like other Semitic languages, Ge'ez (Dillmann and Bezold, 1907), Amharic (Leslau, 2000; Anbessa and Hudson, 2007) and Tigrigna (Mason, 1996; Yohannes, 2002), make use of the root and pattern system. In these languages, a root (which is called a radical) is a set of consonants which bears the basic meaning of the lexical item whereas a pattern is composed of a set of vowels inserted between the consonants of the root. These vowel patterns together with affixes results in derived words. Such derivational process makes these languages morphologically complex.

In addition to the morphological information, some syntactic information are also expressed at word level. Furthermore, an orthographic word may attach some syntactic words like prepositions, conjunctions, negation, etc. which create various word forms (Gasser, 2010; Gasser, 2011). In these languages, nominals are inflected for number, gender, definiteness and case whereas verbs are inflected for person, number, gender, tense, aspect, and mood (Griefenow-Mewis, 2001).

Essentially, unlike the Semitic languages which allow prefixing, Afan-Oromo allows suffixing. Most functional words like postpositions are also suffixed. However, there are some prepositions written as a separate word.

Wolaytta like Afan-Oromo is a suffixing language in which words can be generated from root words recursively by adding suffixes only. Wolaytta nouns are inflected for number, gender and case whereas verbs are inflected for person, number, gender, aspect and mood (Wakasa, 2008).

2.2 Syntactic Features

Ethiopian languages that are under our consideration follow Subject-Object-Verb (SOV) word-order except Ge'ez which allows the verb to come first. In Ge'ez, the basic word-order is Verb-Subject-Object (VSO).

3 Challenges of SMT

Statistical Machine Translation is greatly impacted by the linguistic features of the target languages. The challenges range from the writing system to that of word ordering and morphological complexity.

3.1 Writing System

The Ge'ez writing system, which is used by Amharic, Tigrigna and Ge'ez languages, uses different characters in words that convey the same meaning, especially in Amharic. For example, peace can be written as: ሰላም or ሠላም. Such character variations affect probability values that have direct impact on the performance of SMTs.

3.2 Word Ordering

Most of the languages under consideration have same word order. With this respect, Amharic, Afan-Oromo, Tigrigna and Wolaytta have SOV, while only Ge'ez has VSO. This might challenge machine translation system where Ge'ez is in the pair. Another challenge is the existence of flexibility in word order. For instance, even though Afan-Oromo follows SOV word order, nouns can be changed based on their role in a sentence which makes the word order to be flexible. Such flexibility will pose a challenge for translation from a source to Afan-Oromo.

3.3 Morphological Complexity

While word alignment could be done automatically or with supervision, morphological agreement between words in the source and target are crucial. For instance, Amharic and Geez have subject agreement, object agreement and genitive (possessive) agreement. Each of which is expressed as bound morphemes. In Amharic, for the word ገደልህ/you killed/ the subject "you" is represented by the suffix "+ህ" while the same subject is represented as "+" in the Geez ቀተልህ /you killed/). Most of the morphemes in the considered Ethiopian languages are bound ones.

4 Parallel Corpora Preparation

The development of machine translation more often uses statistical approach because it requires very limited computational linguistic resources compared to the rule based approach. Nevertheless, the statistical approach relies to a great extent on parallel corpora of the source and target languages.

The research team has applied different techniques to collect parallel corpora for the selected Ethiopian language pairs. The domain of the collected data is only religious for which we have data for all the considered language pairs. It includes Holy Bible and different documents written in spiritual theme and collected from Jehovah's Witnesses (JW[1]), Ethiopicbible[2], Ebible[3] and Geez experience[4] which are freely accessible websites.

A simple web crawler was used to extract parallel text from the websites. Python libraries such as requests, and BeautifulSoup were used to analyse the structure of the websites, extract texts

---

[1] available at `https://www.jw.org`
[2] available at `https://www.ethiopicbible.com`
[3] available at `http://ebible.org`
[4] available at `https://www.geezexperience.com`

and combine into a single text file. To collect the bible data, we have generated the structure of the URL so that it shows the book names, chapters and verses of the Bible in each language.

For the "daily text" which is published at JW.org, we tried to use the date information to generate URL for each language. Finally, we extracted the data based on the generated URL information and merged to a single UTF-8 text file for each language.

4.1 Pre-processing

Data preprocessing is an important and basic step in preparing bilingual and multilingual parallel corpora. Since the collected parallel data have different formats and characteristics, it is very difficult and time-consuming to prepare usable parallel corpora manually because it needs to analyse the structure of the collected raw data by applying different linguistic methods. We have, therefore, applied different automatic methods of text pre-processing that requires minimal human interference. As part of the pre-processing unnecessary links numbers, symbols and foreign texts in each language have been removed. During pre-processing the following tasks have been performed: character normalization, sentence tokenization and sentence level alignment.

4.1.1 Character Normalization

As it is indicated in Section 3.1, there are characters in Amharic that have similar roles and are redundant. For example the character (ሀ) can be written as (ሐ, ሓ, ኀ, ኃ and ሃ). Though they used to possess semantic differences in the traditional writings, currently these characters are mostly used interchangeably. To avoid words with same meaning from being taken as different words due to these variations we have replaced a set of characters with similar function into a single most frequently used character.

4.1.2 Sentence Tokenization and Alignment

Lines that contain multiple sentences in both source and target languages are tokenized. The team has set two criteria to check whether the aligned sentences are correct or not. The first criterion is counting and matching the number of sentences in the source language and the target language. In the parallel corpora of the language pairs in which Ge'ez is the target, the source language contains multiple verses in a single line. While on the Ge'ez side, each line contains a single verse. In such cases, we merged different verses of Ge'ez to produce the line that is aligned with that of the source language.

4.2 Corpus Size and Distribution of Words

The corpora have been analysed to see the relationship between languages in the language pairs. As it has been revealed in different literature, the Ethio-Semitic languages have more complex morphology than the other Ethiopian languages. Due to this difference, the same number of sentences in these language pairs is tokenized into significantly different number of tokens and word types. Table 1 clearly shows that the vocabulary of the languages in the Ethio-Semitic language family is much more than the vocabulary of the other two language families.

Sentences	Languages	Token	Type	Average sentence Length
34,349	Amharic	521,035	98,841	15
	Tigrigna	546,570	87,649	15
11,546	Amharic	148,084	38,097	12
	Ge'ez	158,003	33,386	13
11,457	Amharic	163,816	37,283	14
	Afan-Oromo	214,335	24,005	18
10,987	Tigrigna	162,508	32,953	14
	Afan-Oromo	206,844	23,536	18
9,400	Amharic	119,262	32,780	12
	Wolaytta	137,869	25,331	14
	Afan-Oromo	46,340	8,118	15

Sentences	Languages	Token	Type	Average sentence Length
2,923	Wolaytta	33,828	8,786	11
2,504	Tigrigna	34,780	9,864	13
	Wolaytta	29,458	7,989	11

Table 1: Sentence and Word Distribution of the Parallel Corpora

On the contrary the token of the non-Semitic languages is significantly higher than the tokens of the Ethio-Semitic languages. This is because syntactic words like preposition, conjunction, negation, etc are bound in the Ethio-Semitic language group. It is clear, therefore, that such differences between the languages in a language pair makes SMT difficult because it aggravates data sparsity and results into a weakly trained translation model. Although the size of the data we have is much less to draw conclusions, we could also see that the Ethio-Cushitic and Ethio-Omotic languages are morphologically more similar with each other than their similarity with the Ethio-Semitic languages.

We have also observed morphological differences among the Ethio-Semitic languages that is revealed by the difference in the number of token and word type in the same corpus we have for Amharic-Tigrigna and Amharic-Ge'ez language pairs. The data revealed that Amharic is the most morphologically complex language of the family.

5   SMT Experiments and Results

To check the usability of the collected parallel corpora for seven Ethiopian language pairs, we have conducted bi-directional SMT experiments.

5.1   Experimental Setup

To conduct SMT experiments, each parallel corpus has been divided into three sets: 80% for the training, 10% for tuning and 10% for test sets. Moses (Koehn, 2009) has been used along with Giza++ alignment tool (Och and Ney, 2003) for aligning words and phrases. SRILM toolkit (Stolcke, 2002) has been used to develop the language models using target language sentences from the training and tuning sets of parallel corpora. Bilingual Evaluation Under Study (BLEU) is used for automatic scoring.

5.2   Experimental Results

Table 2 presents the experimental results of bi-directional SMT systems developed for the seven Ethiopian language pairs. The Table shows the difference in the performance of the systems developed for the same language pair in different directions.

Sentences	Language pair	BLEU
34,349	Amharic - Tigrigna	21.22
	Tigrigna - Amharic	19.06
11,457	Amharic - Afan Oromo	17.79
	Afan Oromo - Amharic	13.11
10,987	Tigrigna - Afan Oromo	16.82
	Afan Oromo - Tigrigna	14.61
9,400	Amharic - Wolaytta	11.23
	Wolaytta - Amharic	7.17
11,546	Ge'ez - Amharic	7.31
	Amharic - Ge'ez	6.29
2,923	Wolaytta - Afan Oromo	4.73
	Afan Oromo - Wolaytta	2.73
2,504	Tigrigna - Wolaytta	2.2
	Wolaytta - Tigrigna	3.8

Table 2: Experimental Results

The performance of SMT systems decreases when Ethio-Semitic languages are on the target side. This confirms that Ethio-Semitic languages (when they are targets) are more challenging to SMT than the other language families. The only exception being Tigrigna and Wolaytta language pair, where the performance is high when Tigrigna is a target. This could be attributed to the small data we have for this language pair.

The results in the Table 2 also show the effect of data size on the performance of SMT systems. That means as the data increases, the performance also increases. In this view again we have an exceptionally lower BLUE score for the Amharic-Ge'ez language pair than the score we achieved for Amharic-Afan Oromo language pair although the data size used is almost equal. The performances of the Amharic-Wolaytta-Amharic translation systems are better than Amharic- Ge'ez-Amharic systems although the data size used in the former is less than the data size used in the latter. The results confirm that the morphological complexity of the languages severely affect SMT performance than the amount of data. From the difference in results achieved for the Amharic-Ge'ez (6.29) and Ge'ez-Amharic (7.31) language pairs, it is possible to understand that syntactic differences affect the performance of SMT more than the difference in their morphological features. We have seen from their number of word types that Amharic has more complex morphology than Ge'ez which, however, has flexible syntactic structure.

Despite the size of the data, the performance registered in translation towards the Ethio- Semitic languages has less BLEU score than the translations from them. This is because of the fact that, when the Ethio-Semitic languages, specially Amharic, are used as a target language, the translation from other languages with less morphological complexity as a source languages is challenged by one-to-many alignment. On the other hand, better performance is registered the other direction since the alignment is many-to-one. Beside this, the word-based language model favours the non-Semitic languages than Semitic ones due to the complexity of the morphology of the latter language family.

6 Conclusions and Future Work

This paper presents the attempt made in the preparation of usable parallel corpora for Ethiopian languages. The corpora have been collected from the web in the religious domain. Then, they are further pre-processed and normalized. We have now usable parallel corpora for seven Ethiopian language pairs. Using the corpora, bi-directional statistical machine translation experiments have been conducted. The results show that translation systems from Ethio-Semitic languages to either Omotic or Cushitic language families achieve better BLEU score than those in the other directions. That leads us to conclude that the Ethio-Semitic language family has the most complex morphology which greatly affects the performance of SMT.

Finding solutions that minimize the negative effect of morphological complexity of the Ethio-Semitic languages on the performance of SMT is therefore a future endeavour. We considered a previous work by (Mulu, 2017) who gained a significant improvement by the application of morphological segmentations to guide us in utilizing the use of morphemes instead of words as units for both the translation and the statistical language models. The most attractive solution to the problems of machine translation that is the trend of the time is the use of ANN modelling, which however, requires more data than what we have. So we will use our experience of corpus preparation and work towards the application of the state of the art technologies to develop usable machine translation systems for the Ethiopian languages.

As it is well known, domain is the most important factor on the performance of SMT. Thus, we are also working on the development and organization of parallel corpora for the Ethiopian languages in different domains.

Acknowledgement

We would like to acknowledge Addis Ababa University for the thematic research fund and NORHED (Linguistic Capacity Building-Tools) for sponsoring conference participation.

References

Gebremariam Akubazgi. 2017. *Amharic-Tigrigna machine translation using hybrid approach*. Master's thesis, Addis Ababa University.

Teferra Anbessa and Grover Hudson. 2007. *Essentials of Amharic*. Rüdiger Köppe, Verlag, Köln.

August Dillmann and Carl Bezold. 1907. *Ethiopic grammar, enlarged and improved by c. Bezold*. Translated by JA Crichton. London: Williams & Norgate.

Teshome Eleni. 2013. *Bidirectional English-Amharic machine translation: An experiment using con- strained corpus*. Master's thesis, Addis Ababa University.

Michael Gasser. 2010. A dependency grammar for Amharic. In *Proceedings of the Workshop on Language Resources and Human Language Technologies for Semitic Languages*, Valletta, Malta. `ftp://html.soic.indiana.edu/pub/gasser/sem_ws10.pdf`

Michael Gasser. 2011. Hornmorpho: a system for morphological processing of Amharic, Oromo, and Tigrinya. In *Conference on Human Language Technology for Development*, pages 94-99, Alexandria, Egypt.

Catherine Griefenow-Mewis. 2001. *A grammatical sketch of written Oromo*, volume 16. Rüdiger Köppe.

John Hutchins. 1995. Machine translation: A brief history. In *Concise history of the language sciences*, pages 431–445. Elsevier.

John Hutchins. 2005. The history of machine translation in a nutshell, `http://www.hutchinsweb.me.uk/Nutshell-2005.pdf`.

Daba Jabesa. 2013. *Bi-directional English-Afaan oromo machine translation using hybrid approach*. Master's thesis, Addis Ababa University.

Philipp Koehn. 2009. *Statistical machine translation*. Cambridge University Press.

Wolf Leslau. 2000. *Introductory grammar of Amharic*, volume 21. Otto Harrassowitz Verlag.

John S Mason. 1996. *Tigrinya grammar*. Red Sea Press (NJ).

Melese Michael and Meshesha Million. 2017. Experimenting Statistical Machine Translation for Ethiopic Semitic Languages : The case of Amharic-Tigrigna. In *LNICST. EAI International Conference on ICT for Development for Africa*, pages 140-149, Springer.

Gebreegziabher Teshome Mulu. 2017. *English-Amharic Statistical Machine Translation*. PhD Dissertation, IT Doctoral Program, Addis Ababa University, Addis Ababa, Ethiopia.

Franz Josef Och and Hermann Ney. 2003. A systematic comparison of various statistical alignment models. *Computational linguistics*, 29(1):19–51.

Gary F Simons and Charles D Fennig. 2017. *Ethnologue: Languages of the world*. SIL, Dallas, Texas.

Adugna Sisay. 2009. *English–Afan Oromo machine translation: An experiment using statistical Approach*. Master's thesis, Addis Ababa University.

Fissaha Sisay. 2004. *Adding Amharic to a Unification-based Machine Translation System: An Experiment*. Peter Lang.

Andreas Stolcke. 2002. SRILM-an extensible language modeling toolkit. In *Seventh international conference on spoken language processing*, `https://www.isca-speech.org/archive/icslp_2002/i02_0901.html`

Tsegaye Tariku. 2004. *English-Tigrigna factored statistical machine translation*. Master's thesis, Addis Ababa University.

Motomichi Wakasa. 2008. *A descriptive study of the modern Wolaytta language*. Unpublished PhD thesis, University of Tokyo.

Tesfay Tewolde Yohannes. 2002. *A modern Grammar of Tigrinya*. Tipografia U. Detti.

Using Embeddings to Compare
FrameNet Frames Across Languages

Jennifer Sikos
IMS, University of Stuttgart
Stuttgart, Germany
sikos@ims.uni-stuttgart.de

Sebastian Padó
IMS, University of Stuttgart
Stuttgart, Germany
pado@ims.uni-stuttgart.de

Abstract

Much of the recent interest in Frame Semantics is fueled by the substantial extent of its applicability across languages. At the same time, lexicographic studies have found that the applicability of individual frames can be diminished by cross-lingual divergences regarding polysemy, syntactic valency, and lexicalization. Due to the large effort involved in manual investigations, there are so far no broad-coverage resources with "problematic" frames for any language pair.

Our study investigates to what extent multilingual vector representations of frames learned from manually annotated corpora can address this need by serving as a wide coverage source for such divergences. We present a case study for the language pair English — German using the FrameNet and SALSA corpora and find that inferences can be made about cross-lingual frame applicability using a vector space model.

1 Introduction

Frame Semantics (Fillmore et al., 2003) is a theory of predicate-argument structure that describes meaning not at the level of individual words, but is instead based on the concept of a scenario or scene called a *frame*. Frames are defined by the group of words that evoke the scene (*frame-evoking elements* or *FEEs*), as well as their expected semantic arguments (*frame elements*). A JUDGMENT frame, for instance, would have FEEs *praise, criticize*, and *boo* and frame elements such as COGNIZER, EVALUEE, EXPRESSOR and REASON. The Berkeley FrameNet project (Baker et al., 1998) is the most well-known lexical resource based on Frame Semantics, and provides definitions for over 1200 frames.

A very attractive feature of Frame Semantics is that it can abstract away from individual words, which makes it a promising descriptive framework for events that generalize across languages (Boas, 2005; Lönneker-Rodman, 2007). However, there is a fundamental tension within Frame Semantics between the characterization of the scene, which is arguably relatively language-independent, and the characterization of the FEEs and frame elements which can vary among even closely related languages. For example, FrameNet distinguishes between the frames OPERATE_VEHICLE (*drive*) and USE_VEHICLE (*ride*) which are often indistinguishable in German, at least for the very frequent verb *fahren (drive/ride)* (Burchardt et al., 2009). Another example is the well-known difference between Germanic and Romance languages regarding the conceptualization of motion events, where manner can be incorporated into the semantics of the FEE - *run into a room*, or externalized - *enter a room running* (Subirats, 2009). In general, some frames are evidently more parallel than others cross-lingually (Tonelli and Pianta, 2008; Torrent et al., 2018; Vossen et al., 2018).

The question of whether a particular frame transfers across languages is often determined by linguists on the basis of large corpora, comparing either frames assigned to direct translations (Padó, 2007) or extracting "typical" uses of frames in the languages under consideration. Identifying the degree of applicability can, however, be a long process that must be repeated for each new frame and language.

In this paper, we investigate to what extent this problem can be alleviated by the use of computational methods. More concretely, we build distributional representations, also known as embeddings, of frames

Proceedings of the First Workshop on Linguistic Resources for Natural Language Processing, pages 91–101
Santa Fe, New Mexico, USA, August 20, 2018.

(Turney and Pantel, 2010; Baroni and Lenci, 2010; Hermann et al., 2014) which build a compact representation of a frame's meaning from the entire corpus. These embeddings are constructed for each language separately on the basis of expert-labeled corpora but are represented in a joint space, which enables us to automatically measure the cross-lingual similarity of language-specific frames (e.g., AWARENESS in English and AWARENESS in German). Our hypothesis is that frames which generalize well across languages will show a high similarity, while frames which do not generalize well will yield a low similarity. In this sense, we can see the set of frames that show the lowest self-similarity across languages as a repository of cases of potential generalization failure. Concretely, we carry out a case study for the language pair English–German, which is relatively well-studied in terms of Frame Semantics.

This paper is organized as follows. First, we describe distributional semantic models (*DSMs*) and their utility in capturing cross-lingual lexical semantics. We give an overview of the annotated corpora that we use for our experiments for English – German frames, followed by an overview of the model structure and input for training our DSMs. Finally, we present results of our frame embeddings in both English and German data and interpret output of our computational model through findings from the theoretical literature. To our knowledge, our work is the first to explore interoperability of frames across languages with embeddings. We present results that demonstrate how DSMs can capture latent semantic relationships between frames and speculate about the conclusions that can be drawn when using DSMs for frame semantic analysis.

2 Background

2.1 Word Embeddings

Vector representations of word meanings, generally known as distributional semantic models (DSMs) or embeddings, have become a popular tool for research in lexical semantics within the Natural Language Processing community. The distributional hypothesis (Harris, 1954) forms the basis for DSM models, which claims that similar words should be expected to appear in similar contexts. Building on this assumption, current DSMs represent words as vectors in a low-dimensional space in which similarity is supposed to indicate semantic relatedness. DSMs can either be computed using count-based methods, which directly count word context co-occurrences and optionally apply dimensionality reduction, or prediction-based methods, where the representations are the parameter vectors of an underlying optimization task (Baroni et al., 2014).

A widely-used prediction-based model is the word2vec model (Mikolov et al., 2013c). Word2vec produces word vectors by predicting the target for a window of context, a setup known as the continuous bag-of-words (CBOW) model. In the CBOW architecture, an input for the target verb "cook" with a context window of 2 might appear as ['the','chef','a','meal'], and embeddings would accordingly be generated for each token in the vocabulary. The model is trained over a neural network with negative sampling, where noisy words are selected from a noise distribution and the model learns to approximate word meaning by discriminating the difference between the true and noisy word.

While the use of embeddings to model meaning at the word level is the most widespread application, they can in fact be applied to linguistic units of almost any granularity, from morphemes to word senses to sentences and even paragraphs and documents. In this study, we apply them to modeling the meaning of frames, i.e., semantically motivated predicate classes, following Hermann et al. (2014).

2.2 Cross-lingual Embeddings

The goal of a cross-lingual DSM is to make meaning representations from different languages comparable, either by learning mutilingual embeddings in the same space or by mapping monolingual embeddings into a joint space (Ruder et al., 2017; Upadhyay et al., 2016). Mikolov et al. (2013b) introduced a particularly simple version that takes advantage of a vocabulary of shared bilingual seed words to map embeddings from a source language onto the vector space of a target language. They learn a transformation matrix $\mathbf{W}$ by minimizing the mean squared error (MSE) between the source seed words and their translations from the bilingual dictionary:

$$\mathrm{MSE} = \sum_{i=1}^{n} \parallel \mathbf{W} x_i^s - x_i^t \parallel^2$$

where x^s represents the seed words from the source language, and x^t are seed words from the target. The transformation matrix can then be applied to an embedding from the source space to project it onto the target language space. This can be achieved by solving $z = \mathbf{W}x$, where x is the source embedding and z is the same vector transformed into the target language space. This results in a shared space where semantic units that evoke similar concepts in one language are close to their translations in another.

Conceptually, the bilingual seed words is a set of words that are assumed, a priori, to have the same meaning in both languages. A good choice for this set appear to be named entities, which are less prone to semantic problems like polysemy and vagueness, and which are furthermore easy to collect for most language pairs. We will adopt this choice in the present study.

3 Annotated Corpora

The popularity of the Berkeley FrameNet project has inspired the Multilingual FrameNet project, where frame-semantic resources have emerged in multiple languages across the world (Torrent et al., 2018). In our work, we focus on two languages that are relatively well-represented in the Frame Semantics literature, English and German, using the FrameNet and SALSA corpora, respectively.

3.1 FrameNet Corpus

The FrameNet corpus (release 1.5) provides over 173k annotated datasets with manually-curated sentences, drawn from the 100 million word British National Corpus (BNC)[1], which is balanced across multiple genres, including novels and news reports. FrameNet's FEEs can range from verbal, nominal, adjectival, and even adverbial and prepositional in some cases. In FrameNet's v1.5 complete annotation set, there are over 11k FEEs, where each FEE attestation is labeled. This produced sentences in which multiple FEEs are present, and lexical units are annotated on average 20.7 times in the current annotated corpus.

3.2 SALSA Corpus

SALSA (Erk et al., 2003; Burchardt et al., 2009) is a German corpus with frame semantic annotations. It was constructed over the syntactic annotations in the German TIGER (version 2.1), and is composed of 1.5 million words from German newswire text. SALSA (release 2.0) provides 24,184 sentences with frame annotations, and the corpus has labels for 998 unique FEEs. Each unique FEE is annotated on average 36.9 times.

3.3 Parallelism

For the purposes of our study, it is important that the corpora are as comparable as possible. Comparability must be considered on two levels: corpus composition and annotation. With regard to corpus composition, we note that SALSA is based on a corpus consisting exclusively of newswire, while FrameNet is based on the much broader BNC. Nevertheless, we maintain that the match is good, albeit not perfect. As for the semantic annotation schema, SALSA adopted the annotation scheme of the Berkeley FrameNet project fairly directly (Ellsworth et al., 2004). The main difference is that SALSA proceeded predicate-by-predicate instead of frame-by-frame, which required the introduction of "pseudo-frames" for senses that were not covered by FrameNet at the time of annotation (Burchardt et al., 2009). We exclude these from our analysis. Finally, another small difference regards the annotation of multi-word expressions, which we address further in Section 4.

4 Methods

To build frame embeddings for English and German, we pre-process the two corpora introduced in the previous section. Below, we describe the steps we took to format the input for the model, and then we elaborate on how specifically we build the frame embeddings.

---

[1] `http://www.natcorp.ox.ac.uk/`

4.1 Preprocessing the FrameNet corpus

We use the FrameNet 1.5 corpus, which provides tokenized and lemmatized sentences (Bauer et al., 2012). We perform three pre-processing steps. First, multi-word frame-evoking elements (FEEs) are concatenated into a single token. This is motivated by the presence of multi-word FEEs that evoke different frames from the single-word FEEs that they contain. One such case is the lexical unit *ride*, which evokes the RIDE_VEHICLE frame, and the multi-word FEE *ride out*, which evokes SURVIVING. We keep instances of MWE FEEs such as *ride out* as single units in the vector space.

The second step is a detection of named entities using the pretrained English model from spaCy's named entity recognition (NER) package[2]. We later use these entities as seed words for the cross-lingual mapping of embeddings (cf. Section 2). Again, for simplicity, we concatenate entities that span multiple tokens into a single span, e.g., "San Francisco" would be converted to "San_Francisco".

The third step optionally replaces each occurrence of a FEE by the name of the frame it evokes to produce the "Frame Corpus". By applying the word2vec embedding algorithm to the Frame Corpus, we can generate a monolingual embedding for each frame. Without this replacement, we retain the so-called "FEE Corpus", from which we can generate standard word-level representations for the FEEs. An example of the FEE Corpus and Frame Corpus model inputs are shown below in Table 1.

Original	"The Washington Post reported on the country's biological weapons labs"
FEE Corpus	[The_Washington_Post, *report*, on, the, country, 's, *biological_weapon*, lab]
Frame Corpus	[The_Washington_Post, STATEMENT, on, the, country, 's, WEAPON, lab]

Table 1: Example of original FrameNet sentence and the FEE Corpus and Frame Corpus versions

4.2 Preprocessing the SALSA corpus

Similar to FrameNet, the SALSA corpus provides pre-tokenized and lemmatized sentences (Erk et al., 2003). Multi-word predicates are prevalent in the SALSA data but cannot be concatenated as easily as they are in English; SALSA decided to annotate some constructions as FEEs that are arguably more syntactically than semantically motivated. Table 3 shows the three most frequent MWE patterns. The first class, separated prefix verbs, are merged into a single word. The second class, combinations of verbal FEEs with modals, and the third class, combinations of verbal FEEs with the particle *zu (to)*, we decided not to concatenate. Like English, we recognize named entities using spaCy (using the pretrained German model in this case), and convert any named entities that span over multiple words into a single token ("Volksrepublik China" becomes "Volksrepublik_China"). Also identical to the English FrameNet input, we build two corpora using the German data, a FEE Corpus and a Frame Corpus, to generate embeddings for frames and FEEs, respectively. An example in shown in Table 2.

Original	"Konzernchefs lehnen den Milliardär als US-Präsident ab"
	(CEOs reject the billionaire as US President)
FEE Corpus	[Konzernchef, *ablehnen*, der, Milliardär, als, US-Präsident]
Frame Corpus	[Konzernchef, JUDGMENT_COMMUNICATION, der, Milliardär, als, US-Präsident]

Table 2: Example of original SALSA sentence and the FEE Corpus and Frame Corpus versions

4.3 Frame Embeddings

For both English and German, we first learn 300-dimensional monolingual FEE-level and frame-level embeddings from the respective corpora, using the word2vec CBOW method (see (Mikolov et al., 2013a) for more in-depth details). Then, we employ Mikolov (2013a)'s method based on a shared bilingual vocabulary to learn a linear projection from the source to the target vector space. As a bilingual vocabulary, we use the intersection of the recognized named entities of the standard classes (organizations; persons

---

[2]https://spacy.io/

VVFIN+PTKVZ	$\rightarrow$	PTKVZ_VV
Example: gehört an	$\rightarrow$	angehören
VM* VV*	$\rightarrow$	no change
Example: müssen rechnen		
PTKVZU	$\rightarrow$	no change
Example: zu sagen		

Table 3: Rules for combining multi-word predicates in German SALSA corpus

Bill Clinton	Mussolini
Netanyahu	Vegas
Pentagon	CIA
Intel	IBM
San Francisco	McDonald's
Apple	Bill Gates
Mao Zedong	Reuters
Washington Times	New York Times

Table 4: Examples of named entities occurring in both FrameNet and SALSA

and person groups; locations and geopolitical entities) from FrameNet and SALSA. In other words, we first match on named entities whose surface form is identical between English and German – so *New York / New York*. To increase the size of the seed entities, we use a bilingual dictionary for English–German (Conneau et al., 2017) to further match any named entities where the surface form varies but reflects the same individual or location, for example *President Clinton / Präsident Clinton*. Overall, 40,262 entities were detected in the English FrameNet sentences, while 15,398 entities were detected in the German SALSA. The intersection of entities that appeared in both corpora was 2,899. The list in Table 4 gives a sample of the entity names that appear in both FrameNet and SALSA.

The models are trained on the pre-processed corpora. This results in a total of 230 frame embeddings for both EN and DE, 11,830 English FEE embeddings, and 998 German FEE embeddings.[3]

5   Experiment 1: Hyperparameter optimization and sanity check

Producing embeddings with word2vec's CBOW algorithm involves choices regarding several hyperparameters, notably the number of negative samples (*neg*), the learning rate (*alpha*), the size of the context window (*win*), and the number of iterations (*iter*) – cf. Section 2. We use the same hyperparameter values for the Frame Corpus-based and FEE Corpus-based embeddings.

It is common practice to choose the values for these hyperparameters based either on performance on a development set or on some auxiliary task, such as word similarity prediction. In order to validate the FrameNet/SALSA frames that we use in our subsequent analysis, we decided to define an auxiliary task; namely, a check for the quality of the monolingual frame embeddings. An added benefit of this auxiliary task is that it can also be understood as a form of sanity checking for the monolingual embeddings before using them for cross-lingual comparison.

More concretely, we ask how well the embedding we obtain for each frame corresponds to the centroid of all FEE embeddings of that frame. For example, we would expect that the COMMERCE_BUY frame embedding should be highly similar to the centroid of the embeddings of the FEEs *buy, purchase*, but dissimilar to centroid of embeddings for predicates such as *tell* or *beat*. Formally, let $c_{FEE}(\phi)$ denote the *FEE centroid* for a frame ϕ, defined as

$$c_{FEE}(\phi) = \frac{1}{||\{\text{fee} \mid \text{fee} \in \phi\}||} \sum_{\text{fee} \in \phi} \overrightarrow{\text{fee}}.$$

We can now assemble, for each frame f, the list of FEE centroids c_{FEE} of all frames ranked by their cosine similarity to the frame embedding $\overrightarrow{f}$. This list enables us to define the accuracy of the model using standard evaluation measures for ranked retrieval. We report the percentage of frames whose most similar FEE centroid is their own (R@1), the percentage whose FEE centroid is among the five most similar ones (R@5), and the percentage whose FEE centroid is among the ten most similar ones (R@10).

5.1   Results

Tables 5 and 6 give a sampling of the some of the hyperparameters that were used to evaluate the frame embeddings. The numbers indicate that the choice of hyperparameters is in fact important. Furthermore, the behavior of the embeddings with respect to the hyperparameters is relatively parallel between English and German: too few iterations and too few negative samples result in noisy embeddings. Setting *neg* to

---

[3]The embeddings are available at `http://www.ims.uni-stuttgart.de/data/XLFrameEmbed.html`.

neg	alpha	win	iter	R@1	R@5	R@10
5	.025	2	10	0.481	0.701	0.766
10	.025	5	20	0.832	0.951	0.970
10	.05	2	20	0.733	0.923	0.957
20	.025	2	30	**0.931**	0.987	0.993
20	.025	2	35	0.929	0.990	0.994
30	.025	2	30	0.912	0.988	0.993

Table 5: FrameNet (EN): Evaluation of Frame Embedding Quality

neg	alpha	win	iter	R@1	R@5	R@10
5	.025	2	10	0.408	0.591	0.653
10	.025	2	20	0.843	0.925	0.938
10	.05	2	20	0.938	0.986	0.993
20	.025	5	20	0.904	0.972	0.979
20	.025	2	35	**0.965**	0.979	0.986
30	.025	2	30	0.931	0.993	0.993

Table 6: SALSA (DE): Evaluation of Frame Embedding Quality

Frame	Top 10 Most Similar Frame Embeddings	
	FrameNet (EN)	SALSA (DE)
COMMERCE_BUY	COMMERCE_SELL, GETTING, SUPPLY, IMPORTING, DEGREE_OF_PROCESSING, TRANSFER, IMPORT_EXPORT, RECEIVING, AMASSING, CAUSE_MOTION	GETTING, IMPORT_EXPORT, RECEIVING, CAUSE_MOTION, REMOVING, MANUFACTURING, ACTIVITY_START, USING, COMMITMENT, BRINGING
DECIDING	COMMUNICATION_RESPONSE, ASSESSING, SOLE_INSTANCE, ACTIVITY_ONGOING, ATTEMPT, TELLING, GIVING, ARRIVING, DESIRING	COMMUNICATION_RESPONSE, ASSESSING, ACTIVITY_ONGOING, ATTEMPT, TELLING, GIVING, ARRIVING, DESIRING, RESPONSE, PERCEPTION_ACTIVE

Table 7: Top 10 nearest neighbors for FrameNet/SALSA frame embeddings

20 and running for 30 to 35 iterations, however, yields arguably good embeddings with R@1 values of over 90%, that is, the vast majority of frame embeddings are located closest to their own FEE centroid. For R@10, the numbers approach (for German) or even exceed (for English) 99%. Note that these tables include all frames that appear in the corpora. When we prune our scoring to only frames that occur >5 times in the corpus, we obtain R@1 scores of over 97% for both languages. For the remainder of the paper, we adopt the hyperparameters that yield the highest accuracy.

We complement these results with a more qualitative analysis, were we find the top ten nearest neighbor frame embeddings for two frames in the same, monolingual space. This determines to what extent the frame embeddings form sensible semantic neighborhoods: We would expect a frame like COMMERCE_BUY to have COMMERCE_SELL as one of its nearest neighboring frames, while a frame like GIVING_BIRTH would not. The results are shown in Table 7 and demonstrate that essentially all nearest neighbors are semantically related to the target frame, expressing a wide range of concepts. For example, for COMMERCE_BUY, we find the inverse perspectivization COMMERCE_SELL, entailments (GETTING, RECEIVING, CAUSE_MOTION), preconditions (COMMITMENT), scenarios and narrative chains (IMPORTING, IMPORT_EXPORT, MANUFACTURING), and aspectual class (ACTIVITY_START). At the same time, the lists are sufficiently dissimilar to motivate our second experiment which assesses to which extent these differences reflect cross-lingual differences in frame usage and applicability.

6 Experiment 2: Analysis of Cross-Lingual Frame Correspondences

As described in Section 4, we project the FrameNet and SALSA frame embeddings into the same space. This means we can compare them via a simple distance metric such as cosine similarity, and we can visualize them via dimensionality reduction to two dimensions. We start our analysis by confirming that the joint space respects the monolingual similarities and introduces reasonable cross-lingual ones. For clarity, we will affix -EN to English (FrameNet) frames and -DE to German (SALSA) frames.

Figure 1 shows the nearest frame neighbors for VERDICT in English and a joint FrameNet-SALSA space. The joint space, while introducing related frames in the German space, still preserves the relationships on the source side; namely, ARREST, NOTIFICATION_OF_CHARGES, and TRIAL. Additional related frames emerge from the German data, including CRIMINAL_INVESTIGATION and PROCESS_START.

We now proceed to analyze our embeddings through the perspective of prior cross-lingual studies

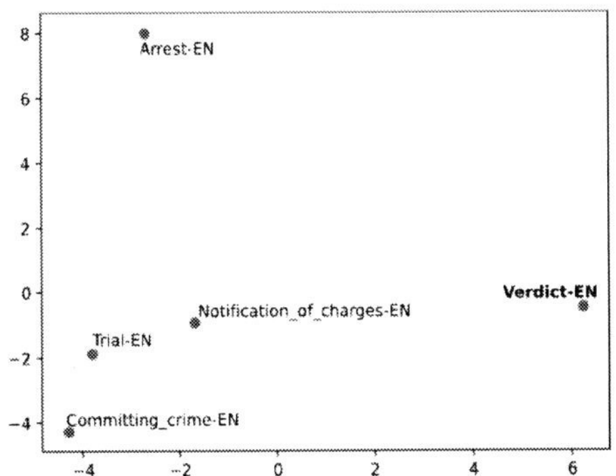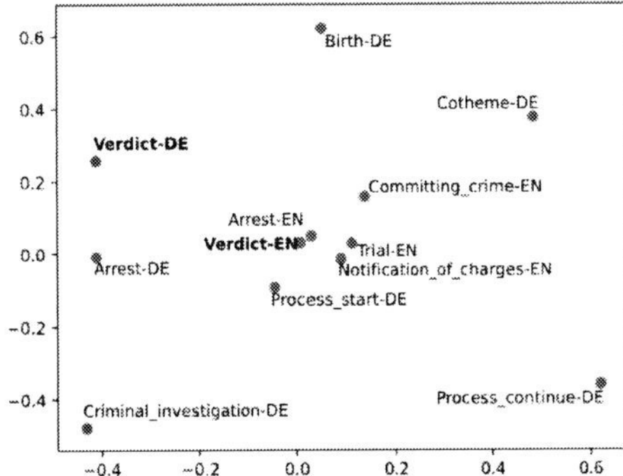

Figure 1: English space around VERDICT-EN (left), and joint space (right). Many semantic relationships are preserved in the cross-lingual mapping.

from the linguistics literature. We focus in particular on the frames and frame properties that diverge in English and German, and compare these findings with results from our corpus-based frame embeddings. Conversely, we explore frames that have a high potential for universality and compare their similarities in the cross-lingual vector space.

6.1 Specificity vs. Cross-lingual Frame Applicability

FrameNet frames form a hierarchy with more abstract, schematic, often scenario-like frames at the top and more specific and more constrained frames at the bottom (Fillmore et al., 2003). Arguably, the more specific a frame is, the higher is the risk that its constraints do not carry over well to other languages, while frames that are higher on the FrameNet hierarchy should be more universally applicable (Padó, 2007).

As two examples for such general frames, consider COMMUNICATION and MOTION, which apply to general speaking and moving events (with FEEs such as *speak, communicate, say* and *move, come, go*, respectively). Both frames are extended by more specific child frames, such as COMMUNICA-TION_RESPONSE, COMMUNICATION_MANNER, MOTION_DIRECTIONAL and SELF_MOTION. We now test whether the specificity of the frames correlates with the cross-lingual similarities of the frame embeddings. We expect MOTION-DE and MOTION-EN to be highly similar while MOTION_DIRECTIONAL-DE and -EN are less similar when mapped into a joint, multilingual vector space.

The results are visualized in Figure 2: in general, both coarsely defined frames have a higher similarity than their respective child frames, although this tendency is much more pronounced for COMMUNICATION than MOTION. The one exception to this trend is the SELF_MOTION frame, which can also be argued is a general frame for self-propelled movement; in fact, the SELF_MOTION is annotated more in the SALSA corpus (count=76) with a greater variety of FEEs (31 unique FEEs for SELF_MOTION in SALSA) than MOTION (count=32), which has significantly fewer unique FEE annotations (10 unique FEEs).

6.2 Most and Least Similar Frames

Next, we computed the frames that were most and least similar across FrameNet and SALSA. Our expectation was that the list of most similar frames would be dominated by very general frames (as per the previous analysis) and that the list of least similar frames would contain mostly cases known as problematic from the lexicographic literature.

These expectations were only confirmed to an limited extent. Amongst the very similar frames, frames tend to be belong to abstract domains such as Cognition (GRASP, JUDGMENT, MEMORY) or describing abstract properties of events (ACTIVITY_RESUME, LIKELIHOOD). Two concrete frames are also prominent: VERDICT and ARREST. This was a surprising result, given the differences in the judicial systems of the USA and Germany.

Even for very similar frames, it is striking now little correlation there is between the FrameNet and SALSA frequencies for certain frames, and the imbalance is more pronounced for the least similar frames.

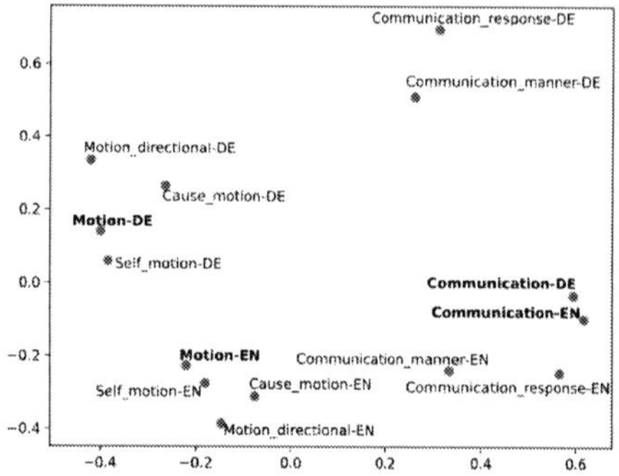

Figure 2: Cross-lingual similarity scores for COMMUNICATION and MOTION.

Frame	Similarity DE-EN
COMMUNICATION	0.54
COMMUNICATION_RESPONSE	0.17
COMMUNICATION_MANNER	0.14
MOTION	0.39
CAUSE_MOTION	0.15
MOTION_DIRECTIONAL	0.27
SELF_MOTION	0.46

Figure 3: Cross-lingual similarity between the less-specific COMMUNICATION and MOTION frames and more specific child frames.

Most Similar Frames	Similarity	Freq EN/DE	Least Similar Frames	Similarity	Freq EN/DE
GRASP	0.66	287/21	ORIGIN	-0.14	194/8
COMMUNICATION	0.54	84/25	PEOPLE_BY_VOCATION	-0.11	586/12
VERDICT	0.51	215/77	UNDERGOING	-0.07	38/136
ARREST	0.51	189/103	INGEST_SUBSTANCE	-0.02	187/7
BUILDING	0.49	393/52	EMPLOYING	0.00	151/428
ACTIVITY_RESUME	0.49	37/8	TEXT	0.03	1080/4
JUDGMENT	0.48	1212/33	SENSATION	0.03	471/1
MEMORY	0.48	209/41	TAKING_SIDES	0.04	189/18
COTHEME	0.48	665/7	COMMITTING_CRIME	0.07	48/55
LIKELIHOOD	0.48	577/6	SENTENCING	0.07	77/39

Table 8: Most and least similar English–German frame pairs in joint space.

In fact, we believe that for a number of frames in this list (e.g., SENSATION), the reason for low similarity is that SALSA provides so few annotations that no reliable embeddings can be learned, irrespective of any linguistic or lexicographic considerations. For the remaining frames, the low similarity appears to result from large differences in the FEEs that were chosen for annotation. For example, FrameNet's ORIGIN contains many nationalities and ethnicities (*American, Assyrian, Byzantine*) while SALSA annotated family terms like *Kind, Sohn, Enkel (child, son, grandson)*. Similarly, PEOPLE_BY_VOCATION, which in FrameNet covers a wide range of professions, only contains one FEE in German, *Kumpel (miner)*. These appear to be artifacts of SALSA's strategy of annotating lemma by lemma, as a result of which some frames end up being annotated only for a single, or very few, FEEs (Ellsworth et al., 2004). So, the least similar frames provide information about annotation choices rather than conceptual applicability.

Note that the definition of abstract/general frames can be made more concrete by considering FrameNet's frame-to-frame relations "X is Inherited by/is Used by/has Subframe Y". All relations share the common property that X is a more abstract frame than Y. Thus, if there is a high number of relations in which a frame occurs in position X, then it should be a more abstract frame, and behave more similar across languages. This turns out to be true in our sample: the ten most similar frames listed in Table 8 filled a high average number of relations in position X (4.89) while the ten least similar frames had a comparably low average (1.7).

6.3 Monolingual Annotation Choices

Nevertheless, the previous analysis raises the question of how monolingual annotation choices influence cross-lingual comparability. As an example, let us consider the English verb *announce*, which is relatively flexible regarding its subcategorization behavior; Boas (2009) analyzed instances of the verb and found

FEE	Annotated German frames	Count	Most similar English frames
ankündigen	HERALDING-DE	85	**STATEMENT-EN**, REPARATION-EN,
	OMEN-DE	1	OMEN-EN, REST-EN
	EVIDENCE-DE	1	

Table 9: SALSA FEEs and frames for translations of the English STATEMENT FEE *announce* (left), and most similar English frame embeddings (right)

that the STATEMENT-EN frame, which can express the SPEAKER, MEDIUM, and MESSAGE roles, is able to cover all of the following uses (Boas, 2009):

(1)   a.   [The CEO SPEAKER] *announced* [that the company would be acquired MESSAGE].

       b.   [The press report MEDIUM] *announced* [that the company would be acquired MESSAGE].

       c.   [The CEO SPEAKER] *announced* [that the company would be acquired MESSAGE] [by email MEDIUM].

The closest German translation of *announce* is *ankündigen*, which can likewise express each of the alternations above. Consequently, we would expect the instances of *ankündigen* in SALSA to be annotated with STATEMENT-DE.

However, as the left-hand cell of Table 9 shows, SALSA decided to annotate the overwhelming majority of the *ankündigen* instances with the frame HERALDING. HERALDING is a specific frame involving a COMMUNICATOR informing the public about a future course of action (EVENT), and in English HERALDING can only be evoked by the verb *herald*. Presumably, the reason for the German annotation is that the very typical use of *ankündigen* with a direct object NP expresses not just a statement event but a commitment by the speaker to carry out the action described by the NP:

(2)   [Regierung in Rom COMMUNICATOR] *kündigt* [Preisstopp und Sparprogramm EVENT] *an.*   (s1494)
       (Government in Rome announces price stop and austerity program)

Unfortunately, in FrameNet, there is no direct connection of any type between STATEMENT and HERALD-ING. What our cross-lingual embeddings can provide in this case in an insight into the relationship between these two frames. We do this by retrieving the most similar English frame embeddings for the SALSA *ankündigen* embedding. The result that we find is the most similar frame to *ankündigen* is STATEMENT-EN. This indicates that the usage of *ankündigen* in the SALSA corpus is, even if not labeled as such, semantically still very similar to STATEMENT-EN. Arguably, this pattern - a predicate and its direct translations that belong to two different frames, provides evidence that the involved frames share some kind of conceptual relationship (Sikos and Padó, 2018). In other words, the cross-lingual model has identified a potential gap in the FrameNet frame relations.

7   Conclusion

In this paper, we have looked at the question of the cross-lingual applicability of FrameNet semantic frames. Our starting hypothesis was that multilingual vector spaces can serve as a rich source of information on this topic. A frame vector space can represent frame-evoking elements and frames as vectors, which are readily comparable by geometric distances, thus providing similarity judgments between them.

In our experiments, we have constructed a joint, bilingual space by applying word embedding methods to the annotations of the English FrameNet corpus and the German SALSA corpus. The outcome of three specific analyses that we have carried out – specificity, frame similarity, and translational variation – provides overall positive evidence for this hypothesis: In many cases, our findings correspond well to previous linguistic findings reported, for example, in Boas (2009). Based on our results, we believe that vector space models can be used to help the linguistic/lexicographic work on cross-lingual frame semantics by guiding lexicographers towards potential frame mismatches and cross-lingual applicability.

That said, the picture that emerged is somewhat more nuanced than we anticipated. As usual in corpus-based research, one must be aware that the similarity structure of the embeddings is not always directly interpretable in terms of frame generalizability. Among the factors that impact embeddings are "usual suspects" like frequency (low-frequency embeddings are potentially noisy, cf. Table 9) and polysemy (the sense distribution of FEEs influences vectors), but also the annotation decisions of individual annotation projects (cf. SALSA's incomplete coverage of frames in terms of FEEs, and the decision to annotate *ankündigen* with HERALDING-DE). A deeper investigation of these factors is a topic for future work.

Another clear avenue for future investigation is to apply our analysis to compare semantic annotations in multiple languages, which is fast becoming a possibility as new, multilingual FrameNets emerge.

References

Collin F Baker, Charles J Fillmore, and John B Lowe. 1998. The Berkeley FrameNet project. In *Proceedings of ACL/COLING*, pages 86–90, Montreal, QC.

Marco Baroni and Alessandro Lenci. 2010. Distributional memory: A general framework for corpus-based semantics. *Computational Linguistics*, 36(4):673–721.

Marco Baroni, Georgiana Dinu, and Germán Kruszewski. 2014. Don't count, predict! a systematic comparison of context-counting vs. context-predicting semantic vectors. In *Proceedings of ACL*, pages 238–247, Baltimore, MD.

Daniel Bauer, Hagen Fürstenau, and Owen Rambow. 2012. The dependency-parsed FrameNet corpus. In *Proceedings of LREC*, pages 3861–3867.

Hans C Boas. 2005. Semantic frames as interlingual representations for multilingual lexical databases. *International Journal of Lexicography*, 18(4):445–478.

Hans C Boas. 2009. *Multilingual FrameNets in computational lexicography – Methods and applications*. De Gruyter.

Aljoscha Burchardt, Katrin Erk, Anette Frank, Andrea Kowalski, Sebastian Padó, and Manfred Pinkal. 2009. Using FrameNet for the semantic analysis of German: Annotation, representation, and automation. In Hans C. Boas, editor, *Multilingual FrameNets in Computational Lexicography – Methods and Applications*, pages 209–244. De Gruyter.

Alexis Conneau, Guillaume Lample, Marc'Aurelio Ranzato, Ludovic Denoyer, and Hervé Jégou. 2017. Word translation without parallel data. *arXiv:1710.04087*.

Michael Ellsworth, Katrin Erk, Paul Kingsbury, and Sebastian Padó. 2004. PropBank, SALSA and FrameNet: How design determines product. In *Proceedings of the LREC workshop on Building Lexical Resources From Semantically Annotated Corpora*, pages 17–23, Lisbon, Portugal.

Katrin Erk, Andrea Kowalski, Sebastian Padó, and Manfred Pinkal. 2003. Towards a resource for lexical semantics: A large German corpus with extensive semantic annotation. In *Proceedings of ACL*, pages 537–544, Sapporo, Japan.

Charles J Fillmore, Christopher R Johnson, and Miriam R L Petruck. 2003. Background to FrameNet. *International Journal of Lexicography*, 16(3):235–250.

Zellig S Harris. 1954. Distributional structure. *Word*, 10(2-3):146–162.

Karl Moritz Hermann, Dipanjan Das, Jason Weston, and Kuzman Ganchev. 2014. Semantic frame identification with distributed word representations. In *Proceedings of ACL*, pages 1448–1458, Baltimore, MD.

Birte Lönneker-Rodman. 2007. Multilinguality and FrameNet. Technical report, International Computer Science Institute.

Tomas Mikolov, Kai Chen, Greg Corrado, and Jeffrey Dean. 2013a. Efficient estimation of word representations in vector space. *arXiv:1301.3781*.

Tomas Mikolov, Quoc V Le, and Ilya Sutskever. 2013b. Exploiting similarities among languages for machine translation. *arXiv:1309.4168*.

Tomas Mikolov, Ilya Sutskever, Kai Chen, Greg S Corrado, and Jeff Dean. 2013c. Distributed representations of words and phrases and their compositionality. In *Advances in neural information processing systems*, pages 3111–3119.

Sebastian Padó. 2007. Translational equivalence and cross-lingual parallelism: The case of FrameNet frames. In *Proceedings of the NODALIDA workshop on building Frame semantics resources for Scandinavian and Baltic languages*, pages 39–46, Tartu, Estonia.

Sebastian Ruder, Ivan Vulić, and Anders Søgaard. 2017. A survey of cross-lingual word embedding models. *arXiv:1706.04902*.

Jennifer Sikos and Sebastian Padó. 2018. Framenet's 'using' relation as source of concept-driven paraphrases. *Constructions and Frames*, 10(1). In press.

Carlos Subirats. 2009. Spanish FrameNet: A frame semantic analysis of the Spanish lexicon. In Hans C. Boas, editor, *Multilingual FrameNets in Computational Lexicography – Methods and Applications*, pages 135–162. De Gruyter.

Sara Tonelli and Emanuele Pianta. 2008. Frame information transfer from English to Italian. In *Proceedings of LREC*, pages 2252–2256, Marrakech, Morocco.

Tiago Timponi Torrent, Lars Borin, and Collin Baker, editors. 2018. *Proceedings of the LREC 2018 International FrameNet Workshop on Multilingual Framenets and Constructicons*, Miyazaki, Japan.

Peter D Turney and Patrick Pantel. 2010. From Frequency to Meaning: Vector Space Models of Semantics. *Journal of Artificial Intelligence Research*, 37(1):141–188.

Shyam Upadhyay, Manaal Faruqui, Chris Dyer, and Dan Roth. 2016. Cross-lingual models of word embeddings: An empirical comparison. In *Proceedings of ACL*, pages 1661–1670, Berlin, Germany.

Piek Vossen, Antske Fokkens, Isa Maks, and Chantal van Son. 2018. Towards an open Dutch FrameNet lexicon and corpus. In *Proceedings of the LREC 2018 Workshop International FrameNet Workshop 2018 : Multilingual Framenets and Constructicons*, pages 75–80, Miyazaki, Japan.

Construction of a Multilingual Corpus Annotated with Translation Relations

Yuming Zhai
LIMSI-CNRS
Univ. Paris-Sud
Univ. Paris-Saclay, France
zhai@limsi.fr

Aurélien Max
LIMSI-CNRS
Univ. Paris-Sud
Univ. Paris-Saclay, France
amax@limsi.fr

Anne Vilnat
LIMSI-CNRS
Univ. Paris-Sud
Univ. Paris-Saclay, France
anne@limsi.fr

Abstract

Translation relations, which distinguish literal translation from other translation techniques, constitute an important subject of study for human translators (Chuquet and Paillard, 1989). However, automatic processing techniques based on interlingual relations, such as machine translation or paraphrase generation exploiting translational equivalence, have not made use of these relations explicitly until now. In this work, we present a categorization of translation relations and then we annotate a parallel multilingual (English, French, Chinese) corpus of oral presentations, the *TED Talks*, with these relations. Our long-term objective will be to automatically detect these relations in order to integrate them as important characteristics for the search of monolingual segments in relation of equivalence (paraphrases) or of entailment. The annotated corpus resulting from our work will be made available to the community.

1 Introduction

Human translators have studied translation relations since a long time (Vinay and Darbelnet, 1958; Chuquet and Paillard, 1989), which categorize different translation techniques apart from literal translations. But to the best of our knowledge, no automatic processing techniques explicitly implement these interlingual relations.

As an important natural language understanding and generation task, machine translation (MT) has been seriously improved with first phrase-based statistical machine translation (PBMT) then recently with neural machine translation (NMT). MT has also been exploited to generate paraphrases from bilingual parallel corpus, which was originally proposed by Bannard and Callison-Burch (2005). The assumption is that two segments in the same language are potential paraphrases if they share common translations in a foreign language. Currently the largest resource of paraphrases, PPDB (Paraphrase Database) (Ganitkevitch et al., 2013), has been built following this method exploiting translational equivalence. Nonetheless, the work of Pavlick et al. (2015) revealed that there exist other relations than strict equivalence (paraphrase) in PPDB (*i.e. Entailment (in two directions), Exclusion, Other related and Independent*). The existence of these other relations in PPDB reflects the lack of semantic control during the paraphrasing process.

We propose a categorization of translation relations which model human translators' choices, and we annotate a multilingual (English, French, Chinese) parallel corpus of oral presentations, the *TED Talks*[1], with these relations. The annotation is still ongoing and we are developing a classifier based on these annotations to conduct automatic detection. Our further goal is to integrate this information as important characteristics for the search of monolingual segments in relation of equivalence (paraphrases) or of entailment.

After presenting the related work in section 2, we describe our parallel corpus of *TED Talks* (section 3) and the translation relations (section 4). The annotation process and the statistics follow in section 5. Contrastive study between target languages is presented in section 6. Finally, we conclude in section 7.

[1] https://www.ted.com/

Proceedings of the First Workshop on Linguistic Resources for Natural Language Processing, pages 102–111
Santa Fe, New Mexico, USA, August 20, 2018.
">

2 Related work

Deng and Xue (2017) have studied the divergences present in English-Chinese machine translation, by using a hierarchical alignment scheme between the parse trees of these two languages. Seven types of divergences have been identified, and some of them cause important difficulties for automatic word alignment. In particular, we can underline lexical differences resulting from non-literal translations, and structural differences between languages (with or without change of types of syntagms). In order to supply a particular dataset of multiword expressions (MWE) for evaluating machine translation, Monti et al. (2015) have annotated specifically these expressions in the English-Italian *TED Talks* corpus, associated with their translation generated by an automatic system. The phenomena discussed in these two studies are included in the translation relations that we present in this article.

PARSEME (PARSing and Multiword Expressions) [2] is a European scientific network built up to elaborate universal terminologies and annotation guidelines for MWEs in 18 languages (Savary et al., 2015). Its main outcome is a multilingual 5-million word annotated corpus, which underlies a shared task on automatic identification of verbal MWEs (Savary et al., 2017). Our trilingual annotated corpus focuses on bilingual relation between translations, and we annotate all words in the corpus, including continuous and discontinuous MWEs.

As a complement of MT evaluation metrics, which reflect imperfectly systems' performance, Isabelle et al. (2017) have introduced a challenge set based on difficult linguistic materials. The authors could hence determine some remaining difficulties for recent NMT systems. The problems include, in particular, incomplete generalizations; translating common and syntactically flexible idioms, or crossing movement verbs *e.g. swim across X → traverser X à la nage*. The annotated corpus that we present here could also constitute a challenge set, for the purpose of evaluating MT systems when human translators resort to different translation relations.

3 Corpus

In order to study translation relations for several pairs of languages, we have worked on a multilingual parallel corpus. This corpus is available from the Web inventory *WIT³* (Cettolo et al., 2012), which gives access to a collection of transcribed and translated talks, including the corpus of *TED Talks*[3]. This corpus was released for the evaluation campaign IWSLT 2013 and 2014.[4] The source language, *i.e.* the original language in which the speakers expressed themselves, is English. We have calculated the intersection of a parallel corpus with translations in French[5], Chinese, Arabic, Spanish and Russian. The translation of subtitles for *TED Talks* is controlled by volunteers and language coordinators per language[6], which generally ensures good quality translations. The corpus to be annotated contains 2 436 lines of parallel sentences for each pair of languages (the English corpus contains 51 926 tokens). For the moment, we annotate English-French and English-Chinese corpora to validate our hierarchy of translation relations, since these two target languages are very dissimilar in several linguistic aspects: morphology, grammar, expression, etc.

For English and French languages, the corpus has been tokenized by Stanford Tokenizer[7], and lemmatized by TreeTagger (Schmid, 1995) while keeping the tokenization of Stanford Tokenizer. The capital letters at the beginning of each sentence are kept only if these words always appear with capital initials elsewhere in the corpus, otherwise they are lowercased. We have used the tool THULAC (Li and Sun, 2009) for the segmentation of the Chinese corpus, and proceeded to several corrections before annotation. The words are automatically aligned by training FastAlign (Dyer et al., 2013), with its default parameters on each entire parallel corpus (*i.e.* 163 092 lines and 3 303 660 English tokens). We import

---

[2]`http://www.parseme.eu/`

[3]`https://wit3.fbk.eu/`

[4]We have used training corpus of 2014 (160 656 lines), development corpus (880 lines) and test corpus (1 556 lines) of 2010.

[5]The sentence boundaries have been corrected in French test corpus to calculate the intersection.

[6]`https://www.ted.com/participate/translate/get-started`

[7]`http://nlp.stanford.edu/software/tokenizer.shtml`

these automatic alignments before annotation to accelerate the process, in particular for the words which are literally translated. The annotators should correct these alignments if necessary.

4 Translation relations

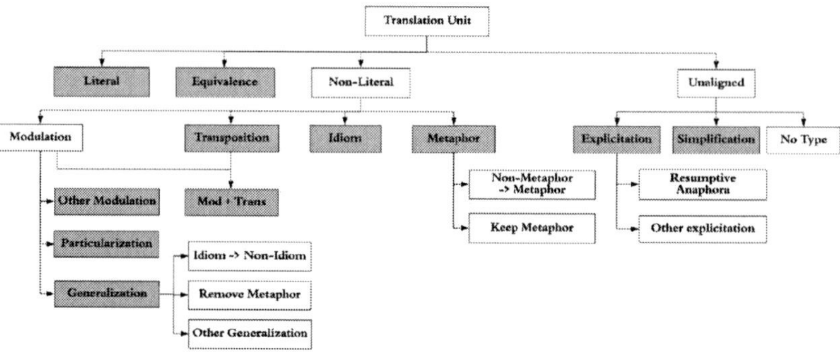

Figure 1: Hierarchy of translation relations.

The first attempt to establish a taxonomy of translation procedures has been carried out by Vinay and Darbelnet (1958). The hierarchy of translation relations that we propose here is based on theories clarified in the work of Chuquet and Paillard (1989), and on phenomena found during our initial study of the corpus (see figure 1).

The colored nodes represent our categories, the other nodes present the hierarchy (*i.e. Non-Literal, Unaligned, Modulation, No Type*) or the phenomena more specific but for which there is no dedicated label (*e.g. Remove Metaphor, Other Generalization*). We present below their definition and typical examples:

1. Literal translation: word-for-word translation (including insertion or deletion of determiners, changes between singular and plural forms), or possible literal translation of some idioms:

    What time is it? → Quelle heure est-il ?, facts are stubborn → les faits sont têtus

2. Equivalence:

    i) non-literal translation of proverbs, idioms, or fixed expressions:

    Birds of a feather flock together. → Qui se ressemble s'assemble.

    ii) semantic equivalence in supra-lexical level, translation of terms:

    magic trick → tour de magie, hatpin → épingle à chapeau

3. Modulation: consists in changing the point of view, either to circumvent a translation difficulty or to reveal a way of seeing things, specific to the speakers of the target language. This category could result in semantic shift between source text and target text. Apart from its two sub-types *Particularization* and *Generalization*, all the other phenomena are represented by the sub-type *Other Modulation*:

    this is a completely unsustainable pattern → il est absolument impossible de continuer sur cette tendance, I had an assignment → on m'avait confié une mission

4. Particularization: the translation is more precise or presents a more concrete sense:

    *the director **said** → le directeur **déclara**, language loss → l'extinction du langage*

5. Generalization: this category contains three sub-types, but we annotate them with the same label:

    i) the translation is more general or neutral; in other cases, this translation technique makes the sense more accessible in the target language:

look carefully at → *regardez, as we **sit here** in ... → alors que nous **sommes à** ...*

ii) translation of an idiom by a non-fixed expression:

trial and error → *procéder par tâtonnements*

iii) removal of a metaphorical image:

*ancient Tairona civilization which once **carpeted** the Caribbean coastal plain → anciennes civilisations tyranniques qui **occupaient** jadis la plaine côtière des Caraïbes*

6. Transposition: translating words or expressions by using other grammatical categories than the ones used in the source language, without altering the meaning of the utterance:

   astonishingly inquisitive → dotée d'une curiosité stupéfiante

   *patients **over** the age of 40 → les malades **ayant dépassé** l'âge de 40 ans*

7. Modulation plus Transposition: this category can contain any sub-type of *Modulation* combined with *Transposition*:

   *this is a people **who cognitively do not distinguish** → c'est un peuple **dont l'état des connaissances ne permet pas de faire la distinction***

8. Idiom: translate non-fixed expression by an idiom (frequently used when translating English to Chinese):

   at any given moment → à un instant "t"

   died getting old → 行将就木 *"getting closer and closer to the coffin"*

9. Metaphor: this category contains two sub-types reduced to only one label:

   i) keep the same metaphorical image by using a non-literal translation:

   *the Sun begins to **bathe** the slopes of the landscape → le soleil qui **inonde** les flancs de ce paysage*

   ii) introduce metaphorical expression to translate non-metaphor:

   *if you **faint** easily → si vous **tombez dans les pommes** facilement*

10. Unaligned - Explicitation:

    i) resumptive anaphora (Charolles, 2002): add a phrase or sentence summarizing the preceding information (which could be present in previous sentence), to help understanding the present sentence.

    ii) introduce in the target language clarifications that remain implicit in the source language but emerge from the situation; add language-specific function words:

    *feel their past in the wind → ressentent leur passé **souffler** dans le vent*

    an entire book → 一 本 完整 的 书 (add the Chinese classifier 本)

11. Unaligned - Simplification: remove deliberately certain content words in translation:

    *and you'll **suddenly** discover what it would be like → et vous découvrirez ce que ce serait*

12. Unaligned and no type attributed: function words necessary in one language but not in the other; segments not translated but which don't impact the meaning; segments giving repeated information in context; translated segments which don't correspond to any source segment:

    *minus 271 degrees, colder than → moins 271 degrés, **ce qui est** plus froid*

    *the last example I have time to → le dernier exemple **que** j'ai le temps de*

5 Annotation

5.1 Annotation tool and configuration

We have used the Web application Yawat[8] (Germann, 2008), which allows us to align words or segments (continuous or discontinuous), and then to assign labels adapted to our task on monolingual or bilingual units (see figure 2).

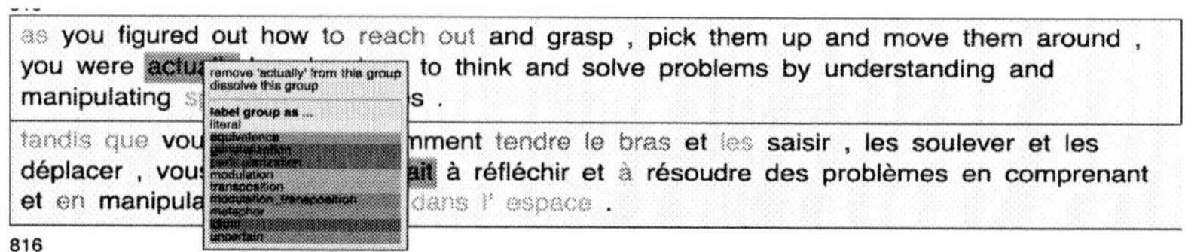

Figure 2: Annotation interface of Yawat.

Here is a trilingual example from our corpus:

well, we use that great euphemism, "trial and error", which is exposed to be meaningless.

eh bien, nous employons cet euphémisme, procéder par tâtonnements, qui est dénué de sens.

我们 *"we"* 普通人 *"ordinary people"* 会 *"particle for future tense"* 做 *"do"* 各种各样 *"diverse"* 的 *"particle for attribute"* 实验 *"experience"* 不断 *"continuously"* 地 *"particle for adverb"* 犯错误 *"make a mistake"* 结果 *"consequently"* 却 *"however"* 一无所获 *"have gained nothing"*

The segments *well* and *we use that great euphemism* are translated literally in French (with *"great"* omitted), but they are omitted in Chinese. The idiom *trial and error* is translated by a generalization in the two languages. The segment *which is exposed to be* is translated by a generalization in French (*est "is"*) and by a modulation in Chinese (结果 *"consequently"* 却 *"however"*). The adjective *meaningless* is translated by a transposition in French (*dénué de sens "lacking meaning"*) and by an idiom of four characters in Chinese (一无所获 *"have gained nothing"*).

The spelling errors in the original corpus have not been corrected, because on one hand, there are not many of them, on the other hand, generally they don't prevent us from assigning labels. Nonetheless, we have included a category *Uncertain* for pairs for which the annotators don't know which label to assign, or for those which contain obvious translation errors.

Three annotators [9] have participated in the annotation. The training of annotators relies on an annotation guide which defines all categories illustrated by giving characteristic examples. The hierarchy of relations provides a general view of relations between these categories. To better understand the context, the annotators could watch the corresponding video of talks[10] before annotating.

5.2 Control study

We have evaluated in a conventional way the feasibility of our annotation task, by measuring the inter-annotator agreement on a control corpus, which contains 100 pairs of trilingual parallel sentences (3 055 English tokens, 3 238 French tokens and 4 195 Chinese characters). For each pair of languages (EN-FR and EN-ZH), two annotators have independently annotated the corpus.

Since there exist disagreements on the boundary of certain segments, we have calculated the agreement of Cohen's Kappa (Cohen, 1960) only for the segments annotated with exactly the same boundaries by two annotators. The value 0.672 signifies a substantial agreement for the pair EN-FR, while EN-ZH has a lower agreement (0.61, the minimum value to be considered as substantial). The number of tokens

---

[8]Yet Another Word Alignment Tool, which is available for research under the license GNU Affero General Public License v3.0.

[9]One French annotator and one Chinese annotator for the whole corpus, and another Chinese annotator for only the English-Chinese control corpus.

[10]The corpora to be annotated are transcriptions of *TED Talks* and their translations.

annotated in segments with same boundaries represent 72.60% of English tokens for EN-FR, but only 52.76% for EN-ZH.

We also calculate another inter-annotator agreement in a more flexible way, by including the pairs with different but compatible boundaries (i.e. without overlap of boundaries), and with a common category.[11] In this scenario, while the coverage of English tokens increase to 85.56% for EN-FR and 74.10% for EN-ZH, the Kappa decreases to 0.617 for EN-FR and to 0.60 (moderate) for EN-ZH. The remaining tokens belong to segments with incompatible boundaries (see table 1 and table 2).

	κ	%EN tokens
strict	0.672	72.60%
flexible	0.617	85.56%

Table 1: EN-FR inter-annotator agreement.

	κ	%EN tokens
strict	0.61	52.76%
flexible	0.60	74.10%

Table 2: EN-ZH inter-annotator agreement.

We have compared the annotations of two annotators in a confusion matrix. There exist certain disagreements between *Literal* and these categories: *Equivalence (e.g. in this way → de cette façon), Modulation (e.g. this entire time → tout ce temps), Particularization (e.g. snuff → tabac)* and *Transposition (e.g. their prayers **alone** → **seulement** leurs prières)*. However, our categories *Equivalence* and *Literal* are very close, and *Particularization* is a sub-type of *Modulation*, consequently we could consider these confusions as acceptable in a more flexible measure. *Modulation* presents the majority of confusions with *Literal* and *Transposition (e.g. from the forest floor → tombées par terre)*, which indicates that it is necessary to better explain their differences when training annotators. *Mod+Trans* is a combined type for which certain annotators perceive sometimes only one of these two types *(e.g. a great distance → de loin)*. *Metaphor* is the origin of several disagreements *(e.g. at the **base** of glaciers → aux **pieds** des glaciers)*, which could mainly be explained by the difficulty of the annotation task for a non-native annotator of the target language.

5.3   Annotation scheme with several passes

The calculation of inter-annotator agreement enables certain standard interpretations on the control corpus, and the confusion matrix helps us to identify the difficulties of the task. For the purpose of converging on boundaries of segments and on attributions of labels, we have adopted an annotation scheme with several passes to ensure a better annotation quality. For each subcorpus[12], the first annotator conducts a first annotation of all categories, then the second annotator takes over, which allows him/her to modify the alignments and/or the categories in case of disagreement. Each annotation file is saved at the end of each pass to document the differences in annotation. This alternation can be repeated until the convergence of all annotations. In practice, we limit ourselves to 3 passes, the third one being accomplished by the first annotator. We observe that the number of modifications in the third pass drop gradually with the documents annotated, which reflects a progressive and fast adaptation of annotators to the task. This annotation scheme is cost-intensive, but has been made necessary by the quality intended, as well as by the inherent difficulties of segmentation observed in the control corpus.

5.4   Statistics of annotated subcorpora

Apart from two control corpora, we have annotated six English-French subcorpora and three English-Chinese subcorpora. Their statistics are presented in table 3. Table 4 shows a distribution of number of tokens annotated in different translation relations for English-French corpus.

---

[11]For example, *I was asked by* and *I was asked by my professor at Harvard* have both been annotated by *Modulation*, and *my professor at Harvard* has been annotated with *Literal* by the first annotator. Here we consider that the two boundaries are compatible, and there is an agreement between the two annotators on one segment (the longest one), because of the common category *Modulation*.

[12]Each subcorpus represents one or several complete speeches of *TED Talks*, in order to ensure better understanding of the context.

	Nb lines	Nb EN Tokens	Nb FR Tokens	Nb ZH Characters
control	100	3 055	3 238	4 195
1	95	1 792	1 774	2 388
2	106	2 282	2 545	3 851
3	101	2 189	2 357	3 380
4	92	1 381	1 489	-
5	133	2 566	2 766	-
6	120	2 691	2 919	-
Total	747	15 956	17 088	13 814

Table 3: Statistics of annotated subcorpora.

	English	French	% EN tokens
Literal	8 701	9 086	67.44%
Equivalence	690	874	5.35%
Modulation	1 671	1 734	12.95%
Transposition	208	297	1.61%
Mod+Trans	250	301	1.94%
Generalization	198	159	1.53%
Particularization	391	560	3.03%
Idiom	4	6	0.03%
Metaphor	16	19	0.12%
Simplification	166	0	1.29%
Explicitation	0	165	0.00%
Uncertain	127	148	0.98%
All types	12 422	13 349	96.29%
No Type	479	501	3.71%
Total nb tokens	12 901	13 850	-

Table 4: Statistics of English-French annotations (number of tokens).

6   Contrast between target languages

We present comparative statistics based on three annotated trilingual subcorpora (see table 5). English and French languages are very similar in grammar and syntax, but Chinese translators should often change word or even phrase order to adapt the translation.

We can see that there are fewer English tokens translated into Chinese using literal translation. For *Equivalence, Modulation* and *Transposition*, the proportions are not so different, but the boundaries of segments could be different. Chinese translations use less complicated *Modulation+Transposition*, but they resort much often to *Generalization* and *Particularization*. In general, *Idiom* and *Metaphor* are under-represented in both target languages, but translating by using a Chinese idiom in four characters is considered as a good practice, which result in a concise language style and translations adapted to Chinese culture. *Simplification* and *Explicitation* show clear differences with French translations. Chinese translations often render only the most important information and leave some other content phrases non-translated. Concerning *Explicitation*, this includes adding necessary Chinese classifiers; inserting content words (e.g. subject noun phrase) to keep the phrase grammatical instead of translating literally word by word and some instances of resumptive anaphora (see section 4). There exist also more instances of *Uncertain*, together with *Simplification*, these phenomena reflect that the quality of Chinese translations are not as good as French translations. Many more English words do not have any type attributed because of the big differences in grammar. At the same time, Chinese translations are more concise than the transcriptions of oral English, which results in the omission of many English transition words.

Here are some examples:

1) EN: *We had to worry about the lawyers and so on.*

FR: *On a dû se préoccuper des avocats et des trucs dans le genre.*

"We had to worry about the lawyers and things like that." (Literal, Modulation+Transposition)

ZH: 要 顾及 到 很多 法律 问题 *"have to worry about many legal issues"* (Generalization)

2) EN: *pressured the people a little bit about it*

FR: *obliger le peuple à en parler "force the people to talk about it"* (Modulation)

ZH: 刨根问底 *"inquire into the root of the matter"* (Idiom)

3) EN: *and it doesn't matter how much information we're looking at, how big these collections are or how big the images are.*

FR: *et ce quelle que soit la quantité d'informations que l'on visionne, la taille de ces collections ou la taille des images.*

"regardless of the amount of information viewed, the size of the collections or the size of the images." (Modulation+Transposition)

ZH: 不管 所 见到 的 数据 有 多少 、 图像 集 有 多大 以及 图像 本身 有 多 大 ， *Seadragon* 都 拥有 这样 的 处理 能力 。

"it doesn't matter how much data we're looking at, how big the collections of images are, and how big the images themselves are, Seadragon possesses this processing ability"

(Explicitation for the last phrase: resumptive anaphora which refers to information in the previous sentence)

	English	French	%EN tokens	English	Chinese	%EN tokens
Literal	4 267	4 423	68.13%	3 307	5 311	52.80%
Equivalence	406	514	6.48%	426	629	6.80%
Modulation	589	617	9.40%	615	863	9.82%
Transposition	142	195	2.27%	166	258	2.65%
Mod+Trans	188	225	3.00%	90	134	1.44%
Generalization	90	65	1.44%	200	208	3.19%
Particularization	197	256	3.15%	273	661	4.36%
Idiom	4	6	0.06%	10	21	0.16%
Metaphor	10	15	0.16%	6	10	0.10%
Simplification	92	-	1.47%	314	-	5.01%
Explicitation	-	58	-	-	929	-
Uncertain	79	79	1.26%	157	277	2.51%
All types	6 064	6 453	96.82%	5 564	9 301	88.84%
No type	199	223	3.18%	699	318	11.16%
Total nb tokens	6 263	6 676	-	6 263	9 619	-

Table 5: Contrasts between translations towards different target languages (number of tokens).

7 Conclusion and perspectives

In this work we are interested in translation relations, to our best knowledge, they have never been taken into account in machine translation as well as in paraphrase generation by exploiting translational equivalence. We categorized these relations and annotated them in a multilingual parallel corpus of *TED Talks*. We chose this specific genre (transcribed and translated speech) in order to obtain more diversity than with the technical corpora. The measured inter-annotator agreement is strong for segments with the same boundaries, but we have adopted a more time-consuming annotation process with three passes to ensure better annotation quality.

A parallel task with our corpus annotation is the development of a classifier to automatically detect these relations. Our long-term objective will be to have a better semantic control using this information as important characteristics to exploit translational equivalence, for the search of monolingual segments in relation of equivalence (paraphrases) or of entailment.

We think that there exist many other types of applications for this corpus, for example: evaluate machine translation or automatic word alignment for different translation relations, like the work of Isabelle et al. (2017); understand what are the characteristics of non-literal translations in order to improve machine translation to generate natural and native expressions; provide a concordancer for translation studies to investigate different translation relations. We could also supply pre-processed parallel corpora in other languages (Arabic, Spanish and Russian) for those who are interested to enrich annotation and comparative studies.

Acknowledgements

This work is founded by a scholarship from Paris-Sud University. We thank Yaqiu Liu for her annotation of English-Chinese control corpus and for her valuable insights in corpus analysis. We are grateful to our anonymous reviewers for their thoughtful and constructive comments.

References

Colin J. Bannard and Chris Callison-Burch. 2005. Paraphrasing with bilingual parallel corpora. In *ACL 2005, 43rd Annual Meeting of the Association for Computational Linguistics, Proceedings of the Conference, 25-30 June 2005, University of Michigan, USA*, pages 597–604.

Mauro Cettolo, Christian Girardi, and Marcello Federico. 2012. Wit^3: Web inventory of transcribed and translated talks. In *Proceedings of the 16th Conference of the European Association for Machine Translation (EAMT)*, pages 261–268, Trento, Italy, May.

Michel Charolles. 2002. *La référence et les expressions référentielles en français*. Ophrys.

Hélène Chuquet and Michel Paillard. 1989. *Approche linguistique des problèmes de traduction anglais-français*. Ophrys.

Jacob Cohen. 1960. A coefficient of agreement for nominal scales. *Educational and Psychological Measurement*, 20:37–46.

Dun Deng and Nianwen Xue. 2017. Translation Divergences in Chinese-English Machine Translation: An Empirical Investigation. *Computational Linguistics*, 43(3):521–565.

Chris Dyer, Victor Chahuneau, and Noah A. Smith. 2013. A simple, fast, and effective reparameterization of IBM model 2. In Lucy Vanderwende, Hal Daumé III, and Katrin Kirchhoff, editors, *Human Language Technologies: Conference of the North American Chapter of the Association of Computational Linguistics, Proceedings, June 9-14, 2013, Westin Peachtree Plaza Hotel, Atlanta, Georgia, USA*, pages 644–648. The Association for Computational Linguistics.

Juri Ganitkevitch, Benjamin Van Durme, and Chris Callison-Burch. 2013. PPDB: The Paraphrase Database. In *Human Language Technologies: Conference of the North American Chapter of the Association of Computational Linguistics, Proceedings, June 9-14, 2013, Westin Peachtree Plaza Hotel, Atlanta, Georgia, USA*, pages 758–764.

Ulrich Germann. 2008. Yawat: Yet Another Word Alignment Tool. In *ACL 2008, Proceedings of the 46th Annual Meeting of the Association for Computational Linguistics, June 15-20, 2008, Columbus, Ohio, USA, Demo Papers*, pages 20–23. The Association for Computer Linguistics.

Pierre Isabelle, Colin Cherry, and George F. Foster. 2017. A Challenge Set Approach to Evaluating Machine Translation. In Martha Palmer, Rebecca Hwa, and Sebastian Riedel, editors, *Proceedings of the 2017 Conference on Empirical Methods in Natural Language Processing, EMNLP 2017, Copenhagen, Denmark, September 9-11, 2017*, pages 2476–2486. Association for Computational Linguistics.

Zhongguo Li and Maosong Sun. 2009. Punctuation As Implicit Annotations for Chinese Word Segmentation. *Computational Linguistics*, 35(4):505–512, December.

Johanna Monti, Federico Sangati, and Mihael Arcan. 2015. TED-MWE: a bilingual parallel corpus with MWE annotation. Towards a methodology for annotating MWEs in parallel multilingual corpora. In *Proceedings of the Second Italian Conference on Computational Linguistics CLiC-it*, pages 193–197, Trento.

Ellie Pavlick, Johan Bos, Malvina Nissim, Charley Beller, Benjamin Van Durme, and Chris Callison-Burch. 2015. Adding semantics to data-driven paraphrasing. In *Proceedings of the 53rd Annual Meeting of the Association for Computational Linguistics and the 7th International Joint Conference on Natural Language Processing of the Asian Federation of Natural Language Processing, ACL 2015, July 26-31, 2015, Beijing, China, Volume 1: Long Papers*, pages 1512–1522.

Agata Savary, Manfred Sailer, Yannick Parmentier, Michael Rosner, Victoria Rosén, Adam Przepiórkowski, Cvetana Krstev, Veronika Vincze, Beata Wójtowicz, Gyri Smørdal Losnegaard, Carla Parra Escartín, Jakub Waszczuk, Matthieu Constant, Petya Osenova, and Federico Sangati. 2015. PARSEME – PARSing and Multi-word Expressions within a European multilingual network. In *7th Language & Technology Conference: Human Language Technologies as a Challenge for Computer Science and Linguistics (LTC 2015)*, Poznań, Poland, Nov. Available at https://hal.archives-ouvertes.fr/hal-01223349/document.

Agata Savary, Carlos Ramisch, Silvio Cordeiro, Federico Sangati, Veronika Vincze, Behrang QasemiZadeh, Marie Candito, Fabienne Cap, Voula Giouli, Ivelina Stoyanova, and Antoine Doucet. 2017. The PARSEME shared task on automatic identification of verbal multiword expressions. In Stella Markantonatou, Carlos Ramisch, Agata Savary, and Veronika Vincze, editors, *Proceedings of the 13th Workshop on Multiword Expressions, MWE@EACL 2017, Valencia, Spain, April 4, 2017*, pages 31–47. Association for Computational Linguistics.

Helmut Schmid. 1995. Improvements In Part-of-Speech Tagging With an Application To German. In *Proceedings of the ACL SIGDAT-Workshop*, pages 47–50.

Jean-Paul Vinay and Jean Darbelnet. 1958. *Stylistique comparée du français et de l'anglais: méthode de traduction*. Bibliothèque de stylistique comparée. Didier.

Towards an Automatic Classification of Illustrative Examples in a Large Japanese-French Dictionary Obtained by OCR

Mutsuko Tomokiyo
UGA, LIG-GETALP
Grenoble
mutsuko.tomokiyo@imag.fr

Christian Boitet
UGA, LIG-GETALP
Grenoble
christian.boitet@imag.fr

Mathieu Mangeot
UGA, LIG-GETALP
Grenoble
mathieu.mangeot@imag.fr

Abstract

This paper focuses on improving the Cesselin, a large, open source Japanese-French bilingual dictionary digitalized by OCR, available on the web, and contributively improvable online. Labelling its examples (about 226,000) would significantly enhance their usefulness for language learners. Examples are proverbs, idiomatic constructions, normal usage examples, and, for nouns, phrases containing a quantifier. Proverbs are easy to spot, but not the other types. To find a method for automatically or at least semi-automatically annotating them, we have studied many entries, and hypothesized that the degree of lexical similarity between results of MT into a third language might give good cues. To confirm that hypothesis, we sampled 500 examples and used Google Translate to translate into English the Cesslin Japanese expressions and their French translations. The hypothesis holds well, in particular for distinguishing examples of normal usage from idiomatic examples. Finally, we propose a detailed annotation procedure and discuss its future automatization.

1 Introduction

The Cesselin Japanese-French bilingual dictionary was edited by a French missionary, Gustave Cesselin (1873-1944), and published in 1939 and 1957 in Japan (82,703 entries and 2,345 pages)[1]. We have converted it to an electronic form by using an OCR (optical character reader) and made some improvements. An example of the entry for 飲む *nomu* "drink" in original and online form on the Jibiki platform is given in Figure 2 below (before the references).

Our aims are to improve, update and complete the Cesselin to make it available as a modern on-line dictionary for Japanese or French language learners or researchers in Japanese studies, and also to contribute to some improvement in the translation performance of Japanese↔French machine translation (MT) systems. About 60,000 other articles have already been added from other free sources.

The Cesselin includes knowledge on spoken and written Japanese[2], and rich illustrative examples containing the headwords. It is however not satisfactory for modern users, because it contains outdated

---

[1]A few other on-line Japanese-French dictionaries exist: the Diko (3000 entry words, Diko), the *Dictionnaire français-japonais* (15,000 entry words, Lexilogos), the *Dictionnaire japonais* (24,000 entry words, Assimil), and the *Dictionnaire Glosbe* (entry words unknown, Glosbe), etc. The number of words in these dictionaries may change, because they are going to be edited and extended in a collaborative way.

[2]The Japanese writing system has been fixed by the Japanese government in 1986, in order for the writing form to conform to pronunciation.

Proceedings of the First Workshop on Linguistic Resources for Natural Language Processing, pages 112–121
Santa Fe, New Mexico, USA, August 20, 2018.

phonetic descriptions, old Chinese characters and old forms of Okurigana.[3] Also, its examples are given without any indication[4] concerning their types. As in many dictionaries, the examples are given to help understanding various meanings and usages of words, and to show their grammatical constructions, and their usages in collocations, proverbs, and quantified phrases. Information on the exact type of each example would help users looking for specific information such as numerical quantifiers, and enable MT developers to methodically deal with lexical ambiguities (Tomokiyo et al., 2016). It would also help language learners or researchers to practice Japanese or French, and to deepen their understanding of the Japanese culture.

In Section 2, we explain an experiment made in order to investigate what kinds of examples are included in the Cesselin. After getting a general impression while correcting the OCR results of about 15,000 entries, we have manually analyzed 500 examples (out of about 226,000), taken from 25 complex entries, established a classification of examples, and proposed classification criteria. In Section 3, we propose an automatable step by step procedure to classify and annotate the remaining 225,500 examples according to these criteria. In Section 4, we briefly present the Universal Networking Language (UNL) Universal Words (UW) dictionary we used to test words in English translations for synonymy. We also examine some technical aspects of the automatization of our procedure. That step, now beginning, will likely save much human expert time, because it will only be needed to "post-edit" automatically generated annotations, and, we hope, to correct less than 5% of them.

2   Case studies on using results of Google Translate[5] for the classification

To find a classification of the examples that would be useful and amenable to automatic or at least semi-automatic annotation, we have studied many entries, and hypothesized that the degree of lexical similarity between results of MT into a third language might give good cues. To confirm that hypothesis, we selected 500 examples from complex entries (having more than 25 examples in average) and used Google Translate (GT) to translate into English both their Japanese expressions and their French translations.[6] We then compared the two translation outputs from the point of view of lexical similarity. Figure 1 illustrates the process.

That comparison confirmed the assumption[7] that, if an example is a proverb or if a word in an example is employed in a collocation, the J→E translated example (Ej) usually contains lexemes that completely differ from those of the F→E MT-translated example (Ef), because in proverbs and collocational expressions including classifiers/quantifiers, words have a tendency to be used in figurative meaning, and GT does not in general produce adequate translation outputs for them, but very often literal and incorrect translations. Thus, the two outputs contain different lexemes,[8] and one can consequently distinguish proverbs and collocations from other usage examples.

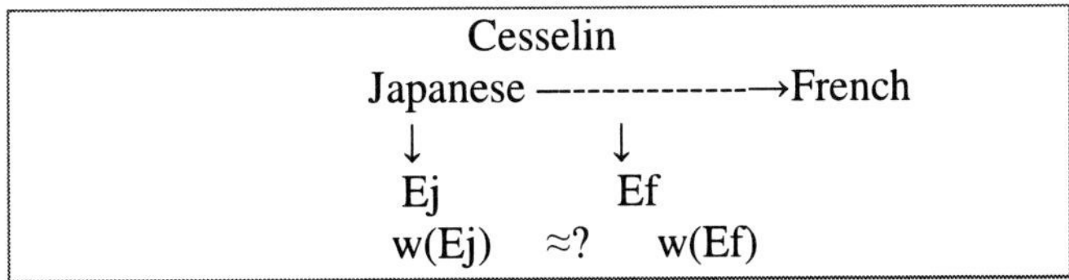

Figure 1: Assumption: according to the similarity of the bag of words w(Ej) and w(Ef), the example is collocational, proverbial, idiomatic, or concerns a quantifier/classifier

---

[3] A Japanese word is written in Kanji (漢字, Chinese character) and Hiragana (平仮名, Japanese character), in Kanji only, or in Hiragana and/or Katakana (片仮名) only. Okuriganas (送り仮名) are hiragana suffixes following Kanji stems. The rules for Okuriganas changed several times, and were standardized by the Japanese government in 1973.

[4] Excepting indications for figurative meaning usage by the label {fig} and for some domain-specific names.

[5] `https://translate.google.fr/?hl=fr - fr/ja/La démocratie n%27a plus de cote`.

[6] We have the premise underlying that translations into French proposed by the Cesselin are correct.

[7] The assumption is grounded on our studies on Japanese, French and English classifiers and quantifiers (Tomokiyo et al., 2017).

[8] We don't consider the fillers such as *John* and *Mary* in *John pulled Mary's leg*, only *pulled* and *leg*.

2.1 Japanese-English and French-English translation of the 500 examples by GT system

The structure of an entry in the Cesselin is as follows: head word (in Japanese), pronunciation given in two different forms (in Japanese and in transliteration in Latin characters, called ローマ字 (Ro-maji)), conjugated forms for verbs and adjectives, part of speech label, definitions (in French), and examples in Japanese, with their transliteration in ローマ字, and their translation or translations into French. Here is an extract of the entry for the verb *nomu* "drink" from the Cesselin dictionary.

```
nomu[ma, mi, me] 飲む - 呑む【のむ】v.t.
1. Boire, avaler.⁹
2. Aspirer, sucer, fumer.¹⁰
3. Prendre.¹¹
4. 飲まねば薬も効能なし(Nomaneba kusuri mo kônô nashi) "Qui veut
la fin veut les moyens.¹²"
5. 飲まぬ酒には酔はぬ (Nomanu sake ni wa yowanu) "II n'y a point
de fumée sans feu.¹³"
```

We have submitted to GT 500 input examples[14] contained in about 20 complex entries of the Cesselin (Table 1): 飲む *nomu* "drink," 買う *kau* "buy," 走 *hashiru* "ran," 居る *iru* "stay, be," 来る *kuru* "come," 思う *omou* "think," 言う *iu* "say," 可愛い *kawaii* "pretty," 強い *tsuyoi* "strong," 安い *yasui* "cheap," すぐ *sugu* "soon, immediately," から *kara* "because, from, since," 家 *ie* "house, family," 夜 *yoru* "night," 足 *ashi* "leg," 車 *kuruma* "car," 年 *nen* "year," 何時 *nanji* "what time," だけ *dake* "only," ながら *nagara* "while," 必要 *hitsuyou* "necessity," もう *mou* "already," 事 *koto* "thing."

(a) Japanese examples in the Cesselin	(b) GT J→E translations	(c) GT F→E translations	(d) Cesselin French translations	(e) Matching results for J-E and F-E[15]
水を飲む。(Mizu wo nomu)	Drink water.	Drink water.	Boire de l'eau.	100%
飲まぬ酒には酔わぬ。(Nomanu sake niha yowanu.)	I'm not intoxicated with drinking alcohol.	There is no smoke without fire.	II n'y a point de fumée sans feu.	(Ø P)
飲んだり吐出したりする。(Nondari hakidashitari suru.)	It drinks or spits out.	Swallow and turn in turn.	Avaler et rendre tour à tour.	Ø
飲んだり吐出したりする。(Nondari hakidashitari suru.)	It drinks or spits out.	Accept and refuse.	{fig} Accepter et refuser.	Ø {fig} (collocation)

Table 1: Excerpt of translations obtained by GT (J→E and F→E)

---

[9]To drink, to swallow

[10]To inhale, to suck, to smoke

[11]To take

[12]He who wills the end wills the means.

[13]There is no smoke without fire.

[14]The chosen words belong to the 200 most frequent words in the frequency list except for 助詞 *joshi* "postpositions": 『現代日本語書き言葉均衡コーパス (Gendai Nihongo kakikotoba kinkou ko-pasu』』語彙表 (Giohyou, The Balanced Corpus of Contemporary Written Japanese (BCCWJ) (http://pj.ninjal.ac.jp/corpus_center/bccwj/freq-list.html))

[15]Matching results are judged by a linguist in the experiment.

2.2 Comparison and contrast of the two translations results

We have asked the following questions concerning the two outputs by GT:

- do the two outputs include totally the same lexemes?

- when they include different lexemes, what kind of lexemes are common to both?

Column (e) in Table 1 shows a manual comparison of the J→E translations (Column (b)) outputs with the F→E translations (Column (d)) from the point of view of lexemes in an example.

Table 2 shows the comparison of the two translation outputs.

items	explanation	count	percentage
(1) 100% concordance (100%)	GT J→E and F→E translations of an example include exactly the same words.	63/500	12.6%
(2) 100%* concordance (100%*)	GT J→E and F→E translations of an example include synonym words	79/500	15.8%
(3) Concordance of words with ⊆ or ⊇ (100%⊆ or ⊇)	The lengths of the GT J→E translation and the GT F→E translation differ significantly, but the two include almost the same words.	26/500	5.2%
(4) Concordance by morphosyntactic analysis (100%**)	GT J→E and F→E translations of an example include the same words for the predicate verb and its principal actants.	15/500	3.0%
(5) No-concordance with {fig} label (Ø{fig.})	GT J→E and F→E translations of an example don't include any common words and the French example is marked by the {fig.} label.	8/500	1,6%
(6) No concordance (Ø)	GT J→E and F→E translations of an example don't include any common word except articles.	269/500	53.8%
(7) No concordance and proverbs (Ø P)	GT J→E and F→E translations of an example don't include any common content word and the example appears in a Japanese proverbs dictionary.	32/500	6.4%
(8) No concordance with usage domain (Ø D)	GT J→E and F→E translations of an example having an indication of usage domain don't include any common word.	4/500	0.8%
(9) Zero output (x)	Zero output by GT.	4/500	0.8%

Table 2: Comparison of J-E and F-E translations outputs for the 500 examples: different cases

According to this experiment, the examples in the Cesselin can be classified into 5 classes:

- ordinary usage examples to give grammatical information or a context where headwords are used

- proverbs

- collocational expressions

- classifiers/quantifiers, which depend on signified entities

- domain-specific examples

2.3 Explanations for examples annotation

In the following examples for the verb 飲む *nomu* "drink" in Table 3, (a) is a proverb, (b) is a sentence including the form 飲む in a figurative meaning, and (c) is a sentence that is not a proverb nor a collocation, but ordinary usage. When one compares the lexemes in the J→E and F→E translations by GT, while (a) and (b) don't contain any common word in their predicative part, in (c), the two translations contain two common words (*drink* and *water*).

That confirms that examples showing ordinary usages have a tendency to be translated as sentences having many words (or synonyms) in common. We thought this phenomenon could be a trump card to classify all examples in the Cesselin, because J→E translations by GT[16] of polylexical expressions are almost always word-for-word translations. We suggest that this comes from a lack of information on the figurative usages of words in GT resources (bilingual dictionary and parallel corpus). Hence, when a word in a Japanese example is used in a figurative meaning depending on the context, the translation result almost never lexically matches the F→E translation result.

	Japanese examples	**GT J-E translations**	**GT F-E translations**	**Cesselin translations of Japanese examples**
(a) Proverb	飲まぬ酒には酔わ ぬ[17] (Nomanu sake ni-ha yowanu)	I'm not intoxicated with drinking alcohol.	There is no smoke without fire.	Il n'y a point de fumée sans feu.
(b) Collocation	彼は妻君に飲まれ ている。(Kare ha saikun ni nomare-teiru)	He is being drunk by his wife.	His wife is bowing him.	Sa femme le berne.[18]
(c) Ordinary usage	水を飲む。(Mizu wo nomu)	Drink water.	Drink water.	Boire de l'eau.

Table 3: Examples for a proverb, a collocational expression and an ordinary usage

Among ordinary usage examples, proverbs, collocational expressions, classifier/quantifiers and domain-specific examples, we have distinguished proverbs from other types of examples by using a proverb dictionary. Using also labels such as {fig} (in Table 4) and {botanic, zoology....} which are attached to some examples in the Cesselin, we have been able to distinguish collocational expressions and domain-specific examples from other examples, respectively.

3   Examples annotation procedure

We propose the following procedure for classification and annotation of the examples in the Cesselin.

Step 1) Differentiation of proverbs from others
We distinguish proverbs from other examples, using the proverb dictionary.[19]
When Japanese examples appear in this Japanese proverbs dictionary, they are annotated as {prov} for *proverb*.

Step 2) Differentiation of ordinary usage examples from others
When lexemes in two translation outputs have 100 percentage of concordance, the example is annotated as {ordusg} for *ordinary usage*.

Step 3) Differentiation of collocational expressions and expressions in specific domains
In the Cesselin, the label {fig} indicates a figurative usage of headwords, but is not used consistently. When the translation for an example is marked with that label (see {fig} in Table 4), we annotate it as {colexp} for *collocations*[20], and when the French translation is labelled by {botanic, zoology, etc.}, we annotate it as {domexp} for *domain-specific usage*.

---

[16]Of course, translation performance of commercial systems depends on the considered language pair.

[17]A word-to-word translation would be: *One doesn't get drunk on Sake which one doesn't drink.*

[18]In modern French, one would say *Sa femme le trompe* — another illustration of the need to update the content.

[19]新明解故事ことわざ辞典 (Sinmeikai koji-kotowaza jiten, Dictionary of legends and proverbs), 三省堂編修所 (Sanseido Editions), Tokyo. That dictionary contains 7,300 items.

[20]Note that phrases or sentences which include words used in figurative meaning are not always collocational expressions.

items	Japanese examples	GT **J-E** translations	GT **F-E** translations	**French translation of Japanese examples**
Collocation without indication	人を飲んで掛かる(Hito wo non de kakaru)[21]	I'm drinking people and hanging.	Miss someone, look down.	Manquer à quelqu'un, regarder de haut.
Collocation with indication {fig}	飲んだり吐出したりする[22] (Nondari hakidashitari suru)	To drink or to spit.	Accept and refuse.	{fig} Accepter et refuser.

Table 4: Examples of words having a figurative meaning, with and without the label {fig}

Step 4) Differentiation of collocational expressions without any label in Cesselin

There are cases where French translations in Cesselin have no label {fig}, but are used in figurative meaning (Table 5). When their English translations haven't any common lexeme (w(Ej) ∩ w(Ef) = ∅), we classify them as collocational expressions, after referring to a KWIC (Keywords in context) list[23] obtained by using the Sketch Engine[24] software. When an example appears many times in the KWIC list, it is considered as a collocation or a classifier/quantifier (Alda, 2011) and we annotate it as {colexp} for *collocational usage*. We compare with the KWIC list, and, if the example is a noun phrase of type "number + noun," or "noun + のような (no-youna, like) + noun,"[25] we annotate it as {quant} for *classifiers/quantifiers* (Tomokiyo et al., 2017; Miyagawa, 1989).

headword	**Japanese example**	GT **J→E** translation	GT **F→E** translation	**French translation for the Japanese example**
足 (ashi, foot)	足を洗う[26] (ashi wo arau)	Wash your feet.	Rise from a lower class.	S'élever d'une classe inférieure.

Table 5: Examples of collocational expressions without any label in the Cesselin

Step 5) Checking on synonymy relationship between the main words in the two translated examples

In Table 6, the J→E translation of the example 必要費 *hitsuyou hi* "necessary cost" is different from the F→E translation of *cost* and *expenses*, and the J→E translation of the example 車に乗る *kuruma ni noru* "to get on a car" is different from the F→E translation for *ride* and *get in*, which are the predicative verbs of the sentences. In these cases, we check whether a synonymy relationship holds between the two words by using a (UNL) UW dictionary (see 4.1). If the two words (rather, word senses) are synonymous, the two translated examples are considered to have 100% concordance, and the example is annotated as {ordusg} for *ordinary usage*.

---

[21]To catch the person, drinking him.

[22]The concrete meaning of 飲んだり吐出したりする : *Drinking and spitting alternately.*

[23]The input is a corpus developed by Mathieu Mangeot (Mathieu's corpus) in the framework of the Jibiki project since 2014 (`http://jibiki.fr`). It is a Japanese-French parallel corpus coming from newspapers, novels, the Bible, etc., and contains 9268785 words at the moment.

[24]The Sketch Engine is a corpus management tool, containing 400 ready-to-use corpora. We have added Mathieu's ccorpus to it. See `https://www.sketchengine.co.uk`

[25]E.g. 山のような問題 *yama no youna mondai* "problems like mountain" → a lot of problems

[26]The concrete meaning of 足を洗う is: *Wash one's feet.* By the way, the expression 足を洗う makes sense in concrete as well as figurative usage. We have not yet solved this problem.

headword	Japanese examples	GT J→E translations	GT F→E translations	French translations	comparison
必要 (hitsuyou)[27]	必要費 (hitsuyou hi)	Necessary cost	Necessary expenses.	Dépenses nécessaires.	100%*[28]
車 (kuruma)[29]	車に乗る (kuruma ni noru)	I ride a car.	Get in the car	Monter en voiture.	100%*

Table 6: Two translated examples having synonymous lexemes

Step 6) Analyzing translated examples having different lengths

Examples translated into English have different lengths because of the nominalization[30] of a predicative verb, like (a) in Table 7, as well as difference of registers (formal vs. informal setting, degree of politeness), as in utterances (b) in Table 7, etc.

In example (b), *Excuse me, are not you*, and *Mr. Yamada* are common to the two translated examples, and only *Please* and *but* are added in the F→E translation. In this case, the example is syntactically analyzed, and if the predicative verb and its main actants are the same, the two examples are considered to have 100% concordance, and we annotate it as {ordusg} for *ordinary usage*.

Expression in the Cesselin	Japanese examples	GT J→E translations	GT F→E translations	French translation for the Japanese examples
a) もう (mou) (J ⊇ F)	もう休みましょう (Mou yasumi masyou)[31]	Let's have a rest now.	Let's rest now!	Reposons-nous maintenant!
b) ながら (nagara) (J ⊆ F)	失礼ながら山田様ではございませんか (Shitsurei nagara Yamada san deha gozaimasen ka)[32]	Excuse me, are not you, Mr. Yamada?	Please excuse me, but are not you Mr. Yamada?	Veuillez bien m'excuser, mais n'êtes-vous pas monsieur Yamada?

Table 7: Two translated examples having different lengths

4 Towards automatic classification

4.1 Usage of a UW dictionary as a pivot of interlingual lexemes

In order to get information on the synonymy relationship between English words in the two translated examples, and also morphosyntactic information, we have used a UW dictionary[33] made available by the UNL project,[34] as a pivot of "interlingual lexemes."

---

[27]*hitsuyou* = "necessary"

[28]The symbol 100 %* stands for the matching of 100 % of the two translation outputs with synonymy information.

[29]A car

[30]We are not yet engaged in this case.

[31]Let's take a rest now.

[32]Excuse me, are not you Mr.Yamada?

[33]The UNL-UW dictionary contains at the moment 126,9421 headwords for Japanese, 520,305 headwords for French and 1,458,686 headwords for English. The semantic attributes consist of 58 labels and 39 semantic relation labels.

[34]The UNL (Universal Networking Language) project was launched at the Institute of Advanced Studies (IAS) of the United Nations University in Tokyo (UNU) in April 1996 under the aegis of the United Nations University in Tokyo, with financial

A Universal Word (UW) is a character-string which represents a sense of a word. It is made of a headword (usually an English word or term) followed by a list of semantic restrictions between parentheses. A UNL semantic representation of an utterance is a hypergraph, where nodes are UWs having semantic attributes, and arcs bear semantic relations between two nodes or scopes. One node has to bear the `@entry` attribute. A scope is an arc-connected subgraph having an entry node and may be referred to as origin or extremity of an arc.

Here are some examples of entries in the UW dictionary:

(a) `expense(icl>cost)`   [expense is "included" in `cost`, hence `cost` has its nominal sense here]

(b) `look(agt>thing, equ>search, icl>examine(icl>do, obj>thing))`
[here:

- `icl` in (a) gives synonym information (`examine`)
- `agt` and `obj` in (b) denote the nature of the 2 main actants of this predicative verb (in discourse)
- `equ` in (b) expresses the fact that `look` (maybe the headword should be `look_for`) is linked to `search` by an `equ` path in the UNL ontology map[35] (Uchida et al., 2006).]

4.2 Mechanisms needed for automatic annotation

Before starting this research, we produced a morphosyntactic analysis of the Cesselin examples by using MeCab (Mangeot 2016).[36] Hence, the Japanese examples are already segmented in words and annotated according to a grammar based on Hashimoto's grammar.[37]

In order to build an automatic classifier/annotator of the Cesselin examples, we further need:

(1) a mechanism to match examples in the Cesselin with proverbs contained in one or more proverb dictionaries. As no Japanese proverb dictionary is available in electronic form (at least .epub), a first challenge is to build an online Japanese proverb database. We envisage to use the same method as that used for computerizing the Cesselin.

(2) a mechanism to call GT on an example and its translation, and to evaluate the lexical similarity of the two translation outputs. The first part is easy, while the second needs the three following resources.

(3) a mechanism to call an English morphosyntactic analyzer on the translated examples, to get the lemmas and possibly other attributes (e.g., number, determination). PhpMorphy would be a possibility (`http://phpmorphy.sourceforge.net/dokuwiki/`).

(4) a mechanism to check the synonymy between two words by comparing the UWs having their lemmas as headwords in the UW dictionary. For this, we intend to put the UW dictionary in the form of a lexical network (it has been made with an earlier version using the PIVAX/Jibiki lexical database).

(5) a mechanism to access a KWIC list produced from the set of Japanese proverbs.

5 Conclusion and perspectives

Labelling the examples (about 226,000) of the Cesselin would significantly enhance their usefulness for language learners. We have hypothesized that the degree of lexical similarity between results of MT (by GT) into English might give good cues. That hypothesis has been confirmed by manually applying a procedure derived from it on 500 examples, and getting 100% correct annotations. Incidentally, that success confirms that handling of polylexical expressions by MT systems (even neural ones) is still very

---

support from the ASCII corporation and IAS. See `http://www.undl.org/unlsys/unl/unl2005/attribute.htm` (Uchida et al., 2006).

[35]The semantic relation labels are created from UNL ontology, which stores all relational information in a lattice structure, where UWs are interconnected through relations including hierarchical relations (10 levels) such as `icl` (a-kind-of) and `iof` (an-instance-of), and mean headword's sub-meaning, respectively. See `http://www.undl.org/unlexp/`.

[36]Spoken Japanese has no space between words in a sentence.

[37]Hashimoto's grammar was introduced by the linguist Shinkichi Hashimoto (1946), and is widely adopted in the educational field in Japan.

poor. We hope our work could help improve them, at least for the J-F pair. We are working towards automating that procedure and applying it to the remaining 265,500 examples. Of course, we don't hope to get 100% correct annotations on this large set, but we hope that corrections done by cooperative online post-editing, will be limited to 5% or 10%.

We are also planning to study whether that method could spot corresponding proverbs, collocational expressions and quantified expressions in bilingual aligned J-F corpora. It will be a good surprise if it works, because sentences in usual texts tend to be quite longer than dictionary examples, which are in general not very long. Also, they rarely include proverbs, which are frequent in dictionary examples, and easy to spot. However, our method of differentiating collocational expressions from other types of expressions might also work in general documents. We plan to test this in the future. Also, it might be possible to disambiguate polylexical expressions by describing the context where a word appears in the UW dictionary (Uchida et al., 2006).

nomu [ma, mi, me.] (飲 – 呑む) v.t:1. Boire, avaler. 2. Aspirer, sucer, fumer. 3. Prendre. 4. Régler. 5. Mépriser, faire peu cas de. 6. Cacher dans son sein, dissimuler. 7. Faire du courtage sans titre ni commission. **Nomaneba kusuri mo kōnō nashi** (-- 薬も効能なし) " Qui veut la fin veut les moyens." **Nomanu sake ni wa yowanu** (--酒には酔はぬ) "Il n'y a point de fumée sans feu." **Nome ya utae ya** (--や唄へや) Faisons la noce et soyons joyeux ! **Nomu ni herazu suu ni heru** (--に減らす吸ふに減る) Ce n'est pas à force de boire, mais bien à force de sucer que ça diminue. fig: Les dépenses les plus répétées, quoique peu sensibles à chaque fois, restent les plus inquiétantes. **Nondari hakidashitari suru** (--吐出したりする) Avaler et rendre tour à tour. fig:Accepter et refuser. **Nonde hakidashita yō** (--吐き出した様) Comme si on avait rendu ce que l'on vient d'avaler. fig: Avoir une figure pâle et comme subitement boursouflée. **Nonde kanashimi wo wasureru** (--悲しみを忘れる) Noyer ses chagrins, laisser ses peines au fond du verre.

Hito wo nonde kakaru (人を--掛る) Manquer à quelqu'un, regarder de haut. **Ippai nomi-nagara keiyaku shita** (一杯--乍ら契約した) Ils passèrent un marché entre deux verres. **Kare wa saikun ni nomarete iru** (彼に妻君に--ゐる) Sa femme le berne. **Mikkakan nomazu kuwazu de** (三日間--食はず で) Sans boire ni manger trois jours durant. **Mizu wo—** (水を--) Boire de l'eau. **Nami ni nomareru** (波に--) Être englouti par les vagues. **Nemuku naru made—** (眠くなる迄--) Boire jusqu'à s'assoupir. **Tabako wo—** (煙草を--) Fumer du tabac. **Tantō wo futokoro ni—** (短刀を懐に--) Dissimuler un poignard dans son sein. **Teki ni nomareru** (敵に--) S'en laisser imposer par l'ennemi. **Urami wo—** (恨を--) Avaler une humiliation.

<table>
<tr><td>Provenance : Cesselin</td><td>MODIFIÉ par CONSTANCE | Éditer | Voir l'historique | Scan | Corpus</td></tr>
</table>

nomu 飲む 【のむ】 nomu 呑む 【のむ】 [動 verbe transitif]

1. Boire, avaler.

2. Aspirer, sucer, fumer.

3. Prendre.

4. Régler.

5. Mépriser, faire peu cas de.

6. Cacher dans son sein, dissimuler.

7. Faire du courtage sans titre ni commission.

- 飲まねば薬も効能なし (Nomaneba kusuri mo kōnō nashi) " Qui veut la fin veut les moyens."
- 飲まぬ酒には酔はぬ (Nomanu sake ni wa yowanu) "Il n'y a point de fumée sans feu."
- 飲めや唄へや (Nome ya utae ya) Faisons la noce et soyons joyeux !
- 飲むに減らず吸ふに減る (Nomu ni herazu suu ni heru) Ce n'est pas à force de boire, mais bien à force de sucer que ça diminue, {fig:} Les dépenses les plus répétées, quoique peu sensibles à chaque fois, restent les plus inquiétantes.
- 飲んだり吐出したりする (Nondari hakidashitari suru) Avaler et rendre tour à tour, {fig:} Accepter et refuser.
- 飲んで吐き出した様 (Nonde hakidashita yō) Comme si on avait rendu ce que l'on vient d'avaler, {fig:} Avoir une figure pâle et comme subitement boursouflée.
- 飲んで悲しみを忘れる (Nonde kanashimi wo wasureru) Noyer ses chagrins, laisser ses peines au fond du verre.
- 人を飲んで掛る (Hito wo nonde kakaru) Manquer à quelqu'un, regarder de haut.
- 一杯飲み乍ら契約した (Ippai nomi-nagara keiyaku shita) Ils passèrent un marché entre deux verres.
- 彼に妻君に飲まれている (Kare wa saikun ni nomarete iru) Sa femme le berne.
- 三日間飲まず食はず (Mikkakan nomazu kuwazu de) Sans boire ni manger trois, jours durant.
- 水を飲む (Mizu wo nomu) Boire de l'eau.
- 波に飲む (Nami ni nomareru) Être englouti par les vagues.
- 眠くなる迄飲む (Nemuku naru made nomu) Boire jusqu'à s'assoupir.
- 煙草を飲む (Tabako wo nomu) Fumer du tabac.
- 短刀を懐に飲む (Tantō wo futokoro ni nomu) Dissimuler un poignard dans son sein.
- 敵に飲まれる (Teki ni nomareru) S'en laisser imposer par l'ennemi.
- 恨を飲む (Urami wo nomu) Avaler une humiliation.

Figure 2: The *nomu* "drink" entry in the original Cesselin and the online Cesselin/Jibiki (18 examples).

References

Mathieu Mangeot. 2016. Collaborative construction of a good quality, broad coverage and copyright free Japanese-French dictionary. HAL-01294566.

Alda Mari. 2011. *Quantificateurs polysémiques.* Université Paris-Sorbonne, Vol.23, France.

Sigeru Miyagawa. 1989. *Structure and case marking in Japanese.* Syntax and Semantics, Vol. 22, New York.

Mutsuko Tomokiyo, Mathieu Mangeot, and Christian Boitet. 2016. Corpus and dictionary development for classifiers/quantifiers towards a French-Japanese machine translation, COLING, CogALex 2016, pages 185-192, Japan.

Mutsuko Tomokiyo, Mathieu Mangeot, and Christian Boitet. 2017. Development of a classifiers/quantifiers dictionary towards French-Japanese MT, MT-Summit 2017, Research Track, Vol 1, pages 216-226, Japan.

Hiroshi Uchida, Meihyin Zhu, and Tarcisio Della Senta. 2006. *Universal Networking Language.* UNDL Foundation, Japan.

Contractions: To Align or Not to Align, That Is the Question

Anabela Barreiro
INESC-ID, Rua Alves Redol 9
1000-029 Lisboa
Portugal
anabela.barreiro@inesc-id.pt

Fernando Batista
Instituto Universitário de Lisboa (ISCTE-IUL)
INESC-ID, Rua Alves Redol 9
1000-029 Lisboa, Portugal
fernando.batista@inesc-id.pt

Abstract

This paper performs a detailed analysis on the alignment of Portuguese contractions, based on a previously aligned bilingual corpus. The alignment task was performed manually in a subset of the English-Portuguese CLUE4Translation Alignment Collection. The initial parallel corpus was pre-processed and a decision was made as to whether the contraction should be maintained or decomposed in the alignment. Decomposition was required in the cases in which the two words that have been concatenated, i.e., the preposition and the determiner or pronoun, go in two separate translation alignment pairs (*PT* - [*no seio de*] [*a União Europeia*] *EN* - [*within*] [*the European Union*]). Most contractions required decomposition in contexts where they are positioned at the end of a multiword unit. On the other hand, contractions tend to be maintained when they occur at the beginning or in the middle of the multiword unit, i.e., in the frozen part of the multiword (*PT* - [*no que diz respeito a*] *EN* - [*with regard to*] or *PT* - [*além disso*] *EN* - [*in addition*]. A correct alignment of multiwords and phrasal units containing contractions is instrumental for machine translation, paraphrasing, and variety adaptation.

1 Introduction

The past decade has seen a significant advance in the field of machine translation mainly due to the growth of publicly available corpora, from which an enormous amount of translation alignments have been extracted. Alignments of multiword units and other phrases represent the driving force in the development of translation systems and the success of systems like Google Translate, which has a great deal to do with huge lexical coverage available in the large amounts of corpora that they have access to (Barreiro et al., 2014b) and from which translation alignments are extracted. But the quality of these alignments is also very important. For example, several authors have pointed out that the integration of multiword units in translation models based on linguistic knowledge is considered as an impact factor in obtaining better quality translations (cf. (Chiang, 2005), (Marcu et al., 2006), or (Zollmann and Venugopal, 2006), among others). Expert participation extends to the gathering, enhancement and integration of language resources including non-contiguous multiword unit alignments (Barreiro and Batista, 2016). Above all, high quality machine translation depends on the quality of the alignments used in the processes of machine learning. Some systems use unsupervised learning, in which the machine itself decides which segments of a source-language phrase align with which target language phrase segments (Och and Ney, 2000), while others use supervised learning based on previous alignments made manually by linguists (Blunsom and Cohn, 2006). In this paper, we focus on the **alignment of multiword units where contractions occur**, a challenge that has been overlooked in the existing literature and can be responsible for grammatical errors in translations.

A contraction is a word formed from two or more words of different parts-of-speech (most frequently) or the same part-of-speech (more seldom) that would otherwise appear next to each other in a sequence. For example, in English the most common contractions are those where the word *not* is added to an

Proceedings of the First Workshop on Linguistic Resources for Natural Language Processing, pages 122–130
Santa Fe, New Mexico, USA, August 20, 2018.

auxiliary verb in negative sentences, with omission of internal letters (e.g., *is not* → *isn't*) or those consisting of combinations of pronouns with auxiliary verbs, in which a word or a syllable is substituted by an apostrophe (e.g., *it is* → *it's*). These contractions are mainly used in speech and informal writing, but not in formal writing as in the Romance languages, where contractions are non-optional. The most common contractions in the Romance languages are those where prepositions are contracted with articles or pronouns with addition, replacement, or omission of letters. For example, in Portuguese the contraction *nas* "in, at the" results from the concatenation of the preposition *em* with the feminine plural definite article *as*; in Italian, the contraction *degli* "of" results from the concatenation of the preposition *di* with the masculine plural definite article *gli*; in Spanish, the contraction *al* "to, at the" results from the concatenation of the preposition *a* with the masculine singular definite article *el*; in French, the contraction *aux* "at, for, to the" results from the concatenation of the preposition *à* with the masculine plural definite article *les*. However, contractions can also be composed of two words with the same part-of-speech, e.g., two determiners (*la une* → *l'une*) or two prepositions (*de après* → *d'après*), as in French.

We describe a linguistically motivated approach to the alignment of multiword units where contractions occurring in these multiword units are required to be decomposed, except in specific circumstances determined by the context, such as when they constitute a non-variable (non-inflecting) element of a frozen multiword unit. Decomposition allows the correct alignment of a multiword unit, such as the prepositional compound *apesar de* "in spite of", in the sense that it separates the preposition *de* "of" that is part of the multiword from a concatenated element, in this case, the feminine singular definite article *a* "the" that is not part of the multiword, but rather belongs to the phrase or expression that immediately follows it (e.g., *apesar **da*** → [*apesar **de***] [***a*** NP]. Similarly, the masculine plural definite article *os* "the" in the expression *à luz de* "in light of" requires to be split from the preposition *de* (e.g., [*à luz **dos***] → [*à luz **de***] [***os*** NP). However, the contraction of the preposition *a* "at" with the feminine singular definite article *a* in this expression is not decomposed from its composed form *à*, because it represents a fixed element of the multiword unit, never changing its form. Failure to align and process correctly these multiword units involving contractions containing elements that are external to them leads to errors in the translated texts. Even if these errors do not affect the understanding of the translated text, they may compromise the quality of the translation leading to greater post-editing efforts.

In our experiment, a linguist has pre-processed manually a subset of the reference Europarl parallel corpus (Koehn, 2005) containing 400 Portuguese-English parallel sentences. From this subset corpus, the EN–PT CLUE4Translation Alignment Collection was achieved by adopting the methodology described in Section 3 for the alignment of Portuguese multiwords and other phrasal units involving contractions in the original corpus. This methodology was achieved during the development of the CLUE Alignment Guidelines, a set of linguistically-informed guidelines for the alignment translation or paraphrastic units in bitexts. In other words, the Guidelines were developed in two separate sets of documents containing statements by which to determine courses of action regarding the alignment of multiwords and other phrasal units, depending on whether these linguistic units are used in translation (CLUE4Translation Alignment Guidelines) or in paraphrasing (CLUE4Paraphrasing Alignment Guidelines). The approach reinforces the weight of multiwords as objects of representation in the alignment between the source and the target languages. This is independent of the source-target being two different languages (e.g., translation), two language varieties (e.g., variety adaptation), or the same language (e.g., paraphrases). The annotation of the subset corpus was performed with the CLUE-Aligner tool (Barreiro et al., 2016), a paraphrastic and translation unit aligner built to provide an efficient solution in the alignment of non-contiguous multiword units. CLUE-Aligner was developed within the eSPERTo project[1], whose objective is to develop a context-sensitive, linguistically enhanced paraphrase system that can be used in natural language processing applications, such as intelligent writing aids, summarization tools, smart dialogue systems, language learning, among others. Our broader research aims to contribute to new ma-

---

[1] eSPERTo stands for **S**ystem of **P**araphrasing for **E**diting and **R**evision of **T**ext (in Portuguese, **S**istema de **P**arafraseamento para **E**dição e **R**evisão de **T**exto). eSPERTo's core linguistic resources were extracted from OpenLogos bilingual resources (Barreiro et al., 2014a), the free open source version of the Logos System (Scott, 2003) (Barreiro et al., 2011) (Scott, 2018), adapted and integrated into NooJ linguistic engine (Silberztein, 2016). eSPERTo is available at https://esperto.l2f.inesc-id.pt/esperto/esperto/demo.pl

chine translation systems that produce high quality translation for which linguistically-based alignments
are extremely important.

2 Related Work

In NLP tasks, contractions are problematic for several reasons, among them: (i) two or more function
words[2] mostly with different parts-of-speech overlap, which makes syntactic analysis and generation
difficult; (ii) in cross-language analysis, the contrast between languages that have contractions and languages that do not have them, or do not have them in the same contexts, may present additional difficulties. Although, most parsers and part-of-speech taggers can process contractions successfully, the
alignment of segments in a parallel pair of sentences, where one particular segment corresponds to a
contraction in one language and to more than one segment (no contraction) in the other language has not
been adequately addressed in alignment annotation guidelines or alignment research (cf. (Och and Ney,
2000), (Lambert et al., 2005), (Graça et al., 2008), or (Tiedemann, 2011), among others). For example,
the Portuguese contraction of the preposition *em* and the demonstrative pronoun *este* in *neste* corresponds
to two words in English (*in this*) and in Spanish (*en esta*), as illustrated in example (1).

(1) *EN - to make further progress* **in this** *area*
    ES - a fin de avanzar **en esta** *dirección*
    PT - com o intuito de conseguir um avanço **neste** *(***em + este***) domínio*

In addition, the freely available parallel corpora most used in alignment tasks (Koehn, 2005) have
not been pre-processed in order to make possible the correct alignment of the pairs of multiword units
involving contractions. These shortcomings and lack of adequate directives to guide annotators in alignment tasks are responsible for machine translation errors, but they also affect negatively other NLP tasks
involving alignment resources, such as paraphrasing, among others. Our contraction pre-processing task
aims to advance the state of the art alignment taking into consideration the correct alignment of multiword units where contractions existed in the original corpus.[3] The methodology used to decide whether
contractions need to be decomposed for the alignment of their canonical forms or whether they are required to be maintained inside the multiword unit is presented in Section 3.

The Romance languages have peculiar behaviour with regards to the use of contractions. Some languages require a particular contraction, other languages require another type of contraction. Our methodology is consistent with regards to decomposition of contractions when they refer to aligning canonical
forms, i.e., separate words like a preposition and a determiner cannot align with a contraction or when
they are part of a frozen compound or fixed expression. For example, the English lexical bundle ***in that
sense*** requires the contraction in the Portuguese translation ***nesse*** *sentido* to be maintained. The equivalents in the remaining Romance languages do not contain contractions (***en ese*** *sentido* in Spanish, and
en ce *sens* in French).

3 Methodology

In our alignment task, the PT–EN CLUE4Translation parallel corpus was pre-processed for a framework
decision regarding whether its contractions should be decomposed or maintained. Sections 3.1 and 3.2
discuss the alignment issues specific to each one of the decisions, with a set of real-world alignment
examples, which aid in the understanding of the issues raised. Initially, the pre-processing task consisted
of a semi-manual decomposition by a linguist of all contractions. Decomposition allowed for the correct
alignment of multiword units where contracted forms required to be split so that those multiwords and
the phrases that follow them could be mapped to the corresponding elements in the source language, as
illustrated in Section 3.1. Subsequently, all the decomposed forms were reviewed and the decomposed

---

[2]Function or structure words, such as prepositions, determiners, auxiliary verbs and pronouns, among others, have little
lexical or ambiguous meaning, and are used to express grammatical (or structural) relationships with other words within a
sentence. They are extensively described in grammars. Function words are in contrast with content or lexical words, which
include nouns, verbs, adjectives, and most adverbs, normally containing very specific meanings listed in the dictionaries.

[3]This topic has been only superficially described in earlier work (Barreiro and Mota, 2017).

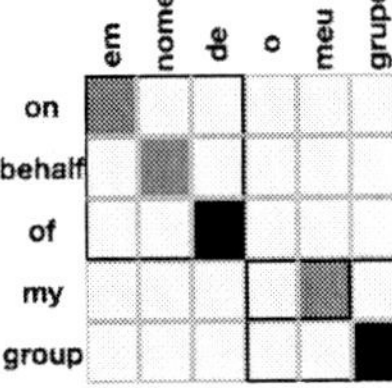 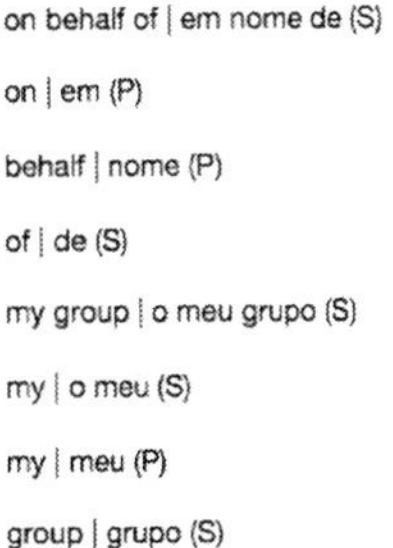

Figure 1: Alignment of the compound word *em nome de* "on behalf of" and the noun phrase *o meu grupo* "my group" with their internal elements (individual words)

forms in multiwords and frozen expressions were changed back to contractions, as described in Section 3.2. This methodology prioritized decomposition for statistical reasons only. The number of contractions that need to be decomposed in the corpus is much greater than the number of contractions that require to be maintained.

3.1 Decomposed Contractions

The Portuguese word *do* "of the" occurring in the original corpus corresponds to the contraction of the preposition *de* with the masculine definite article *o* that agrees with its masculine noun modifier *grupo* in the phrase *em nome do meu grupo* "on the behalf of my group". This contraction was decomposed in two elements, the preposition *de* "of" and the masculine singular definite article *o* "the" (*de + o*) in order to align correctly both the canonical form (lemma) of the compound word *em nome de* "on behalf of", and the noun phrase *o meu grupo* "my group", where the preposition of the contraction goes with the compound and the definite article goes with the noun phrase, i.e., the decomposition is required to make possible that the two concatenated words go in two different alignment pairs, as illustrated in Figure 1. Similar decomposition has taken place in contractions such as those illustrated in examples (2)–(5).

(2) *EN* - **across** + [the Atlantic]
    PT - **do outro lado de** (do = [de+o]) [o Atlântico]

(3) *EN* - **issues like** + [the NP]
    PT - **questões como a de** (dos = [de+os]) [os NP]

(4) *EN* - **with respect to** + [the N]
    PT - **quanto a** (ao = [a+o]) [o N]

(5) *EN* - **fully approves** [NP: the joint position of the council]
    PT - **dá a sua total aprovação a** (à = [a+a]) [NP: *a posição comum do conselho*]

Decomposition of contractions also has implication in coordination. For example, the coordinated noun phrases *o parlamento* "the parliament" and *o conselho* "the council" illustrated in Figure 2 are direct complements of the Portuguese prepositional verb *realizado por* "carried out by". While in English the preposition *by* of the prepositional verb is not repeated before the second noun phrase, in Portuguese there is repetition of the preposition *por* in the coordination introduced by the prepositional verb *realizado por* [NP] *e por* [NP]. The CLUE-Aligner alignment tool allows the alignment of the non-contiguous coordinating structure, excluding the NP elements (gaps), which are the variable elements of the coordination, and making possible to align them separately. Alignment methodologies require these linguistic nuances captured in translation to be handled correctly.

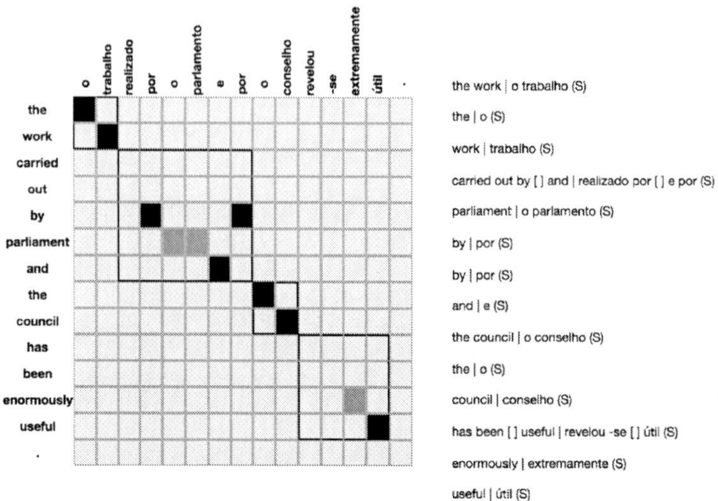

Figure 2: Alignment of the coordinated multiword *realizado **por*** [NP] *e **por*** [NP], implying the double decomposition of the contraction *pelo* into the preposition *por* of the prepositional verb and the masculine singular definite article *o* of the coordinated NP.

3.2 Non-decomposed Contractions

In a second pre-processing step, decomposed contractions *à = a + a* "to + the", *na = em + a* "in + the", and *do = de + o* "of + the" were restored in non-compositional multiword units, such as the fixed expressions *à luz de* "in light of" already mentioned in Section 1, *à data* "at the time" illustrated in Figure 3, and *na ordem do dia* "the next item" in the corpus (better translated as "in the agenda"), illustrated in Figure 4.

4 Analysis of Preliminary Results

Preliminary results confirmed that most contractions require decomposition in contexts where they are part of a multiword unit. For example, the most frequent contractions in the corpus, (*de + a, de + o, de + os*, and *em + a*), with more than 50 occurrences each, establish syntactic relationships between multiwords, such as compounds, prepositional nouns, etc., some of which are discontinuous (e.g. *centrar-se* [] *em* "to deal with"). In these contractions, the preposition establishes the final border of the first phrase (i.e., the last word in the phrase), and the determiner establishes the initial border of the phrase immediately after (i.e., the first word in the phrase). The second noun phrase can be a named entity (e.g., *União Europeia* "European Union", *Ásia* "Asia"), or a term (e.g., *capital de risco* "risk capital", *fundos de pensão* "pension funds"), but, there are also occurrences of contractions that require decomposition in contexts where the preposition is part of a multiword unit (the last word of the multiword, e.g., *em relação a* "with regard to" and the determiner is part of a regular noun phrase, e.g., *as observações* "the comments". Table 1 presents the frequency of contractions in contexts in which they require decomposition.

With regards to contractions that cannot be decomposed, most of them occur in the beginning or in the middle of the multiword unit, seldom in the end. For example, the contractions *no, neste, pelo*, and *às* in the multiwords *no que diz respeito a* "with regard to", *neste momento* "at this time", *pelo contrário* "on the contrary", and *às 12h30* "at 12.30 p.m." cannot be decomposed, because they are not positioned in the border with the next phrase. The same goes for the contraction *à* in the multiword unit *até à data* "so far", which occurs in a middle position. Exceptionally, the contraction *disso* in the multiword *além disso* "in addition" also remains undecomposed, because it corresponds to a fixed adverbial expression. Table 2 presents the frequency of contractions in contexts in which they cannot be decomposed.

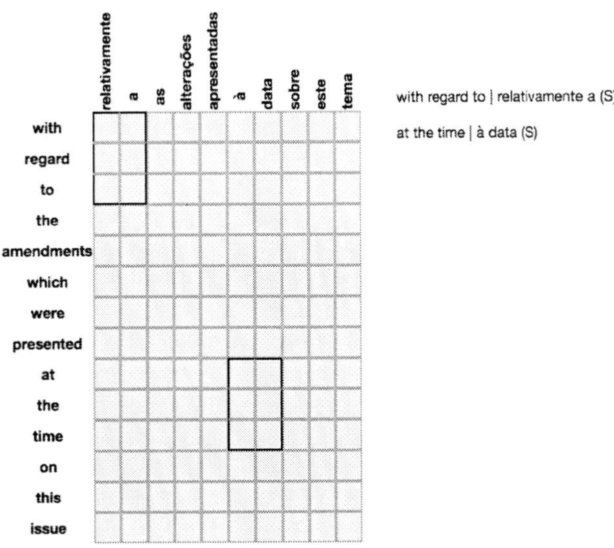

Figure 3: Alignment of the fixed expression *à data*

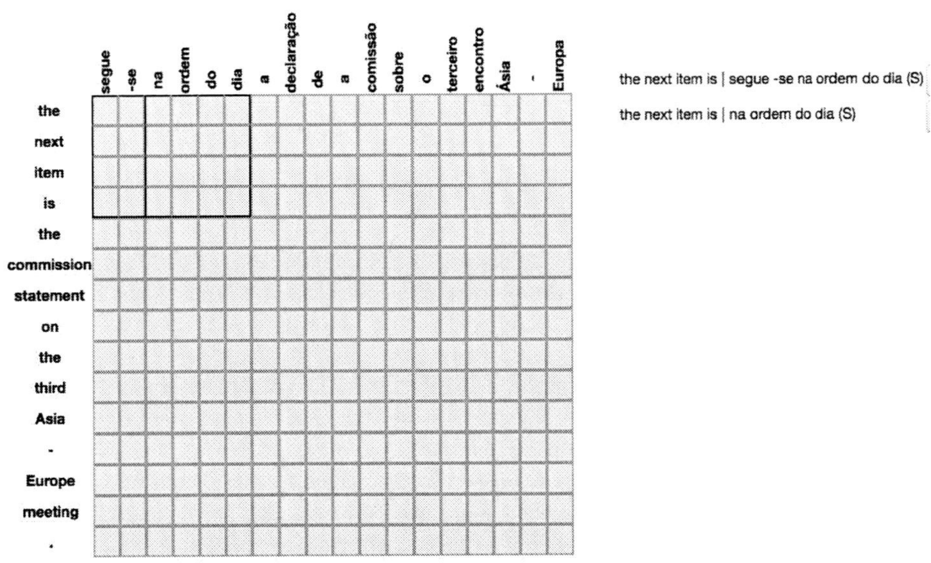

Figure 4: Alignment of the fixed expression *na ordem do dia*

Decomp.	Freq	PT example	EN translation
de a	113	[no seio **de**] [**a** União Europeia]	[within] [the European Union]
de o	93	[a promoção **de**] [**o** capital de risco]	[encouraging] [risk capital]
de os	68	[o favorecimento **de**] [**os** fundos de pensão]	[to favour] [pension funds]
em a	61	[integração **em**] [**a** Ásia]	[integration in] [Asia]
a a	44	[dar prioridade **a**] [**a** extensão de]	[focusing on] [the extension of]
a o	34	[prestar-se [] atenção **a**] [**o** trabalho infantil]	[attention must [] be paid to] [child labour]
de as	29	[o objectivo **de**] [**as** redes transeuropeias]	[the purpose of] [the trans-European networks]
em o	29	[fusões **em**] [**o** mercado de capitais]	[mergers on] [the capital market]
a os	20	[no concernente **a**] [**os** fundos de pensões]	[as for] [pension funds]
em as	16	[centrar-se [] **em**] [**as** questões comuns]	[to deal with] [questions which unite us]
a as	15	[em relação **a**] [**as** observações]	[with regard to] [the comments]
em os	12	[com base **em**] [**os** mesmos critérios]	[to use the same yardstick]
por o	10	[realizado **por**] [**o** parlamento]	[carried out by] [parliament]
por os	10	[angariados **por**] [**os** mercados de capital de risco]	[raised from] [venture capital]
por a	9	[influenciados [] **por**] [**a** instalação de]	[compromised [] by] [fitting]
em uma	7	[assenta **em**] [**uma** relação de igualdade]	[based on] [a relationship of equality]

Table 1: Frequency of contractions in contexts in which they require decomposition

contracted	freq	PT example	EN translation
no	43	**no** que diz respeito a	with regard to
do	34	inclusão [na ordem **do** dia]	added [to the agenda]
da	33	[**da** mesma forma que]	[in the same way that]
nos	17	**nos** dois sentidos	on both sides
dos	17	a carta **dos** direitos fundamentais	the charter of fundamental rights
na	17	**na** sua quase unanimidade	almost unanimously
neste	13	**neste** momento	at this time
à	13	até **à** data	so far
ao	13	**ao** dar prioridade a	by focusing on
disso	7	além **disso**	in addition
pelo	6	**pelo** contrário	on the contrary
das	5	redução [] **das** despesas	reducing [] expenditure
nesse	2	**nesse** sentido	to this effect
às	2	**às** 12h30	at 12.30 p.m.
desse	2	**desse** modo	hence
consigo	2	em paz **consigo** próprio	at peace with itself

Table 2: Frequency of contractions in contexts in which they cannot be decomposed

A few observations are worth noting with regards to undecomposeable contractions. One of them is that there are some semantico-syntactic patterns that function as linguistic constraints. For example, the contractions *às*, *nos*, or *pelos* cannot be decomposed when used with time-related named entities, such as *às seis horas da tarde* "at 6 p.m", *às sextas-feiras* "on Fridays", *nos anos sessenta* "in the sixties", or *pelos anos seguintes* "for all years ahead", among others. Another important observation is that, in normal circumstances, contractions of prepositions with pronouns, such as *consigo* in the expression *consigo próprio* "with itself" should not be decomposed.

The alignment task has given us cause to reflect on how certain linguistic units have been aligned in previous research work. As far as alignments involving the contraction phenomenon, have there been discussions on whether the contraction should be maintained or decomposed in cases such as *muitos dos presentes nesta assembleia* "many in the house", or *pelas mais variadas razões* "for a variety of reasons"? What about other linguistic phenomena? Is there scientific ground to establish "strict" boundaries for aligning paraphrastic units or translation units or are alignment decisions sometimes arbitrary? While this is not the first attempt to establish guidelines for alignment tasks, we have made an attempt to treat contractions in a scientific way, either maintaining the contraction at the beginning and the middle of a multiword unit or decomposing the contraction at the end of the multiword unit. The resulting alignment data may still contain errors, but we tried to make decisions in more than an ad-hoc fashion.

5 Final Remarks

Language experts' involvement in machine translation is essential in pre-editing tasks to improve the quality of the text to be translated (input or source text), and in post-editing tasks to improve the translated text (output or target text). High quality machine translation is directly related to the human factor, namely to the intervention of language specialists involved in translation and their role in the validation of correct translation alignments. When used in machine translation systems, alignments containing linguistic knowledge contribute to improved accuracy, reduced computational complexity and ambiguity, and improved translation quality, as illustrated for the contractions described in this paper. Given that contractions can be a frequent phenomenon in a language, the results that can be obtained through their correct alignment in a system can be significantly better than those obtained in a purely statistic or ad-hoc manner. But, there are other linguistic phenomena that require further examination. Without a suitable linguistic approach to the alignment task, and limited to the capacity of the algorithms, systems will continue to be overloaded with poor quality alignments, which will create translation of limited quality, requiring a greater post-editing effort. However, there is still a shortage of manually annotated alignments that can be used in training and evaluation for many language pairs or language variants, especially those with scarce resources. In this paper, we have used a methodology to align multiword units involving contractions, which pose a challenge to their correct alignment. The proposed alignment methodology does not depend on the application, so the pairs of aligned multiwords and phrases can be used in translation, paraphrasing, variety adaptation and other NLP tasks. We also hope that the linguistic knowledge learned in our alignment task can help solve problems related to the alignment of multiword units, provide better solutions to process and align them, and ultimately serve to build a more sophisticated automatic alignment tool.

Acknowledgements

This work was supported by national funds through Fundação para a Ciência e a Tecnologia (FCT) under project eSPERTo, with reference EXPL/MHC-LIN/2260/2013, and with reference UID/CEC/50021/2013. Anabela Barreiro was also funded by FCT through post-doctoral grant SFRH/BPD/91446 /2012.

References

Anabela Barreiro and Fernando Batista. 2016. Machine Translation of Non-Contiguous Multiword Units. In Wolfgang Maier, Sandra Kübler, and Constantin Orasan, editors, *Proceedings of the Workshop on Discontinuous Structures in Natural Language Processing*, DiscoNLP 2016, pages 22–30, San Diego, California, June. Association for Computational Linguistics (ACL).

Anabela Barreiro and Cristina Mota. 2017. e-PACT: eSPERTo Paraphrase Aligned Corpus of EN-EP/BP Translations. *Tradução em Revista*, 1(22):87–102.

Anabela Barreiro, Bernard Scott, Walter Kasper, and Bernd Kiefer. 2011. OpenLogos Rule-Based Machine Translation: Philosophy, Model, Resources and Customization. *Machine Translation*, 25(2):107–126.

Anabela Barreiro, Fernando Batista, Ricardo Ribeiro, Helena Moniz, and Isabel Trancoso. 2014a. OpenLogos Semantico-Syntactic Knowledge-Rich Bilingual Dictionaries. In Nicoletta Calzolari, Khalid Choukri, Thierry Declerck, Hrafn Loftsson, Bente Maegaard, Joseph Mariani, Asuncion Moreno, Jan Odijk, and Stelios Piperidis, editors, *Proceedings of the 9th International Conference on Language Resources and Evaluation*, LREC 2014, pages 3774–3781, Reykjavik, Iceland, May. European Language Resources Association.

Anabela Barreiro, Johanna Monti, Brigitte Orliac, Susanne Preuss, Kutz Arrieta, Wang Ling, Fernando Batista, and Isabel Trancoso. 2014b. Linguistic Evaluation of Support Verb Constructions by OpenLogos and Google Translate. In Nicoletta Calzolari, Khalid Choukri, Thierry Declerck, Hrafn Loftsson, Bente Maegaard, Joseph

Mariani, Asuncion Moreno, Jan Odijk, and Stelios Piperidis, editors, *Proceedings of the 9th International Conference on Language Resources and Evaluation*, LREC 2014, pages 35–40, Reykjavik, Iceland, May. European Language Resources Association.

Anabela Barreiro, Francisco Raposo, and Tiago Luís. 2016. CLUE-Aligner: An Alignment Tool to Annotate Pairs of Paraphrastic and Translation Units. In Nicoletta Calzolari, Khalid Choukri, Thierry Declerck, Sara Goggi, Marko Grobelnik, Bente Maegaard, Joseph Mariani, Hélène Mazo, Asunción Moreno, Jan Odijk, and Stelios Piperidis, editors, *Proceedings of the 10th Edition of the Language Resources and Evaluation Conference*, LREC 2016, pages 7–13. European Language Resources Association.

Phil Blunsom and Trevor Cohn. 2006. Discriminative Word Alignment with Conditional Random Fields. In *Proceedings of the 21st International Conference on Computational Linguistics and the 44th Annual Meeting of the Association for Computational Linguistics*, ACL-44, pages 65–72, Sydney, Australia. Association for Computational Linguistics.

David Chiang. 2005. A Hierarchical Phrase-based Model for Statistical Machine Translation. In *Proceedings of the 43rd Annual Meeting on Association for Computational Linguistics*, ACL 2005, pages 263–270, Ann Arbor, Michigan, USA. Association for Computational Linguistics.

João Graça, Joana Paulo Pardal, Luísa Coheur, and Diamantino Caseiro. 2008. Building a Golden Collection of Parallel Multi-Language Word Alignment. In Nicoletta Calzolari, Khalid Choukri, Bente Maegaard, Joseph Mariani, Jan Odijk, Stelios Piperidis, and Daniel Tapias, editors, *Proceedings of the 6th International Conference on Language Resources and Evaluation*, LREC 2008, pages 986–993, Marrakech, Morocco, May. European Language Resources Association.

Philipp Koehn. 2005. EuroParl: A Parallel Corpus for Statistical Machine Translation. In *Proceedings of the 10th Machine Translation Summit*, pages 79–86, Phuket, Thailand. AAMT, Asia-Pacific Association for Machine Translation.

Patrik Lambert, Adrià De Gispert, Rafael Banchs, and José B. Mariño. 2005. Guidelines for Word Alignment Evaluation and Manual Alignment. *Language Resources and Evaluation*, 39(4):267–285, Dec.

Daniel Marcu, Wei Wang, Abdessamad Echihabi, and Kevin Knight. 2006. SPMT: Statistical machine translation with syntactified target language phrases. In *Proceedings of the 2006 Conference on Empirical Methods in Natural Language Processing*, EMNLP 2006, pages 44–52, Stroudsburg, PA, USA. Association for Computational Linguistics.

Franz Josef Och and Hermann Ney. 2000. Improved Statistical Alignment Models. In *Proceedings of the 38th Annual Meeting on Association for Computational Linguistics*, ACL 2000, pages 440–447, Hong Kong. Association for Computational Linguistics.

Bernard Scott. 2003. The Logos Model: An Historical Perspective. *Machine Translation*, 18(1):1–72.

Bernard Scott. 2018. *Translation, Brains and the Computer: A Neurolinguistic Solution to Ambiguity and Complexity in Machine Translation*. Machine Translation: Technologies and Applications. Springer International Publishing.

Max Silberztein. 2016. *Formalizing Natural Languages: the NooJ Approach*. Wiley Eds.

Jörg Tiedemann. 2011. *Bitext Alignment*. Synthesis Digital Library of Engineering and Computer Science. Morgan & Claypool.

Andreas Zollmann and Ashish Venugopal. 2006. Syntax Augmented Machine Translation via Chart Parsing. In *Proceedings of the Workshop on Statistical Machine Translation*, SMT 2006, pages 138–141, New York City, June. Association for Computational Linguistics.

Enabling Code-Mixed Translation: Parallel Corpus Creation and MT Augmentation Approach

Mrinal Dhar
IIIT Hyderabad
Gachibowli, Hyderabad
Telangana, India
mrinal.dhar@gmail.com

Vaibhav Kumar
IIIT Hyderabad
Gachibowli, Hyderabad
Telangana, India
vaibhav4595@gmail.com

Manish Shrivastava
IIIT Hyderabad
Gachibowli, Hyderabad
Telangana, India
m.shrivastava@iiit.ac.in

Abstract

Code-mixing, use of two or more languages in a single sentence, is generated by multi-lingual speakers across the world. The phenomenon presents itself prominently in social media discourse. Consequently, there is a growing need for translating code-mixed hybrid language into standard languages. However, due to the lack of gold parallel data, existing machine translation systems fail to properly translate code-mixed text.

In an effort to initiate the task of machine translation of code-mixed content, we present a newly created parallel corpus of code-mixed English-Hindi and English. We selected previously available English-Hindi code-mixed data as a starting point for our parallel corpus, and 4 human translators, fluent in both English and Hindi, translated the 6,096 code-mixed English-Hindi sentences into English. With the help of the created parallel corpus, we analyzed the structure of English-Hindi code-mixed data and present a technique to augment run-of-the-mill machine translation (MT) approaches that can help achieve superior translations without the need for specially designed translation systems. The augmentation pipeline is presented as a pre-processing step and can be plugged with any existing MT system, which we demonstrate by improving code-mixed translations done by systems like Moses, Google Neural Machine Translation System (NMTS) and Bing Translator.

1 Introduction

In the last decade, digital communication mediums like e-mail, Facebook, Twitter, etc. have allowed people to have conversations in a much more informal manner than before. This informal nature of conversations has given rise to a new form of hybrid language, called *code-mixed* language, that lacks a formally defined structure.

Myers-Scotton (1993) defines code-mixing as "the embedding of linguistic units such as phrases, words and morphemes of one language into an utterance of another language". *Code-switching* is a similar concept, except that code-mixing is observed entirely in a single sentence, while code-switching occurs across sentences. For the purposes of this study, however, we will not make a difference between code-mixing and code-switching and treat them both as code-mixing.

Code-mixing of Hindi and English, where sentences follow the syntax of Hindi but borrow some vocabulary from English is very prevalent on social media content in India, where most people are multi-lingual. An example of a code-mixed English-Hindi sentence is presented below:

Proceedings of the First Workshop on Linguistic Resources for Natural Language Processing, pages 131–140
Santa Fe, New Mexico, USA, August 20, 2018.

- *"Main kal* movie *dekhne jaa rahi thi* and *raaste me* I met Sam."

  Gloss : I yesterday [movie] to-see go Continous-marker was [and] way in [I met Sam].

  English Translation : I was going to a movie yesterday and I met Sam on the way.

This phenomenon is present in informal communication in almost every multi-lingual society, as studied by Choudhury et al. (2007). They investigated how language used on these social media platforms, which they have called *texting* language, differs from the standard language that is found in more formal texts like books. It is also more common in the areas of the world where people are naturally bi- or multi-lingual. Usually, these are the areas where languages change over short geo-spatial distances and people generally have at least a basic knowledge of the neighbouring languages (Jamatia et al., 2015). A very good example for this is a country like India which has an extensive language diversity and where dialectal changes frequently instigate code-mixing.

In recent times, we have seen an explosion of Computer Mediated Communication (CMC) worldwide (Herring, 2003). In CMC, language use lies somewhere in between spoken and written forms of a language and tend to use simple shorter constructions, contractions and phrasal repetitions typical of speech (Danet and Herring, 2007). Such conversations, especially in social-media are both multi-party and multilingual, with mixing occurring between two or more languages, where the choice of language-use being highly influenced by the speakers and their communicative goals (Crystal, 2011). With multiple languages coming into play, and the variety of factors which influence the usage of those, the task of processing text becomes quite difficult.

As of now, according to the data of internetworldstats.com, the Internet has four-hundred fifty million English speaking users out of one billion five hundred million total users. This means that the market for English language is slightly less than one third of the total market. In other terms, most current approaches to information extraction exploiting social media and user-generated content (UGC), that are predominantly developed for English, are working with a mere third of the total data available.

The huge part of UGC that is not in English is currently being neglected mostly due to the relatively ephemeral character of UGC in general. Such content remains usually untranslated unless the users themselves so choose, because (i) it expresses opinions, and most users are much more likely to express or look for other opinions in the same language as their own rather than translated from a different one; (ii) it is generated and updated at an extremely fast pace and has a very short lifespan, which rules out in practice the possibility of translation by human subjects; and (iii) it is also produced in immense quantities, which, together with the previous point, ends up rendering translation by human subjects effectively impossible (both in terms of time and cost). All this leads to an enormous body of information being constantly generated which is also being constantly lost behind language barriers: the consolidation of Web 2.0 has caused an unprecedented increase in the amount of data and each individual user is currently being deprived of most of it (Carrera et al., 2009).

These language barriers are intensified by the fact that a huge number of people don't use just one language, but multiple languages simultaneously, in the form of code-mixing. Even if we were able to create a system capable of processing information in every language, or perhaps a system capable of translating text from any given language to another, we would still not be able to break down the language barrier completely, due to the phenomenon of code-mixing. This is where code-mixed translation comes into play.

While translation of code-mixed text has been a requirement for some time, there is a noticeable lack of resources for this task. To tackle this problem, we have created a set of 6096 English-Hindi code-mixed and monolingual English gold standard parallel sentences as an initial attempt to promote generation of data resources for this domain.

However, most MT systems require a significant number of "parallel" sentences to perform well. While we wait for large parallel corpora for code-mixed text to be developed, we could make do by equipping the existing state-of-the-art MT systems to handle code-mixed content. This necessity has motivated us to develop an augmentation pipeline to support code-mixing on existing MT systems.

To summarize, the main contributions of this work are as follows:

- We are releasing [1] a gold standard parallel corpus consisting of 6096 English-Hindi code-mixed and monolingual English that we created.

- We have developed an augmentation pipeline for existing machine translation systems that can boost their translation performance on code-mixed content.

- We carry out experiments involving various machine translation systems like Moses, Google NMTS and Bing Translator to compare their translation performance on code-mixed text, and demonstrate how our augmentation pipeline improves their translation results.

The rest of our paper is divided into the following sections: We begin with a study of research conducted in this domain in Section 2. We discuss the process of creation of the corpus and its features in Section 3. In Section 4, we introduce our augmentation pipeline for machine translation systems and describe the approach in detail. Then in Section 5, we perform experiments with existing machine translation systems, and describe the impact of our augmentation pipeline on their translation accuracy for code-mixed data, proceeded by a discussion of our results.

2 Related Work

In recent times, there has been a lot of interest from the Computational Linguistics community to support code-mixing in language systems and models.

Due to a massive growth of social media content, the usage of noisy non-standard tokens online has also increased. Hence, text normalization systems have become necessary that can convert these non-standard tokens to their standard form. Language identification at the word level was attempted by Nguyen and Doğruöz (2013) on Turkish-Dutch posts collected from an online chat forum. They performed comparisons between different approaches such as using a dictionary and statistical models. They were able to develop a system which had an accuracy of 97.6%, and concluded that language models prove to be better than a dictionary based approach. Barman et al. (2014) explored the same task on social media text in code-mixed Bengali-Hindi-English languages. They annotated a corpus with over 180,000 tokens, and used statistical models with monolingual dictionaries to achieve an accuracy of 95.76%.

Vyas et al. (2014) deal with POS tagging of English-Hindi code-mixed data that they extracted from Twitter and Facebook. Social media is a good source for obtaining code-mixed data as it is the preferred choice of the urban youth as informal platforms for communication. Bali et al. (2014) have done a study of English-Hindi code-mixing on Facebook, and their investigation demonstrates the extent of code-mixing in the digital world, and the need for systems that can automatically process this data. Sharma et al. (2016) have addressed shallow parsing of English-Hindi code-mixed data obtained from online social media. They were the first to attempt shallow parsing of code-mixed data, to the best of our knowledge.

Language identification in code-mixed data is an important step because it might determine how to further process the data in tasks like POS tagging, for example. Chittaranjan et al. (2014) explore a CRF based system for word level identification of languages.

Apart from this, Raghavi et al. (2015) have explored the problem of classification of code-mixed questions. By translating words to English before extracting features, they were able to achieve a greater accuracy in classification. WebShodh, developed by Chandu et al. (2017), is an online web based question answering system that is based on this work.

Gupta et al. (2016) created a dataset of code-mixed English-Hindi sentences along with the associated language and normalization. This was the first attempt to create such a linguistic resource for the language pair. They also presented an empirical study detailing the construction of language identification and normalization system designed for the language pair.

Code-mixed translation has been attempted previously by Sinha and Thakur (2005) from a linguistics perspective. However, we primarily draw our inspiration from the skeleton model presented by Rijhwani et al. (2016). Though they present the broad idea similar to ours, we find that many of the assumptions

---

[1] https://github.com/mrinaldhar/en-hi-codemixed-corpus

made were very simplistic and no evaluation or results were provided and no systems were released. We provide a deeper look into the code-mixed translation process and demonstrate the impact along with benchmark dataset.

3 Corpus creation

3.1 Analysis

We started with the dataset created and released by Gupta et al. (2016). They collected 1,446 sentences from social media, and performed language identification and word normalization on these sentences. We also obtained 771 sentences from the dataset released as part of the ICON 2017 tool contest on POS-tagging for code-mixed social media text, created by collection of Whatsapp chat messages. Additionally, we use the dataset released by Joshi et al. (2016) for the task of sentiment analysis of code-mixed content, which contains 3,879 code-mixed sentences.

For our study, we removed annotations such as sentiment labels, POS tags, etc. from the obtained datasets, and only used raw sentences for the task of corpus creation. For the augmentation pipeline, we also make use of the language identifiers, wherever available in the dataset samples.

The 6,096 code-mixed sentences contain a total of 63,913 tokens. Of these tokens, 37,673 are Hindi words and 16,182 are English words. The rest of the tokens were marked as "Rest". "Rest" would mean that these tokens could be abbreviations, named entities, etc. The tokens in the data were already normalized.

It is very crucial to find the level of code-mixing in data, since if the extent of code mixing is too less, then it is as good as a monolingual corpus and would not provide us much benefit in the task of code-mixed translation. Hence, in order to find the level of code-mixing present in the data, we use the Code-Mixing Index (CMI) (Das and Gambäck, 2014) defined as:

$$CMI = \begin{cases} 100 \times [1 - \frac{max\{w_i\}}{n-u}] & n > u \\ 0 & n = u \end{cases} \tag{1}$$

where, w_i is the number of words tagged with a particular language tag, $max\{w_i\}$ represents the number of words of the most prominent language, n is the total number of tokens, u represents the number of language independent tokens (such as named entities, abbreviations), in our case these would be the words marked as "Rest".

Summarized statistics of the data can be found in Table 1. From the table we can see that the code-mixing index is around 30.5, hence, we can safely assume that the data has a decent variety of code-mixed sentences which could be effectively used for the creation of translation systems.

3.2 Methodology for Annotation

For the task of translation, we selected 4 annotators who were fluent in both English and Hindi. Before starting the process of annotation, we randomly sampled 100 sentences from the corpus. We then asked one of the annotators to translate the given sentences into English. The other three annotators judged the translated sentences into two categories, *Totally Correct (TC)* and *Requires Changes (RC)*. Finally, we use the Fleiss' Kappa measure in order to calculate agreement.

Fleiss' Kappa is a statistical measure for assessing the reliability of agreement between a fixed number of raters when assigning categorical ratings to a number of items or classifying items in order to calculate the agreement. The measure is defined as follows:

Let N denote the number of subjects, n denote the number of ratings per subject, and k be the number of categories into which assignments are to be made. In our case N=100, n=3, k=2. Let the subjects be indexed by $i = 1, ... N$, categories be indexed by $j = 1, ... k$ and n_{ij} be the number of raters who assigned the jth category to the ith subject. Then,

$$P_i = \frac{1}{n(n-1)}[(\sum_{j=1}^{k} n_{ij}{}^2) - (n)] \tag{2}$$

here, P_i denotes the extent to which raters agree to the ith subject,

$$\overline{P} = \frac{1}{N} \sum_{i=1}^{N} P_i \tag{3}$$

$$p_j = \frac{1}{Nn} \sum_{i=1}^{N} n_{ij} \tag{4}$$

$$\overline{P_e} = \sum_{j=1}^{k} {p_j}^2 \tag{5}$$

and finally,

$$\kappa = \frac{\overline{P} - \overline{P_e}}{1 - \overline{P_e}} \tag{6}$$

where κ denotes the Fleiss' Kappa score.

Using this, we found out that the κ score for code-mixed to English translation was close to 0.88. We can consider this score to be in correspondence with almost complete agreement. We speculate that such a high agreement could arise from the fact that the annotators had the same cultural background and shared similar communities.

In Table 2 we provide a few examples of code-mixed English-Hindi translated to English with the help of our pipeline. From the examples we can clearly see that the dataset sentences consist of transliterated Hindi words. Transliterated words usually pose a problem because one needs to come up with a standard form of those words before proceeding to the task of translation. However, Gupta et al. (2016) had already normalized the transliterated words. Hence, we were able to translate sentences without having to normalize the words.

Type	Value
Total no. of code-mixed sentences	6,096
Total no. of tokens	63,913
Total no. of Hindi tokens	37,673
Total no. of English tokens	16,182
Total no. of 'Rest'	10,094
Code Mixing Index	30.5

Table 1: Corpus Statistics

Some examples from the dataset which illustrate code-mixing:

1. I was really trying *ki aajayun*

   Gloss: [I was really trying] I come

   Translation: I was really trying to come

2. Sorrrry, *aaj subah tak pata nhi tha* that I wudnt be able to come today

   Gloss: [Sorrrry], today morning till know not did [that I wudnt be able to come today]

   Translation: Sorrrry, I didn't know until this morning that I wudnt be able to come today.

3. *tu udhar ka* permanent *intezaam karke aa* !

   Gloss: you there is [permanent] arrangement do come !

   Translation: Come over after making a permanent arrangement there !

4. btw i was thinking *mai pehle ghar chale jaungi*, and *sham ko* venue *pe aa jaungi*

   Gloss: [btw i was thinking] i first home walk go, [and] evening [venue] on come go

   Translation: btw I was thinking that I'll first go home and then come to the venue in the evening.

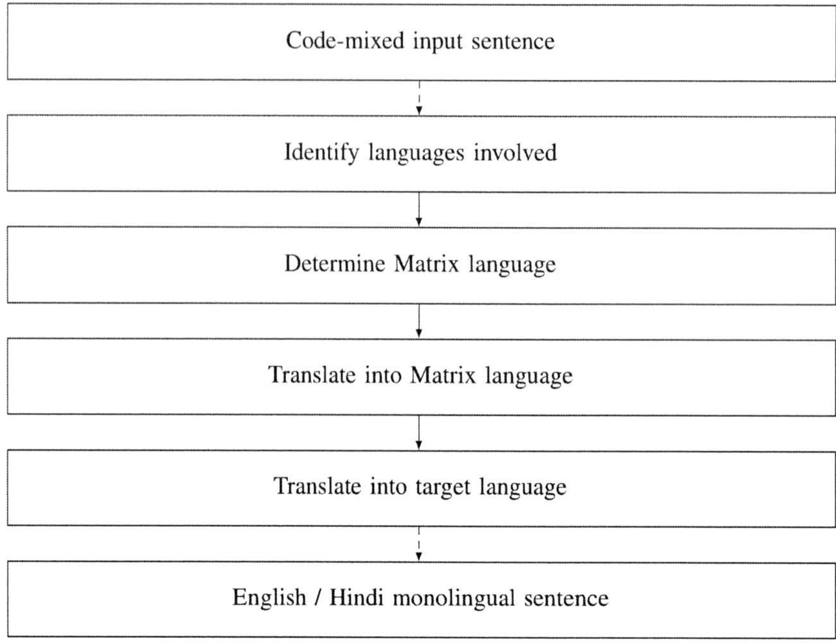

Figure 1: Translation augmentation pipeline

4 MT Augmentation Pipeline

Instead of attempting to create a new machine translation system specifically for code-mixed text, which is not feasible due to lack of abundant gold standard data, we now introduce an approach that will augment existing systems for use with code-mixed languages in the form of the pipeline described in Figure 1.

In order to improve the results of the MT system for code-mixing, we attempt to change the input code-mixed sentence to more closely resemble the kind of input these systems work best for - a monolingual sentence. As the code-mixed sentence follows the structure of the Matrix language, we translate words of the code-mixed sentence that belong to the Embedded language (Em) to the Matrix (Ma) language using a machine translation system (Em-Ma MT). The resulting sentence would be translated to the desired target language (Tgt) using another existing MT system (Ma-Tgt MT), which may or may not be the same as the Em-Ma MT system (depending on what the matrix and target languages are). For our experiments, we have fixed the target (Tgt) to be English, as we attempt to translate English-Hindi code-mixed language into English. The pipeline also recognizes when the target language is the same as the matrix language, and therefore there is no need to perform a translation of respective parts or the whole of the sentence.

4.1 Identification of languages involved

As a pre-processing step, we identify the languages that are involved in creating the hybrid code-mixed language in the text. This step is crucial in determining the pipeline to follow for the rest of the translation.

Gupta et al. (2016) released their dataset with manually annotated language identifiers associated with every word of the sentences in the data. For the other datasets, we make use of the Language Identification (LID) system by Bhat et al. (2015) to identify the corresponding language for each word in a code-mixed sentence.

4.2 Determination of Matrix Language

In the Matrix Language-Frame model proposed by Myers-Scotton (1997), a code-mixed sentence is formed by a Matrix language and an Embedded language. The overall morpho-syntactic structure of the sentence is that of the Matrix language, however, words from the Embedded language are also present in the sentence.

In other words, the Matrix language lends its syntactical structure and the Embedded language lends its vocabulary to the code-mixed sentence. The Matrix language is determined by employing the following heuristics in decreasing order of preference:

1. **The number of words in one language in the sentence**
   The language which has more words in the sentence is likely to be the matrix language.

2. **Determination of the syntactic structure of the text by detecting the language of the verb**
   For example, if the two languages involved in code-mixing are English and Hindi, and a sentence follows SVO structure, in that case English is likely to be the Matrix language of the sentence.

3. **Usage of function words of a particular language in the text**
   The language whose function words exist in the sentence might be the matrix language, since function words are associated with syntax.

4.3 Translation into Matrix Language

While most translation systems are unable to translate foreign (including code-mixed) words due to lack of training, borrowed and commonly used words are often found in parallel corpora. Commercial systems, like Google Translate, can translate frequent short phrases as well. Errors creep in when they have to deal with longer phrases. Keeping this in mind and to reduce the translation cost per sentence, we selected **the longest string of words belonging to the Embedded language** for translation to the Matrix language. This is to ensure the maximal meaningful translation with a single call to the Em-Ma MT engine. This results in a code-mixed sentence that follows the syntax of the Matrix language and also has the majority of its words in this Matrix language.

4.4 Translation into Target Language

Now that the code-mixed sentence has been translated into the matrix language, it can be directly translated into the Target language using the Ma-Tgt MT engine.,

5 Evaluation and Results

In order to evaluate our methods of augmentation, we consider the following existing machine translation systems: **Moses** (Koehn et al., 2007), **Google's Neural Machine Translation System (NMTS)** (Wu et al., 2016), **Bing Translator**.

For training a translation model for Moses, we used the English-Hindi parallel corpus released by Kunchukuttan et al. (2017). This dataset consists of 1,492,827 parallel monolingual English and monolingual Hindi sentences. The Hindi sentences were in the Devanagari script, and required pre-processing for use with our code-mixed dataset, which is entirely in Roman script.

We compare the output translations of these MT systems for code-mixed data, with and without the augmentation by our system. For accuracy metrics, we chose BLEU score, Word Error Rate (WER) and Translation Error Rate (TER) as they are ideal for use with machine translation.

As can be observed from Table 3, our augmentation pipeline significantly improves the translation accuracy of existing machine translation systems. Note that among the systems themselves, Google NMTS performs much better on code-mixed English-Hindi data as compared to traditional phrase based systems like Moses and even neural systems like Bing Translator. Even though Moses does not perform as well as the other systems described here for code-mixed data, our pipeline is still able to boost its performance significantly.

Original sentence	Without Augmentation	With Augmentation
room *mei shayad kal bhi nahi* stay *karungi* , cancel *ho sakti hai uski* booking *abhi* ?	I will not stay in the room tomorrow, can I cancel her booking now?	I will not stay in the room tomorrow, can I cancel her booking now?
Sorrrry , *aaj subah tak pata nhi tha* that I wudnt be able to come today	Sorry , *aaj subah tak pata nahi tha* that I wouldn't be able to come today	Sorry , Did not know until this morning that I wudnt be able to come today
I was really trying *ki aajayun*	I was really trying *ki aajayun*	I was really trying I come
par if its possible and any other guest needs a room , *mera* room *de de kisi ko bhi*	*par* if its possible and any other guest needs a room , *mera* room *de de kisi ko bhi*	*par* if its possible and any other guest needs a room , Give my room to anyone
toh hum aaj train ki ticket karwa lenge .	So we will get a train ticket today.	So we will get a train ticket today.
tu udhar ka permanent *intezaam karke aa* !	You come here by arranging Permanent!	You come here with a permanent arrangement!

Table 2: Augmenting Google Translate with our pipeline

	Without Augmentation			With Augmentation		
	BLEU	**WER**	**TER**	**BLEU**	**WER**	**TER**
Moses	14.9	10.671	2.403	16.9	9.505	2.295
Google NMTS	28.4	5.882	0.692	37.8	4.030	0.537
Bing Translator	18.9	8.940	1.108	25.0	8.054	0.917

Table 3: Comparison of performance with and without using our augmentation pipeline. (Note: BLEU - higher is better, (WER,TER) - lower is better.)

6 Conclusions

In this paper, we have created a set of 6,096 English-Hindi code-mixed and monolingual English gold standard parallel sentences for promoting the task of machine translation of code-mixed data and generation of data resources for this domain.

We have also developed an augmentation pipeline, that can be used to augment existing machine translation systems such that translation of code-mixed data can be improved without training an MT system specifically for code-mixed text. Using the evaluation metrics selected, it is shown that there is a quantifiable improvement in the accuracy of translations with the augmentation proposed.

As part of our study, we have observed that long distance re-ordering of words is still an issue with code-mixed MT. Also, since code-mixed language does not have a standard form, it is difficult to establish a correct version of spelling for a particular word. Language identification is the most critical module for translation augmentation, because the same orthographic form can lead to valid words in multiple languages.

To take this work further, we intend to develop an end-to-end code-mixed MT system which can jointly perform the normalization, language identification, matrix language identification and two-step translation tasks. A hybrid model, partially trained on gold parallel corpus, may also be attempted.

Acknowledgements

A special thanks to Aashna Jena, Abhinav Gupta, Arjun Nemani, Freya Mehta, Manan Goel, Saraansh Tandon, Shweta Sahoo, Ujwal Narayan and Yash Mathne for their help with this study. Thanks to Vatika

Harlalka for proof-reading this paper and ensuring there were as few errors as possible.

References

Kalika Bali, Jatin Sharma, Monojit Choudhury, and Yogarshi Vyas. 2014. i am borrowing ya mixing? an analysis of english-hindi code mixing in facebook. *In Proceedings of the First Workshop on Computational Approaches to Code Switching, EMNLP.*

Utsab Barman, Amitava Das, Joachim Wagner, and Jennifer Foster. 2014. Code mixing: A challenge for language identification in the language of social media. In *Proceedings of The First Workshop on Computational Approaches to Code Switching*, pages 13–23.

Irshad Ahmad Bhat, Vandan Mujadia, Aniruddha Tammewar, Riyaz Ahmad Bhat, and Manish Shrivastava. 2015. Iiit-h system submission for fire2014 shared task on transliterated search. In *Proceedings of the Forum for Information Retrieval Evaluation*, FIRE '14, pages 48–53, New York, NY, USA. ACM.

Jordi Carrera, Olga Beregovaya, and Alex Yanishevsky. 2009. Machine translation for cross-language social media. *PROMT Americas Inc.*

Khyathi Raghavi Chandu, Manoj Chinnakotla, Alan W. Black, and Manish Shrivastava. 2017. Webshodh: A code mixed factoid question answering system for web. In Gareth J.F. Jones, Séamus Lawless, Julio Gonzalo, Liadh Kelly, Lorraine Goeuriot, Thomas Mandl, Linda Cappellato, and Nicola Ferro, editors, *Experimental IR Meets Multilinguality, Multimodality, and Interaction*, pages 104–111, Cham. Springer International Publishing.

Gokul Chittaranjan, Yogarshi Vyas, Kalika Bali, and Monojit Choudhury. 2014. Word-level language identification using crf: Code-switching shared task report of msr india system. page 73–79. Association for Computational Linguistics.

Monojit Choudhury, Rahul Saraf, Vijit Jain, Animesh Mukherjee, Sudeshna Sarkar, and Anupam Basu. 2007. Investigation and modeling of the structure of texting language. *International Journal of Document Analysis and Recognition (IJDAR)*, 10(3):157–174.

David Crystal. 2011. *Internet linguistics: A Student Guide (1st ed.).* Routledge, New York, NY.

Brenda Danet and Susan C Herring. 2007. *The multilingual Internet: Language, culture, and communication online.* Oxford University Press on Demand.

Amitava Das and Björn Gambäck. 2014. Identifying languages at the word level in code-mixed indian social media text. *Proceedings of the 11th International Conference on Natural Language Processing.* pages 169–178.

Sakshi Gupta, Piyush Bansal, and Radhika Mamidi. 2016. Resource creation for hindi-english code mixed social media text. *The 4th International Workshop on Natural Language Processing for Social Media in the 25th International Joint Conference on Artificial Intelligence.*

Susan C Herring. 2003. Media and language change: Introduction. *Journal of Historical Pragmatics*, 4(1):1–17.

Anupam Jamatia, Björn Gambäck, and Amitava Das. 2015. Part-of-speech tagging for code-mixed english-hindi twitter and facebook chat messages. *In Proceedings of Recent Advances in Natural Language Processing 2015 Organising Committee, Association for Computational Linguistics.* pages 239–248.

Aditya Joshi, Ameya Prabhu, Manish Shrivastava, and Vasudeva Varma. 2016. Towards sub-word level compositions for sentiment analysis of hindi-english code mixed text. In *Proceedings of COLING 2016, the 26th International Conference on Computational Linguistics: Technical Papers*, pages 2482–2491. The COLING 2016 Organizing Committee.

Philipp Koehn, Hieu Hoang, Alexandra Birch, Chris Callison-Burch, Marcello Federico, Nicola Bertoldi, Brooke Cowan, Wade Shen, Christine Moran, Richard Zens, Chris Dyer, Ondřej Bojar, Alexandra Constantin, and Evan Herbst. 2007. Moses: Open source toolkit for statistical machine translation. In *Proceedings of the 45th Annual Meeting of the ACL on Interactive Poster and Demonstration Sessions*, ACL '07, pages 177–180, Stroudsburg, PA, USA. Association for Computational Linguistics.

Anoop Kunchukuttan, Pratik Mehta, and Pushpak Bhattacharyya. 2017. The IIT bombay english-hindi parallel corpus. *Under review at LREC 2018, CoRR*, abs/1710.02855.

Carol Myers-Scotton. 1993. Common and uncommon ground: Social and structural factors in codeswitching. *Language in society*, 22(4):475–503.

Carol Myers-Scotton. 1997. *Duelling Languages: Grammatical Structure in Codeswitching*. Clarendon Press.

Dong Nguyen and A Seza Doğruöz. 2013. Word level language identification in online multilingual communication. In *Proceedings of the 2013 conference on empirical methods in natural language processing*, pages 857–862.

Khyathi Chandu Raghavi, Manoj Kumar Chinnakotla, and Manish Shrivastava. 2015. "answer ka type kya he?": Learning to classify questions in code-mixed language. In *Proceedings of the 24th International Conference on World Wide Web*. pages 853–858. ACM.

Shruti Rijhwani, Royal Sequiera, Monojit Choudhury Choudhury, and Kalika Bali. 2016. Translating code-mixed tweets: A language detection based system. In *3rd Workshop on Indian Language Data Resource and Evaluation - WILDRE-3*.

Arnav Sharma, Sakshi Gupta, Raveesh Motlani, Piyush Bansal, Manish Srivastava, Radhika Mamidi, and Dipti M Sharma. 2016. Shallow parsing pipeline for hindi-english code-mixed social media text. *HLT-NAACL The Association for Computational Linguistics*. pages 1340–1345

Rai Mahesh Kumar Sinha and Anil Thakur. 2005. Machine translation of bi-lingual hindi-english (hinglish) text. *10th Machine Translation summit (MT Summit X), Phuket, Thailand*, pages 149–156.

Yogarshi Vyas, Spandana Gella, Jatin Sharma, Kalika Bali, and Monojit Choudhury. 2014. POS tagging of english-hindi code-mixed social media content. In *Proceedings of the 2014 Conference on Empirical Methods in Natural Language Processing (EMNLP)*, pages 974–979. Association for Computational Linguistics.

Yonghui Wu, Mike Schuster, Zhifeng Chen, Quoc V. Le, Mohammad Norouzi, Wolfgang Macherey, Maxim Krikun, Yuan Cao, Qin Gao, Klaus Macherey, Jeff Klingner, Apurva Shah, Melvin Johnson, Xiaobing Liu, ukasz Kaiser, Stephan Gouws, Yoshikiyo Kato, Taku Kudo, Hideto Kazawa, Keith Stevens, George Kurian, Nishant Patil, Wei Wang, Cliff Young, Jason Smith, Jason Riesa, Alex Rudnick, Oriol Vinyals, Greg Corrado, Macduff Hughes, and Jeffrey Dean. 2016. Google's neural machine translation system: Bridging the gap between human and machine translation. *CoRR*, abs/1609.08144.

Author Index

Šojat, Krešimir, 28

Abebe, Tewodros, 83
Abera, Hafte, 78, 83
Andargie, Tsegaye, 83
Assabie, Yaregal, 83
Atinafu, Solomon, 83

Barreiro, Anabela, 122
Batista, Fernando, 122
Boitet, Christian, 112
Boudhina, Safa, 38

Dhar, Mrinal, 131
Dorr, Bonnie, 57

Ephrem, Binyam, 83

Fehri, Héla, 38

Gasser, Michael, 65
Gezmu, Andargachew Mekonnen, 65

H/Mariam, Sebsibe, 78

Kocijan, Kristina, 28
Kumar, Vaibhav, 131

Lemma, Amanuel, 83
Liberman, Mark, 1

Machonis, Peter, 18
Malireddy, Chanakya, 71
Mangeot, Mathieu, 112
Max, Aurélien, 102
Melese, Michael, 83
Meshesha, Million, 83
Moldovan, Dan, 12
Monteleone, Mario, 47
Mulugeta, Wondwossen, 83

Nürnberger, Andreas, 65

Padó, Sebastian, 91
Poljak, Dario, 28

Reyes, Silvia, 47

Rodrigo, Andrea, 47

Seyoum, Binyam Ephrem, 65
Shifaw, Seifedin, 83
Shrivastava, Manish, 71, 131
Sikos, Jennifer, 91
Silberztein, Max, 2
Somisetty, Srivenkata N M, 71

Teferra Abate, Solomon, 83
Tomokiyo, Mutsuko, 112
Tsegaye, Wondimagegnhue, 83

Vilnat, Anne, 102
Voss, Clare, 57

Yifiru Tachbelie, Martha, 83

Zhai, Yuming, 102
Zhang, Linrui, 12